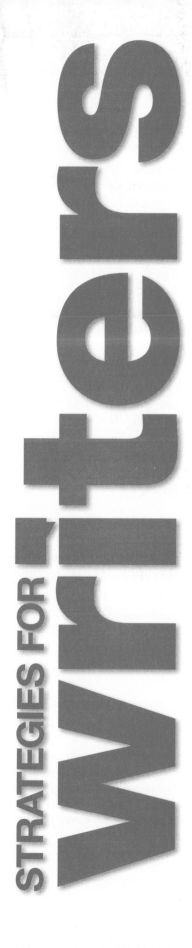

STRATEGIES FOR writers

4

Senior Author
Rebecca Bowers Sipe, Ed.D.
Eastern Michigan University

Consulting Authors
Julie Coiro, Ph.D.
University of Rhode Island

Amy Humphreys, Ed.M., NBCT
Educational Consultant

Sara B. Kajder, Ph.D.
Virginia Tech

Mark Overmeyer, M.A.
Cherry Creek School District, Colorado

Senior Consultant
James Scott Miller, M.Ed.
National Writing Consultant

ZB **Zaner-Bloser**

Program Reviewers

Zaner-Bloser wishes to thank these educators who reviewed portions of this program and provided comments prior to publication.

Joe Anspaugh
Shelbyville Middle School
Shelbyville, IN

Michele Barto, Ed.D.
Fairleigh Dickinson University
Madison, NJ

Jackie Blosser
Lima City Schools
Lima, OH

Kim Bondy
South Arbor Academy
Ypsilanti, MI

Kelly Caravelli
Meadowbrook Middle School
Poway, CA

Cathy Cassy
St. Louis Public Schools
St. Louis, MO

Penny Clare
Educational Consultant
Lee, NH

Mary Dunton
Literacy Consultant
Sparks, NV

Emily Gleason
Beaverton School District
Beaverton, OR

Denise Gray, Ed.D.
Whiteriver Elementary School
Whiteriver, AZ

Laura Hall
Walton Charter Academy
Pontiac, MI

Donna Jett
Rockwood South Middle School
Fenton, MO

Christine Johnson, Ed.D.
Boonton Public Schools
Boonton, NJ

Dr. Roma Morris
Columbia School District
Columbia, MS

Rosanne Richards
Southern Nevada Regional Professional Development Program
North Las Vegas, NV

Sharlene E. Ricks
Alpine School District
American Fork, UT

Debbie Rutherford
Independent National Consultant
Omaha, NE

Melinda Springli
Lawton Public Schools
Lawton, OK

Kerry Stephenson
Pendleton County School District
Butler, KY

Photography: Cover © PHOTO/ananimages/Corbis; Interior models, George C. Anderson; Stopwatch image © Royalty-Free/Corbis; p. 3 © Tim McGuire/Corbis; p. 12 © Tom Walker/Getty Images; p. 99 © Adam Woolfitt/Robert Harding World Imagery/Corbis; p. 106 © Comstock; p. 121 © Toyohiro Yamada/Getty Images; p. 237 © iStockphoto.com/Jill Lang; p. 353 © Catherine Karnow/Corbis; p. 384 © Panoramic Images/Getty Images

Art Credits: pp. 4, 26, 48, 122, 144, 166, 238, 264, 286, 354, 375, 398 Paul Montgomery; pp. 72, 188, 193, 201, 308, 422 Chris Vallo; pp. 69, 70, 71 Heidi Chang

ISBN 978-0-7367-7279-2

Zaner-Bloser, Inc.
1-800-421-3018
www.zaner-bloser.com
Printed in the United States of America   11   12   13   14   15   19840   5   4   3   2   1

SUSTAINABLE FORESTRY INITIATIVE
Certified Chain of Custody
Promoting Sustainable Forest Management
www.sfiprogram.org

Hi, there!

We're your *Strategies for Writers* Writing Partners!

We're here to guide you step-by-step through the stages of the writing process: Prewrite, Draft, Revise, Edit, and Publish.

In each unit, we'll focus on one mode of writing: **narrative, informative/explanatory, opinion,** or **descriptive**.

Have you ever wondered what makes a good personal narrative? Or what the elements of a research report are? How about some reasons for writing an editorial or a descriptive paragraph? We'll answer those questions and more.

We'll focus on these six traits of effective writing: **Ideas, Organization, Voice, Word Choice, Sentence Fluency,** and **Conventions.** We'll explain how to apply the traits to each genre of writing, and we'll show you how the traits work together.

In each chapter, we'll first review a model writing sample. Then we'll use a rubric to score the model. Rubrics are a great way to know exactly what is expected as you plan and evaluate your writing. After that, it's your turn to write!

Narrative writing

Table of Contents

Informative/Explanatory writing

Table of Contents

Opinion writing

Table of Contents

Descriptive writing

Table of Contents

Appendices

Appendix A: Grammar Practice

Table of Contents

Narrative writing

tells a story about real or imaginary events.

Hi, my name is Jack. I'm learning all about narrative writing. I love telling stories to my friends! I also like listening to my grandfather tell me stories about when he was growing up. Now, I'm going to learn strategies for turning stories into good pieces of writing.

IN THIS UNIT

- Personal Narrative
- Biographic Sketch
- Adventure Story
- SOCIAL STUDIES CONNECTION ▷ Play
- Writing for a Test

Name: Jack

Home: Washington

Favorite Sports: soccer and hockey

Favorite Book: *S.O.R. Losers* by Avi

What's a Personal Narrative?

It's a story I write about myself!

What's in a Personal Narrative?

Narrator
That's me! The narrator is the person who tells the story.

Setting
This is where and when the story happens. It could be yesterday at my school or last year in Arizona when we took a family camping trip.

Characters
These are the people in my story. I might be the only character, or I might include other people.

Plot
It's the action! This is what happens in the story.

Tone
This is the mood I want to express to my readers. It could be funny, serious, suspenseful, or sad.

Why write a Personal Narrative?

There are plenty of reasons to write a personal narrative. Here are a few.

To Entertain
Sometimes something happens that is so exciting that I just have to share it with someone else. It's such a good story that my reader will be really entertained.

To Reflect
Sometimes, writing a personal narrative can help me think about things in my life from a different perspective.

To Inform
Some events can be really informative. I can write a personal narrative about something that happened to me. I can share the information about what I've learned.

Linking Narrative Writing Traits to a Personal Narrative

In this chapter, you will write a story about an experience you want to share. This type of narrative writing is called a personal narrative. Jack will guide you through the stages of the writing process: Prewrite, Draft, Revise, Edit, and Publish. In each stage, Jack will show you important writing strategies that are linked to the Narrative Writing Traits below.

Narrative Writing Traits

- a topic that is just the right size, not too big or too small
- details and facts that develop the narrative

- a natural and logical sequence
- a strong beginning and a satisfying ending
- transitions that signal the sequence of events

- a voice and tone that are perfect for the writing
- dialogue that, when used, sounds just right for the characters

- concrete words and phrases that describe the characters and events

- a variety of sentence lengths to make the story flow smoothly

- no or few errors in spelling, grammar, punctuation, and capitalization

Before you write, read Stephen Jensen's personal narrative on the next page. Then use the personal narrative rubric on pages 8–9 to decide how well he did. (You might want to look back at What's in a Personal Narrative? on page 4, too!)

MY LEAP FOR LOONS

Personal MODEL *Narrative*

by Stephen Jensen

first-person narrator

I'm not the outdoors type. Every time my sister Jennifer invited me to go on a canoe trip, I tried my best to get out of it. "I'm busy that weekend," I would say. Jennifer didn't give up, though. One day, I just gave in.

tone in beginning

characters

setting

A few weeks later, Jennifer and I were floating on a lake in northern Minnesota. As our paddles cut through clean waters, we pushed past green, wooded land. We never saw other people. Jennifer went wild every time she saw deer or moose drinking at the shore. One day, we heard a *whoosh* and saw an eagle swoop down to grab a fish. My sister got so excited, I thought she was going to fall out of the boat.

"Wow," I'd say, but I didn't really care. I was counting the hours until we'd pack up the car and drive home. While Jennifer went on and on about moose, I thought about a hot shower followed by a movie.

tone in middle

plot

On our last day, however, even I got excited. We heard a high-pitched wailing sound. Jennifer said "ah" softly, smiled at me, and pointed across the lake. I saw the shadow of a bird gliding slowly over the water. Then we heard a reply. It was coming from right next to our campsite.

In the fading light of day, I spotted my first loon. I couldn't take my eyes off this beautiful creature, whose wail and laugh I would hear in my mind ever after. Before nightfall, we saw many loons. Their backs were delicately etched with a checkered pattern, but their bills were shaped like daggers. Their eyes glowed a spooky red.

These amazing birds dive deep, and they can swim long distances under water. Just when I thought one had disappeared forever, it popped up halfway across the lake!

tone in end

I can't say I went totally loony for loons. However, when we were driving home, I found myself thinking more about those loons than about a shower or a movie.

Personal Narrative Rubric

Use this 6-point rubric to plan and score a personal narrative.

	6	5	4	
Ideas	The writing focuses on one experience. Interesting, descriptive details bring the experience to life for the reader.	The writing focuses on one experience. Most details bring the experience to life for the reader.	The writing focuses on one experience. More details are needed to bring the experience to life for the reader.	
Organization	The events are organized into a clear beginning, middle, and end. The sequence of events is easy to follow.	One or two events may be out of order. Most of the story is easy to follow.	Several events appear to be out of order. Part of the story is hard to follow.	
Voice	The writer uses a first-person voice to engage the reader. The tone sets the right mood.	The writer uses a first-person voice to engage the reader. The tone may not maintain the right mood.	The writer uses a first-person voice at first. The tone sets the right mood at first.	
Word Choice	Concrete, vivid language describes a clear picture for the reader.	Most language is concrete and vivid. The description is clear most of the time.	Many words are vague or too general. They do not form a clear picture.	
Sentence Fluency	Sentences vary in length and structure, making the story enjoyable to read.	Many sentences vary in length and structure. Most of the story flows.	Many sentences are different lengths and sentence structures, but they do not always flow well.	
Conventions	All sentences are complete. There are no sentence fragments.	A few errors are present, but they do not confuse the reader. All sentences are complete.	Some minor errors are noticeable, but the message is clear. A few sentences are incomplete.	

+ Presentation   The narrative is legible and neat. The title and writer's name are at the top of the page.

3	2	1	
The writing introduces one experience. Details may be too general to bring the experience to life for the reader.	The experience is not clear. Details may be weak or unrelated.	The writing is not focused. Details may be unrelated or not provided.	**Ideas**
Events may be out of order. The middle part of the story may be hard to follow.	Events are out of order. The end may be incomplete or missing.	The writing is not organized. It is impossible to follow.	**Organization**
The voice may shift to third-person in several places. The tone may be hard to determine.	The voice and/or tone may not be appropriate. Frequent shifts in voice confuse the reader.	The voice and tone are very weak or absent. The writer does not engage the reader.	**Voice**
Some words are overused or too ordinary to form a clear picture.	The words are ordinary or dull. Some are used incorrectly.	Many words are used incorrectly. The reader cannot form a picture.	**Word Choice**
Several sentences in a row have the same length or structure, making the writing less interesting.	Many sentences are the same length or structure, making the writing choppy in places.	Sentences are incomplete or unclear.	**Sentence Fluency**
Distracting errors make the text difficult to read and understand in some places. Some sentences are incomplete.	Noticeable errors confuse the reader. Some sentences are incomplete.	The writing contains many errors. Sentences are incorrect. Many sentence fragments are present.	**Conventions**

See Appendix B for 4-, 5-, and 6-point narrative rubrics.

Using the Rubric

Personal Narrative

Using the Rubric to Study the Model

Did you notice that the model on page 7 points out some key elements of a personal narrative? As he wrote "My Leap for Loons," Stephen Jensen used these elements to help him write about a personal experience. He also used the 6-point rubric on pages 8–9 to plan, draft, revise, and edit the writing. A rubric is a great tool to evaluate writing during the writing process.

Now let's use the same rubric to score the model. To do this, we'll focus on each trait separately, starting with Ideas. We'll use the top descriptor for each trait (column 6), along with examples from the model, to help us understand how the traits work together. How would you score Stephen on each trait?

Ideas

- **The writing focuses on one interesting experience.**
- **Interesting, descriptive details bring the experience to life for the reader.**

I didn't know anything about loons before I read this story, so I found his story really interesting! All of the details help me imagine Stephen's canoe trip. He paints a vivid picture of his experience by describing how he *cut through clean waters* and *pushed past green, wooded land.*

A few weeks later, Jennifer and I were floating on a lake in northern Minnesota. As our paddles cut through clean waters, we pushed past green, wooded land.

Organization

- The events are organized into a clear beginning, middle, and end.
- The sequence of events is easy to follow.

The writer tells everything in order. He starts with his sister's invitation and ends with the last day of their trip. There is a clear beginning, middle, and end. He also uses transitional words like *on our last day* that help me follow the story.

On our last day, however, even I got excited. We heard a high-pitched wailing sound.

Voice

- The writer uses a first-person voice to engage the reader.
- The tone sets the right mood.

Right from the beginning, the writer draws me into the story by using first-person point of view. It seems like he is speaking directly to me. The feelings that Stephen shares set the tone for the rest of the story.

I'm not the outdoors type. Every time my sister Jennifer invited me to go on a canoe trip, I tried my best to get out of it.

Using the Rubric to Study the Model

Personal Narrative

Word Choice

• Concrete, vivid language describes a clear picture for the reader.

When Stephen describes the loons, he uses very clear and vivid words. Even though I have never seen a loon before, I am able to picture one. Phrases such as *checkered pattern* and *shaped like daggers* give me a clear picture.

Their backs were delicately etched with a checkered pattern, but their bills were shaped like daggers.

Sentence Fluency

• Sentences vary in length and structure, making the story enjoyable to read.

Stephen uses a lot of different kinds of sentences in his personal narrative. For example, some sentences are longer and some are shorter. This helps the story flow smoothly.

In the fading light of day, I spotted my first loon. I couldn't take my eyes off this beautiful creature, whose wail and laugh I would hear in my mind ever after. Before nightfall, we saw many loons.

Conventions

- All sentences are complete.
- There are no sentence fragments.

I looked through the whole story, and every word is spelled correctly. All the sentences are capitalized and punctuated correctly. Every sentence is complete, and there are no sentence fragments.

These amazing birds dive deep, and they can swim long distances under water. Just when I thought one had disappeared forever, it popped up halfway across the lake!

⁺Presentation The narrative is legible and neat. The title and writer's name are at the top of the page.

My Turn!

Now it's my turn to write a personal narrative! I'll use the 6-point rubric on pages 8–9 and good writing strategies to help me. Follow along to see how I do it.

Prewrite

The Rubric Says   The writing focuses on one experience.

Writing Strategy   Make notes about an interesting personal experience.

My teacher said we could write about any experience that we think the rest of the class will find interesting.

I think I'll write about the day the Saddok family moved in next door to us. Many of my classmates live in big apartment buildings like mine. I'm sure they have neighbors from other countries, too. They'll probably be interested in my experience. First I'll jot down some notes on what I remember about that day.

My Notes

✔ Mrs. Saddok did not want to shake Dad's hand.

✔ Mr. Saddok put his right hand over his heart.

✔ No one said anything.

✔ We helped pick up everything.

✔ It all started with a big noise.

Apply

Think about interesting events in your life. Brainstorm some ideas and pick one event you think will be the most interesting. Jot down some notes about the event.

The Rubric Says	The events are organized into a clear beginning, middle, and end.
Writing Strategy	Make a Sequence Chain to organize my notes.

The rubric says the events in my story need to follow each other in order. I'll use a graphic organizer to put my notes in order. I've used graphic organizers before, and I think a Sequence Chain would be the best one for ordering my notes this time. A Sequence Chain helps me to place the events first, second, third, and so on.

Writer's Term

Sequence Chain
A Sequence Chain organizes events in the order in which they happen.

Sequence Chain

The Day We Met Our New Neighbors

First Event	There was a loud noise outside our door.
Second Event	We said hello and offered to help. Nobody said a word to us.
Third Event	Dad told his name and wanted to shake hands with the new neighbors.
Fourth Event	We started picking up all the things. We helped a lot.

Reflect

How does a Sequence Chain help to organize the events in a personal narrative?

Apply

Use your notes to make a Sequence Chain. Be sure to put the events in order.

Draft

Focus on **Ideas**

The Rubric Says Interesting, descriptive details bring the experience to life for the reader.

Writing Strategy Include details about the characters so the reader can form a clear picture.

✏️ **Writer's Term**

Details

Details are words or phrases that give more information about a person or event. Details make writing more interesting.

Now it's time to start writing. I'll use my notes and Sequence Chain to write my draft. I'll make sure that I focus on sharing my experience.

According to the rubric, I also need to use interesting details so my reader will understand what's happening. I'll include descriptive details about my characters that show what they're saying and doing. I want the reader to understand what we experienced.

As usual, I won't worry too much about my grammar, punctuation, and spelling. I know that I can fix errors when I edit my writing.

Proofreading Marks

⌐ Indent	∫ Take out something
≡ Make a capital	⊙ Add a period
/ Make a small letter	⊄ New paragraph
∧ Add something	SP Spelling error

[DRAFT]

The Day We Met Our New Neighbors

Noise outside the door. Jack's dad ran out, and Jack followed him.

Dad said, "Hi, do you need help?" Not a word! They just looked at us.

details

In the hallway were for strangers. The woman wore cloths I'd never seen before. The rest of the family wore unusual cloths too.

Dad held out his hand to the man Dad said, "Hi, I'm Ken Washington, and I live here." The man took Dad's hand. He shook it a little. Didn't say a word. My dad held out his hand to the woman. Turned away.

We could see that a big wooden box had split open. We helped pick up everything.

details

Reflect

Read Jack's draft. Which details help you picture what is happening?

Apply

Use your notes and Sequence Chain to write a draft. Be sure to include details that show the characters and the action in your story.

Revise

The Rubric Says The events are organized into a clear beginning, middle, and end.

Writing Strategy Check to see that the events are in order.

After writing my draft, I looked back at the rubric. It says that the events are organized into a clear beginning, middle, and end. I read my draft again. I'll follow my Sequence Chain to put the events in the correct order.

[DRAFT]

changed order of events

Dad said, "Hi, do you need help?" Not a word! They just looked at us.

In the hallway were for strangers. The woman wore cloths I'd never seen before. The rest of the family wore unusual cloths too.

Apply

Read your draft. Make sure events are in order so the story is easy to follow.

The Rubric Says	The writer uses a first-person voice to engage the reader.
Writing Strategy	Use a first-person point of view.

Writer's Term

First-Person Point of View

Point of view tells the reader who is telling the story. In a personal narrative, the point of view is **first person** because the writer is telling his or her own story. Writers using the **first-person point of view** use words such as **I, me, my, mine, we, us, our,** and **ours** to tell their story.

I have to remember that a personal narrative is my own story. My audience needs to know that I'm actually in the story. This means I need to use personal pronouns such as *I, me,* and *my* to tell my story.

[DRAFT]

My
Noise outside the door. ~~Jack's~~ dad ran out, and

I
~~Jack~~ followed him.

used first-person point of view

Reflect

Why is it important to use first-person point of view in a personal narrative?

Apply

Use personal pronouns (*I, me, my, mine, we, us, our,* and *ours*) to tell your story.

Revise

The Rubric Says   Concrete, vivid language describes a clear picture for the reader.

Writing Strategy   Use clear and specific words to tell the story.

The rubric says to use vivid language to tell my story. That means that I should use words that help the reader "see" and "hear" what is happening. I'll read through my draft again. Then I'll add clear, specific words to describe the scene. For example, the word *trunk* gives the reader a better picture than *box*.

[DRAFT]

used specific words

trunk

We could see that a big wooden ~~box~~ had split

That was the loud

crashing noise we heard.   the books that had spilled out

open. We helped pick up ~~everything~~.

clear words

Apply

Read your draft again. Look for parts that aren't clear. Use clear and specific words to make your writing clearer.

The Rubric Says   All sentences are complete.

Writing Strategy   Make sure there are no sentence fragments.

Next I'll check my spelling, punctuation, and capitalization. I will also check for sentence fragments. A sentence fragment is an incomplete thought. It needs either a subject or a predicate. I'll fix any sentence fragments I find.

[DRAFT]

At the end of the day, Mr. Saddok put his right hand over
                                                nodded
his heart, and then he ~~noded~~. Later, we learned that the
                          ∧   That was their Algerian way to say
Saddoks were from algeria. A sincere thank you.
                        ___   ∧

corrected sentence fragment

Reflect

Look at the words that Jack changed. Do they change the picture you have in your mind? Look at the edits. How did Jack fix a sentence fragment?

Apply   Conventions

Edit your draft for spelling, punctuation, and capitalization errors. Fix any sentence fragments.

For more practice writing complete sentences and fixing sentence fragments, use the exercises on the next two pages.

Complete Subject and Predicate

Know the Rule

The **complete subject** of a sentence tells who or what the sentence is about. It includes the subject and all the words that modify the subject.

> **Example:** My best friend Olivia lives in California.

A **compound subject** (two or more subjects) can share the same predicate.

> **Example:** My best friend Olivia and my cousin met in California.

The **complete predicate** of the sentence tells what happens in the sentence. It includes the verb and all the words that modify the verb.

> **Example:** We drove to the beach with her family.

A **compound predicate** (two or more predicates) can share the same subject(s).

> **Example:** My cousin and I drove to the beach with her family and dug for clams.

Practice the Rule

Number a sheet of paper from 1–10. Then write each sentence below. Circle the complete subject. Underline the complete predicate.

1. My family offered to help our neighbors with their packing.
2. They and their golden retriever were moving to California.
3. Shipping boxes were sorted by size and stacked to the ceiling.
4. My brother and I chose the room with the fewest boxes.
5. We went to the small study at the back of the house.
6. Neither of us had ever seen that many books in one bookshelf.
7. Mysteries, adventure stories, and old comic books lined three shelves.
8. My brother forgot all about packing and read a book about California.
9. I kept packing and filled six boxes.
10. I liked hearing the story and dreamed of heading west someday.

Sentence Fragments

Know the Rule

A **sentence** tells a complete thought. A sentence needs a subject (what the sentence is about) and a predicate (what the subject does).
Example:
I love living in the new apartment.

A **sentence fragment** is a group of words that is missing a subject, a predicate, or both.
Example:
Living in the new apartment.

Practice the Rule

Number a sheet of paper from 1–12. Write **F** for each sentence fragment. Write **C** for complete sentence. If the sentence is a fragment, write **S** if the subject is missing. Write **P** if the predicate is missing.

1. My new neighbors in the next apartment.
2. A huge truck began to unload boxes.
3. Looked out the window at the people outside.
4. Several men carried tables and chairs up the stairs.
5. Rested and ate their lunch under a tree.
6. Everyone came out and welcomed them to the neighborhood.
7. Cookies and lemonade.
8. Moving day turned into a celebration.
9. Played music from other countries.
10. Soon our new neighbors seemed like old friends.
11. Felt very tired.
12. Moving days can be very busy for the people moving in.

Publish

+Presentation

Publishing Strategy   Post narrative on the class bulletin board.

Presentation Strategy   Use neat handwriting or word processing.

My personal narrative is done! Now it's time to publish it. There are all kinds of ways to publish a story. I could turn my story into a book, send it to the school newspaper, or read it aloud to my class. I think I'll post my personal narrative on the class bulletin board. Because I want everyone to be able to read it, I need to make sure my writing is neat and legible. Before posting my story on the bulletin board, I read through it one last time. Here's my final checklist.

My Final Checklist

Did I—

✔ check to see that all sentences have complete subjects and predicates?

✔ make sure there are no sentence fragments?

✔ indent every paragraph?

✔ use neat handwriting or word processing?

✔ put my name on my paper?

Apply

Use the checklist to prepare a final copy. Before posting on your class bulletin board or website, add illustrations or drawings that enhance your personal narrative.

The Day We Met Our New Neighbors
by Jack

There was a loud crashing noise outside our door. My dad ran out, and I followed him.

In the hallway were four strangers. The woman wore clothes I'd never seen before. She was covered from head to toe in brightly colored cloth. The rest of the family wore unusual clothes, too.

Dad said, "Hi, do you need help?" Nobody said a word! They just looked at us as if we were from another planet! Dad held out his hand to the man. Dad said, "Hi, I'm Ken Washington, and I live here." The man took Dad's hand. He shook it a little but didn't say a word. My dad shook the man's hand, and then he held out his hand to the woman. She turned away.

We could see that a big wooden trunk had split open. That was the loud crashing noise we had heard. We helped pick up the books that had spilled out. Then Dad and I helped the family with the rest of the suitcases and trunks. Soon we knew they didn't speak English.

At the end of the day, Mr. Saddok put his right hand over his heart, and then he nodded to us all. Later, we learned that the Saddoks were from Algeria. That was their Algerian way to say a sincere thank you.

Reflect

Use the rubric to check the story. Are all the traits of a good personal narrative there? Don't forget to check your own story against the rubric on pages 8–9.

What's a Biographic Sketch?

It's a story written in third person that tells something important about someone else.

What's in a Biographic Sketch?

Basic Facts
Facts are important pieces of information, such as the person's first and last name, where he or she lives, and specific events that helped the person to become who he or she is.

Characteristics
These are the special qualities that the person has, such as courage, determination, concern for others, or talents.

Accomplishments
This is what the person has achieved. It could be winning at sports, finding success as an artist, helping others, or discovering something new.

Interesting Details
These are interesting facts about the person, such as favorite activities, how the person feels about what he or she does, and any challenges the person has faced.

Why write a Biographic Sketch?

People write biographic sketches for a lot of different reasons. Here are a few of them.

To Inspire
Some people do amazing things that I might like to do, too. It's interesting to learn how they got started, who helped them, and how they became successful.

To Admire
I may not want to do what other people have done, but I can look up to them. I might want to do a biographic sketch of a person who I think is special in some way.

To Inform
I can learn all kinds of things by finding out about another person. I might find out what it feels like to come here from another country or how someone makes music with a computer. Finding out about other people can lead to fascinating discoveries.

Linking Narrative Writing Traits to a Biographic Sketch

In this chapter, you will write a story about something that happened to someone else. This type of narrative writing is called a biographic sketch. Jack will guide you through the stages of the writing process: Prewrite, Draft, Revise, Edit, and Publish. In each stage, Jack will show you important writing strategies that are linked to the Narrative Writing Traits below.

Narrative Writing Traits

	• a topic that is just the right size, not too big or too small • details and facts that develop the narrative
	• a natural and logical sequence • a strong beginning and a satisfying ending • transitions that signal the sequence of events
	• a voice and tone that are perfect for the writing • dialogue that, when used, sounds just right for the characters
	• concrete words and phrases that describe the characters and events
	• a variety of sentence lengths to make the story flow smoothly
	• no or few errors in spelling, grammar, punctuation, and capitalization

Before you write, read Jacob Gadski's biographic sketch on the next page. Then use the biographic sketch rubric on pages 30–31 to decide how well he did. (You might want to look back at What's in a Biographic Sketch? on page 26, too!)

Listening for a Living

by Jacob Gadski

characteristic

Tim Farley should be called "Ears" Farley. That's because <u>he listens</u> all day long. In fact, he listens for a living.

basic facts

Mr. Farley works in a city called Sprintfield. Like many cities, Sprintfield has a lot of noise. Several years ago, in 2003, Mr. Farley saw an ad for a job as a "noise detective." Right away, he decided it was the job for him.

First he went for an interview. He learned the purpose of the job. It was to measure and record exactly how much noise was coming from different places in the city. He would go all around Sprintfield with a sound meter, a little machine that measured decibel levels. Decibels are units that measure sound.

interesting details

Mr. Farley got the job. During the spring of 2004, <u>he worked along the freeway and on other roads.</u> First, <u>he gathered information. Later, he focused on sounds above 80 decibels.</u> These sounds are really loud! In fact, they are louder than in most places in the United States.

accomplishments

After Mr. Farley had been working for a few months, he had a lot of information. By fall of 2004, he knew the city's major sources of noise. The worst source was the sound of car and truck traffic. The second major source was the sound of trains. The third major source was the sound of commercial and industrial activities. Soon, Mr. Farley's job included finding out how to solve the noise problems.

Mr. Farley loved to solve problems. But he learned that some were not easy to fix. In 2005 he recommended that the city put up walls to help block noise. The high walls were ugly. In 2006 he recommended that the city also plant trees and shrubs. These were attractive, but they did not block noise very well.

interesting detail

accomplishments

Mr. Farley keeps listening and looking for the answers to the city's noise problems. When it comes to his job, he is definitely "all ears!"

Biographic Sketch Rubric

Use this 6-point rubric to plan and score a biographic sketch.

	6	**5**	**4**	
Ideas	The sketch tells important events in the person's life. Interesting details make the subject come alive.	Most of the details are interesting. Most make the subject real for the reader.	More memorable details would make the subject real for the reader.	
Organization	Events are arranged in a sequence that unfolds naturally. Transition words make the sequence of events clear.	Events are arranged in a sequence that unfolds naturally. Transition words could be added in one or two places.	A few events are not in a natural sequence. Transition words are too few or are overused.	
Voice	It is clear that the writer respects the subject. The voice connects with the audience.	The voice shows that the writer respects the subject. The voice connects with the audience most of the time.	The voice sounds sincere most of the time. It fails to connect with the audience in places.	
Word Choice	Each word has a job to do, so no unnecessary words are used.	One or two unnecessary words distract the reader.	Some sentences are too wordy, distracting the reader.	
Sentence Fluency	There is a balance of short and long sentences, which makes writing clear and easy to read.	Most sentences vary in length. One or two longer sentences could be shortened.	The sentences are clear, but several sentences in a row are too long or too short.	
Conventions	Subjects and verbs agree. Forms of the verb *be* are used correctly.	There are a few minor errors in agreement and forms of *be*, but they do not confuse the reader.	Some errors in verb agreement and forms of *be* confuse the reader.	

+Presentation The sketch is neat and legible.

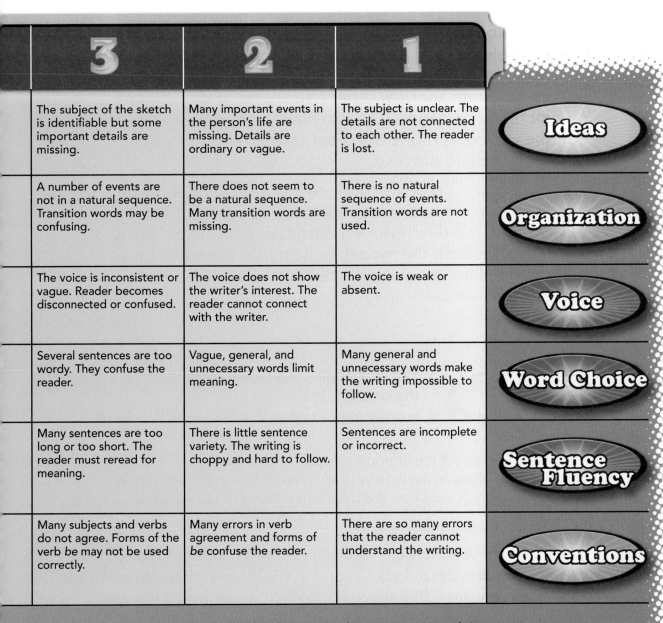

3	2	1	
The subject of the sketch is identifiable but some important details are missing.	Many important events in the person's life are missing. Details are ordinary or vague.	The subject is unclear. The details are not connected to each other. The reader is lost.	**Ideas**
A number of events are not in a natural sequence. Transition words may be confusing.	There does not seem to be a natural sequence. Many transition words are missing.	There is no natural sequence of events. Transition words are not used.	**Organization**
The voice is inconsistent or vague. Reader becomes disconnected or confused.	The voice does not show the writer's interest. The reader cannot connect with the writer.	The voice is weak or absent.	**Voice**
Several sentences are too wordy. They confuse the reader.	Vague, general, and unnecessary words limit meaning.	Many general and unnecessary words make the writing impossible to follow.	**Word Choice**
Many sentences are too long or too short. The reader must reread for meaning.	There is little sentence variety. The writing is choppy and hard to follow.	Sentences are incomplete or incorrect.	**Sentence Fluency**
Many subjects and verbs do not agree. Forms of the verb *be* may not be used correctly.	Many errors in verb agreement and forms of *be* confuse the reader.	There are so many errors that the reader cannot understand the writing.	**Conventions**

See Appendix B for 4-, 5-, and 6-point narrative rubrics.

Using the Rubric to Study the Model

Biographic Sketch

Did you notice that the model on page 29 points out some key elements of a biographic sketch? As he wrote "Listening for a Living," Jacob Gadski used these elements to help him write about another person. He also used the 6-point rubric on pages 30–31 to plan, draft, revise, and edit the writing. A rubric is a great tool to evaluate writing during the writing process.

Now let's use the same rubric to score the model. To do this, we'll focus on each trait separately, starting with Ideas. We'll use the top descriptor for each trait (column 6), along with examples from the model, to help us understand how the traits work together. How would you score Jacob on each trait?

Ideas

- **The sketch tells important events in the person's life.**
- **Interesting details make the subject come alive.**

Jacob tells all about the important events and when they happened. He begins by telling about an interesting person, Mr. Tim Farley, and his job. Notice how the details help bring the story to life.

Mr. Farley works in a city called Sprintfield. Like many cities, Sprintfield has a lot of noise. Several years ago, in 2003, Mr. Farley saw an ad for a job as a "noise detective." Right away, he decided it was the job for him.

- Events are arranged in a sequence that unfolds naturally.
- Transition words make the sequence of events clear.

The writer uses transition words to signal when things happen. The transition words *during*, *first*, and *later* in this example make the sequence of events easy to follow.

Mr. Farley got the job. During the spring of 2004, he worked along the freeway and on other roads. First, he gathered information. Later, he focused on sounds above 80 decibels.

- It is clear that the writer respects the subject.
- The voice connects with the audience.

Right away the reader can see that Jacob respects his subject. He explains why he suggests a different name for the subject.

Tim Farley should be called "Ears" Farley. That's because he listens all day long. In fact, he listens for a living.

Using the Rubric to Study the Model
Biographic Sketch

Word Choice

• Each word has a job to do, so no unnecessary words are used.

The writer does a good job of telling about Mr. Farley without using a lot of unnecessary words. Jacob has chosen his words carefully, and they work well.

Mr. Farley loved to solve problems. But he learned that some were not easy to fix. In 2005 he recommended that the city put up walls to help block noise. The high walls were ugly. In 2006 he recommended that the city also plant trees and shrubs.

Sentence Fluency

• There is a balance of short and long sentences, which makes the writing clear and easy to read.

Jacob uses lots of different kinds of sentences in his biographic sketch. For example, some sentences are longer and some are shorter. Usually, long and short sentences follow each other. This helps the story flow smoothly. It makes the biographic sketch easy to read, too.

First he went for an interview. He learned the purpose of the job. It was to measure and record exactly how much noise was coming from different places in the city.

Conventions

• Subjects and verbs agree.
• Forms of the verb *be* are used correctly.

All the subjects and verbs agree in number. Singular subjects have singular verbs, and plural subjects have plural verbs. In these sentences, the subject, *source*, is singular, so the verb, *was*, is also singular.

The worst source was the sound of car and truck traffic. The second major source was the sound of trains. The third major source was the sound of the commercial and industrial activities.

✚Presentation The sketch is neat and legible.

My Turn!

Now it's my turn to write a biographic sketch! I'll use the 6-point rubric on pages 30–31 and good writing strategies to help me. Read along to see how I do it.

Prewrite

The Rubric Says   Interesting details make the subject come alive.

Writing Strategy   Make a list of interesting questions for an interview.

My mom has a little stone bear carved by an Inuit artist. I have always wondered about the person who made it.

When my teacher asked us to write a biographic sketch, I decided to write about the Inuit artist who made that stone bear. I knew I had to gather information, so I sent the artist an e-mail with interview questions. This will help me get information about the object and give me more than just simple details like the artist's name.

Writer's Term _____

Interview

An **interview** is the process of asking questions of another person and listening to and recording that person's answers.

Questions for My Interview

✔ What kinds of objects do you make?

✔ Why do you like to carve?

✔ When did you first start to carve in stone?

✔ How did you learn to carve?

✔ What skills do you need to be a stone carver?

Apply

Think about a person you would like to write about. List interesting questions you could ask. Then interview the person.

The Rubric Says Events are arranged in a sequence that unfolds naturally.

Writing Strategy Make a Timeline to organize the important events.

I know from the rubric that organization is important. I want to find a natural order for my biographic sketch. During the interview, Mr. Aniksak, the artist, told me when the main events of his life happened and why they are important. If I put the events in the order in which he experienced them, my paper will make sense to the reader. I can put these events on a Timeline to help me stay organized.

Writer's Term

Timeline

A **Timeline** is a graph that shows events in the order in which they happened. A Timeline also shows dates.

Timeline

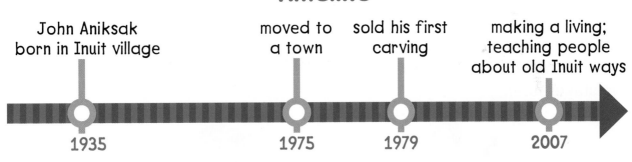

John Aniksak born in Inuit village — 1935

moved to a town — 1975

sold his first carving — 1979

making a living; teaching people about old Inuit ways — 2007

Reflect

Look at Jack's questions and Timeline. Is there enough information? Think of a few more interview questions to ask.

Apply

Look at your interview notes. Use a Timeline to arrange events in a sequence that unfolds naturally.

Draft

Focus on Organization

The Rubric Says   Events are arranged in a sequence that unfolds naturally. Transition words make the sequence of events clear.

Writing Strategy   Organize information using transition words.

Now it's time to tell the whole story. I will use the answers that Mr. Aniksak e-mailed back and my Timeline to write a draft. I am going to use my Timeline to make sure I include all the important events and when they happened. The rubric says I need to arrange the events in a sequence that unfolds naturally. I will use transition words and dates to organize the events.

Right now I'm not going to worry about writing in complete sentences or whether everything I write is spelled perfectly. I know I'll have a chance to fix grammar and spelling mistakes later.

Writer's Term

Transition Words

Transition words make a sequence of events clear. They help the writing move naturally from one event to the next.

Here are some transition words:

**after   during   finally   first   later
now   soon   then   until**

Proofreading Marks

⌐ Indent	ℓ Take out something
≡ Make a capital	⊙ Add a period
/ Make a small letter	¶ New paragraph
∧ Add something	SP Spelling error

[DRAFT]

Carving Art from Stone

John Aniksak carves stone bears, dear, seals, and other animals. He was not always a stone carver, though. Mr. Aniksak was born in an Inuit village in 1935. He and his family are from Canada. The Inuit people have lived in Canada for a very long time. It was a very different kind of life. You would be surprised. He lived very far from roads, stores, and factorys. In 1975, Mr. Aniksak moved to a town. He had to get use to a new way of life. He need a new way to earn a living. He took up carving. He found and chose stone. He learn about carving tools. He is also able to use many skills from his days in the wilderness. His knowledge of artic animals were especially importent. Mr. Aniksak learned his new skill well. In 1979, he sold his first carving, a seal. Everyone who sees his animals really like them. Many of his pieces have be sold. People from all over the country buy his carvings now.

transition words

Reflect

Are the events in Jack's draft organized in a sequence that unfolds naturally? Which transition words helped to make the sequence of events clear?

Apply

Use your interview notes and Timeline to write your own draft. Remember to use transition words.

Revise

The Rubric Says   It is clear that the writer respects the subject. The voice connects with the audience.

Writing Strategy   Use the third-person point of view.

✏️ **Writer's Term** ───

Third-Person Point of View

Writers use **third-person point of view** to tell about the experiences of others and to show that they are not part of the story. For third person, we use the person's name and words such as **he, she, him, her, his, hers, they, them,** and **theirs.**

My biographic sketch is about Mr. Aniksak. That means I need to take myself out of the writing and use third-person point of view. The rubric says that my sketch should show respect for the subject, Mr. Aniksak, and should connect to the audience. So I will use events from Mr. Aniksak's life to show why he is a special artist.

[DRAFT]

used third-person point of view

John Aniksak carves stone bears, dear, seals, and other animals. He was not always a stone carver, though.

Apply

Read your draft. Check that you have used third-person point of view throughout your biographic sketch.

The Rubric Says Each word has a job to do, so no unnecessary words are used.

Writing Strategy Take out any words that are not needed.

I reread my story and noticed that some parts were unclear. I remembered the rubric said that each word has a job to do. I should choose each word carefully. Wordy writing can be confusing to readers. I looked for unnecessary words to take out of my sketch.

[DRAFT]

took out unnecessary words

Today he still loves his work ~~as a carver~~. He ~~still~~ makes his living by
them
carving animals and ~~he also~~ uses ~~his carved animals~~ to teach people

about the old Inuit way of life.

Reflect

How do Jack's revisions improve the writing?

Apply

Read your draft again. Look for places where you can take out words that are not needed.

Revise

Focus on Sentence Fluency

The Rubric Says There is a balance of short and long sentences, which makes the writing clear and easy to read.

Writing Strategy Combine short sentences to improve flow.

The next thing I need to do is check my sentences. The rubric says I shouldn't use all short or all long sentences. So I need to go back to be sure there is variety in my sentences. I'll look for short sentences in a row to see if I can combine them, too.

[DRAFT]

combined set of short sentences

Everyone who sees his animals really like them. Many of his pieces have be, and people

sold. ~~People~~ from all over the country buy his carvings now.

Apply

Check your draft to be sure you have variety in your sentences. Revise sentences for balance and flow.

The Rubric Says	Subjects and verbs agree. Forms of the verb *be* are used correctly.
Writing Strategy	Make sure all verbs are correct.

Now I need to check for errors. I know from the rubric that I always need to check spelling, capitalization, and punctuation. I'll also make sure that all my subjects and verbs agree and that I use the correct forms of the verb *be*.

Writer's Term

Subject-Verb Agreement

Subject-Verb Agreement means that subjects and verbs must agree in number. Singular nouns or pronouns take singular verbs, and plural nouns or pronouns take plural verbs. In the present tense, singular verbs often end in **-s** or **-es**.

corrected subject-verb agreement errors

corrected form of the verb "be"

[DRAFT]

likes

Everyone who sees his animals really ~~like~~ them. Many of his pieces have been

~~be~~ sold, and people from all over the country buy his carvings now.

Reflect

Look at how Jack combined two short sentences. What do you think of the result? Look at the edits. Why did Jack make the changes?

Apply **Conventions**

Reread your work to make sure that subjects and verbs agree.

For more practice with subject-verb agreement and *be*, use the exercises on the next two pages.

Subject-Verb Agreement

Know the Rule

Add **-s** or **-es** to a regular verb in the present tense when the subject is a singular noun or **he, she,** or it.

Examples:

John throws the ball. She catches the ball.

Do not add **-s** or **-es** to a regular verb in the present tense when the subject is a plural noun or **I, you, we,** or **they.**

Examples:

We watch the game. They take pictures.

Practice the Rule

Number a separate sheet of paper from 1–12. Decide which verb in parentheses agrees with the subject. Then write the correct verb.

1. Historians (feel/feels) that art is an important part of history.

2. Civilizations (use/uses) art in many ways.

3. Early art forms (tell/tells) us much about the people who created them.

4. Art (remain/remains) an important part of any culture.

5. Artists sometimes (carve/carves) on cave walls and rocks.

6. They (learn/learns) to use certain tools.

7. Carvers must (know/knows) the final form they wish to create.

8. Carvers cannot (correct/corrects) a mistake.

9. Therefore, they usually (make/makes) a small clay model first.

10. Some artists (do/does) all the stone cutting themselves.

11. Many carvers (give/gives) the simple cutting jobs to an assistant.

12. The style of carving (change/changes) over time.

Forms of *Be*

Know the Rule

The linking verb **be** connects the subject to a noun or an adjective in the predicate. The verb **be** does not show action. It has different forms for different tenses. Use *is* or *was* after a singular subject or with the pronouns *he, she*, and *it*. Remember to use *am* after the pronoun *I*. Use *are* or *were* after a plural subject or with the pronouns *we, you*, or *they*. Remember to use *has* or *have* with *been*.

Examples:
Andy **is** tall. Andy **was** taller than I. Now I **am** taller.
They **are** in Europe. **Were** you there last year?
It **has been** rainy for days. I **have been** in the house.

Practice the Rule

Number a separate sheet of paper from 1–10. Decide which form of **be** agrees with the underlined subject. Then write the correct verb.

1. My <u>grandfather</u> (is/are) the only furniture maker in our town.
2. His furniture <u>designs</u> (is/are) beautiful.
3. Last month, my <u>grandfather and brother</u> (was/were) in England.
4. Many English <u>artisans</u> (is/are) talented wood carvers.
5. A four-poster <u>bed</u> from England (is/are) now for sale at my grandfather's store.
6. Detailed <u>carvings</u> (is/are) on the headboard, footboard, and four posts.
7. <u>Wood carving</u> (is/are) an art.
8. My <u>brother</u> (has been/have been) an apprentice wood carver for a year.
9. At first, <u>he</u> (was/were) interested in cabinet making.
10. <u>Men</u> in my family (has been/have been) furniture makers for six generations.

Publish

⁺Presentation

Publishing Strategy Share your final paper in an author's circle.

Presentation Strategy Use neat handwriting or word processing.

I have finished my biographic sketch. Now I will publish it by sharing it with my class. My classmates will be interested in hearing the story of the artist. The author's circle will be a good way to publish this piece. I need to use neat handwriting or word processing for my final copy to make it legible. I also plan to e-mail a copy to the artist. I'll use a final checklist to make sure it's ready to publish.

My Final Checklist

Did I—

✔ check to see that all subjects and verbs agree?

✔ check to see that I used the correct form of *be*?

✔ indent every paragraph?

✔ use neat handwriting or word processing?

✔ put my name on my paper?

Apply

Use this checklist for your biographic sketch. Then make a neat, final copy to share.

Carving Art from Stone
by Jack

John Aniksak carves stone bears, deer, seals, and other animals. He was not always a stone carver, though.

Mr. Aniksak was born in an Inuit village in 1935. He and his family are from Canada. The Inuit people have lived in Canada for a very long time. It was a very different kind of life. You would be surprised. He lived very far from roads, stores, and factories. His family hunted walrus and seals. They fished for salmon. They gathered roots and berries.

In 1975, Mr. Aniksak moved to a town. He had to get used to a new way of life. First, he needed a new way to earn a living. Soon, he took up carving. He found and chose stone. Then, he learned about carving tools. Now he was also able to use many skills from his days in the wilderness. His knowledge of Arctic animals was especially important.

Mr. Aniksak learned his new skill well. In 1979, he sold his first carving, a seal. Everyone who sees his carvings really likes them. Many of his pieces have been sold, and people from all over the country buy his carvings now.

Today he still loves his work. He makes his living by carving animals and uses them to teach people about the old Inuit way of life.

Reflect

Use the rubric to be sure you've used all the traits of a good biographic sketch. Then use the rubric to score your sketch.

What's an Adventure Story?

It's a tale about a character who does something exciting. It can be something that really happened to someone, or it can be made up. Most adventure stories are fiction—invented by the author.

What's in an Adventure Story?

A Problem
The story is built around a problem or challenge that has to be faced. What happens around the problem is called the **plot**.

Setting
This is when and where the story happens. It could be last week at the soccer field or in 2150 on Saturn.

I'LL SAVE YOU!

A Lead Character
This is the main person in the story. She or he must face dangers or take risks in order to solve the problem. The lead character may not look like a hero at first.

Dialogue
These are the conversations that characters in the story have. Dialogue should sound like how people talk in real life.

Why write an Adventure Story?

People write adventure stories for different reasons. Here are two good reasons to write them.

To Entertain
Adventure stories get you excited and involved. You can imagine yourself as the brave and daring hero. Both the author and the reader can enjoy solving difficult problems in an invented world. Sometimes heroes do things we would never do. This can make it fun and exciting to write about.

To Understand
Stories about heroes can help us understand others. We can learn how different people solve problems and how they find the courage to face danger.

Linking Narrative Writing Traits to an Adventure Story?

In this chapter, you will write a story about something exciting! This type of narrative writing is called an adventure story. Jack will guide you through the stages of the writing process: Prewrite, Draft, Revise, Edit, and Publish. In each stage, Jack will show you important writing strategies that are linked to the Narrative Writing Traits below.

Narrative Writing Traits

- a topic that is just the right size, not too big or too small
- details and facts that develop the narrative

- a natural and logical sequence
- a strong beginning and a satisfying ending
- transitions that signal the sequence of events

- a voice and tone that are perfect for the writing
- dialogue that, when used, sounds just right for the characters

- concrete words and phrases that describe the characters and events

- a variety of sentence lengths to make the story flow smoothly

- no or few errors in spelling, grammar, punctuation, and capitalization

Before you write, read Becky Silver's adventure story on the next page. Then use the adventure story rubric on pages 52–53 to decide how well she did. (You might want to look back at What's in an Adventure Story? on page 48, too!)

The Unexpected Voyage

Adventure **MODEL** Story

by Becky Silver

lead characters

"We never should have gone by ourselves," said Jeremy. "I'll bet we're lost."

"Don't worry," answered Samantha. "Our stop is probably next."

setting

The subway train stopped again. The doors opened. Passengers got off. New people came on. The train started up again.

dialogue

problem

"But it shouldn't take so long to get to the nature museum," said Jeremy. "When we go with Mom and Dad, it doesn't take long at all. If we don't get there soon, we're going to miss Dr. Forrest and his amazing change-of-seasons machine."

Jeremy looked out the window. By twisting a little, he could see where the train was headed. It seemed about to leave the dark underground. In a split second, the train broke into bright daylight. Two things happened at once. Samantha and Jeremy couldn't see for a few seconds because of the blinding sunlight, and the train conductor announced, "We will arrive in Brighton at 11 o'clock. No stops between here and Brighton."

Brighton! Samantha and Jeremy looked at each other in disbelief. Brighton was miles and miles from where they lived. The nature museum was just a few city subway stops from home.

dialogue

"I know!" yelled Jeremy. "We must have gotten on the train in the wrong direction! We should have been traveling south, and instead we've been going north!"

Jeremy thought he should be upset, but instead he felt like laughing. The train was speeding toward Brighton. He and Samantha looked out the window. The train raced along so fast that the sunny world seemed to change color as they moved. Trees that had been green now flamed red and gold. Acorns fell from branches and thudded against the train. Fluffy white clouds danced in an endless, brilliant blue sky.

problem solved

"We can take the train back once we get to Brighton," said Jeremy.

"Meanwhile, we can watch the real change-of-seasons show from right here!" exclaimed Samantha.

Adventure Story Rubric

Use this 6-point rubric to plan and score an adventure story.

	6	**5**	**4**	
Ideas	Story elements work together successfully. Details develop the characters, setting, and plot.	Story elements work together most of the time. Most details develop the characters, setting, and plot.	Story elements work together some of the time. Some details do not develop the characters, setting, and plot.	
Organization	The sequence unfolds naturally. The story builds to a high point, and the problem is solved at the end.	Most of the details build to a high point and problem solution.	Some more details are needed to develop the problem and solution for the reader.	
Voice	The voice is strong and natural. The dialogue makes the characters sound real.	The voice is strong. The dialogue sounds real most of the time.	The voice is clear much of the time. Some dialogue does not sound real.	
Word Choice	The writer uses strong verbs that make the story come to life and convey events precisely.	The writer uses strong verbs most of the time. One or two are weak.	The writer uses weak verbs most of the time. Some events are not conveyed well.	
Sentence Fluency	Sentence beginnings are varied. Transition words connect ideas.	Most of the sentence beginnings are varied and use transition words to connect ideas.	Many sentences are varied. The writer uses a few transition words.	
Conventions	Quotation marks, apostrophes, and other punctuation marks are used correctly.	A few minor errors in punctuation are present, but they do not distract the reader.	Some punctuation errors are noticeable but do not confuse the reader.	

✛ Presentation The story is legible and neat. Illustrations, if used, are complete.

3	2	1	
Story elements don't work together in the middle. Details may not be related in this part of the story.	Story elements don't work together. Details are unrelated or incomplete.	The writing is not a story. Details are not provided.	**Ideas**
Some details do not build to the high point and cause confusion. The solution is not clear.	The story does not build to a high point. The solution does not follow the problem.	The writing is not organized. It is difficult or impossible to follow.	**Organization**
The voice is inconsistent. The dialogue sounds flat or forced at times.	The voice is insincere and/or vague. Dialogue is awkward or missing.	The voice is absent. There is no dialogue.	**Voice**
The writer's verbs are weak or repeated. Events are not conveyed well.	The verbs are weak or confusing. They make the story dull.	Overused, poorly chosen, or repetitive verbs cause confusion.	**Word Choice**
Several sentences sound the same and slow the flow. Few transitions are used.	Some sentences are short and choppy. Some are too long. There are no transitions.	Sentences are incomplete or incorrect. The writing is impossible to follow.	**Sentence Fluency**
Noticeable punctuation errors confuse the reader. Some quotation marks are used incorrectly.	The writing contains many errors. Quotation marks are missing. Apostrophes may be missing or used incorrectly.	Many major errors in punctuation make the text difficult to read and understand. The writer is not in control of conventions.	**Conventions**

See Appendix B for 4-, 5-, and 6-point narrative rubrics.

Using the Rubric to Study the Model

Adventure Story

Did you notice that the model on page 51 points out some key elements of an adventure story? As she wrote "The Unexpected Voyage," Becky Silver used these elements to help her write an exciting story. She also used the 6-point rubric on pages 52–53 to plan, draft, revise, and edit the writing. A rubric is a great tool to evaluate writing during the writing process.

Now let's use the same rubric to score the model. To do this, we'll focus on each trait separately, starting with Ideas. We'll use the top descriptor for each trait (column 6), along with examples from the model, to help us understand how the traits work together. How would you score Becky on each trait?

- **Story elements work together successfully.**
- **Details develop the characters, setting, and plot.**

The beginning of the story sets up everything. I find out that the story has two main characters, Jeremy and Samantha, and that the setting is a subway train. Later on, I find out the problem. The subway train is not taking Jeremy and Samantha to the nature museum. The action of the story shows the train taking Jeremy and Samantha farther and farther away.

The subway train stopped again. The doors opened. Passengers got off. New people came on. The train started up again.

Organization
- The sequence unfolds naturally.
- The story builds to a high point, and the problem is solved at the end.

I know right away that Jeremy and Samantha are worried that something is wrong. They will have to solve the problem by themselves. Their worry builds until they find out just how far from the museum they are. I wonder what I would do if I were alone on a train going the wrong way.

Brighton! Samantha and Jeremy looked at each other in disbelief. Brighton was miles and miles from where they lived. The nature museum was just a few city subway stops from home.

Voice
- The voice is strong and natural.
- The dialogue makes the characters sound real.

I could tell right away that Jeremy and Samantha are about my age. They are trying to get to the museum by themselves. Jeremy reacts the way that I might react if I were lost. The opening dialogue shows that Jeremy is upset. Samantha's words show that she is trying to stay calm.

"We never should have gone by ourselves," said Jeremy. "I'll bet we're lost."
"Don't worry," answered Samantha. "Our stop is probably next."

Using the Rubric to Study the Model

Adventure Story

Word Choice

• The writer uses strong verbs that make the story come to life and convey events precisely.

The writer uses some strong verbs that really pull me into the story. Don't you think that the sentences below are much stronger than *the trees were green and gold* and *acorns fell on the train*?

The train raced along so fast that the sunny world seemed to change color as they moved. Trees that had been green now flamed red and gold. Acorns fell from branches and thudded against the train. Fluffy white clouds danced in an endless, brilliant blue sky.

Sentence Fluency

• Sentence beginnings are varied.
• Transition words connect ideas.

Becky's story moves along at a good pace. The dialogue helps, but she also varies sentences in the narrative part to hold the reader's interest. Look at the way she uses a short sentence to highlight the sudden events. She also uses the transition words *In a split second* to connect her ideas.

By twisting a little, he could see where the train was headed. It seemed about to leave the dark underground. In a split second, the train broke into bright daylight. Two things happened at once.

Conventions

- Quotation marks, apostrophes, and other punctuation marks are used correctly.

I've checked the whole story and can't find any spelling or punctuation errors. All the direct quotations are punctuated correctly. They begin and end with quotation marks. A new paragraph shows when another person is speaking.

"We can take the train back once we get to Brighton," said Jeremy.

"Meanwhile, we can watch the real change-of-seasons show from right here!" exclaimed Samantha.

✛Presentation The story is neat and legible. Illustrations, if used, are complete.

My Turn!

Now it's my turn to write an adventure story! I will use the 6-point rubric on pages 52–53 and good writing strategies to help me. Read along to see how I do it.

Prewrite

The Rubric Says   Story elements work together successfully.

Writing Strategy   Choose a lead character and a problem.

I know that all the parts of an adventure story need to work together. First I need to choose my lead character and a problem to solve. Then I'll think about the setting, other characters, and the plot.

I'd like to make myself the lead character. I know! My problem can be when a little girl in our neighborhood is surrounded by bees. I can make myself the hero of a story about rescuing her! I'll start by writing down the problem I plan to solve in my story.

The Problem

A little girl is surrounded by bees. She is so scared she cannot move.

Apply

Have you ever solved a problem that would make a good adventure story? Write out the problem. Then write out how you solved it.

The Rubric Says	The sequence unfolds naturally. The story builds to a high point, and the problem is solved at the end.
Writing Strategy	Make a Story Map to organize the events.

I have written down a problem for my adventure story. A Story Map can help me organize my story. By focusing on the problem, I can think about using a natural sequence to build my story to a high point, or climax. That's what keeps the reader interested.

Story Map

Setting   **Where** a road near my house
When an August day

Characters Amy Sisson, Mom, Michael, and me

Problem Amy Sisson is scared by bees.

Plot Events Michael and I hear Amy screaming.
We run to help her.
I am scared, but I act like Superkid.
I help Amy get away from the bees.

Ending Amy gets home safely.

Writer's Term

Story Map
A Story Map organizes the setting, characters, problem, events, and ending of a story.

Reflect

Look at Jack's Story Map. How did it help him organize his ideas?

Apply

Make a Story Map to organize your story. List ideas that show the setting, character(s), problem, events, and ending.

Draft

The Rubric Says	The voice is strong and natural. The dialogue makes the characters sound real.
Writing Strategy	Write dialogue that sounds like real people.

I'm ready to start writing my adventure story. I'll use my Story Map to make sure my story has a clear setting, characters, problem, events, and ending.

I will use my story-telling voice to connect with the reader. To make my story come to life, I need to remember to use dialogue. My teacher says, "Your characters should sound like real people talking." I want my readers to understand my characters and hear their voices, too.

I'll do my best with grammar and spelling as I write, but I won't worry about mistakes right now. I know I'll have a chance to fix them later.

Writer's Term

Dialogue
In a story, **dialogue** refers to the conversation between characters.

[DRAFT]

Just Call Me Superkid

setting

It was a hot day. I was playing superhero with my little brother. I was pretending to take on the bad guy when Michael herd something. He yelled, "What's that noise?"

dialogue

"I dont hear anything," I said.

I listened, too. Sure enough, I herd someone. Then I saw little Amy Sisson standing in the road.

event

I saw what was making Amy scream. A beehive had fallen about five feet from her. Bees were everywhere. Amy was frozen with fear. I knew she wouldn't be able to move by herself. I had to help her.

clear problem

high point

I was plenty scared of those bees, too, but I was five years older than Amy. More important, I felt like Superkid.

Reflect

Read Jack's draft. In what ways does it hold your interest?

Apply

Use your Story Map to write your own draft. Don't forget to include dialogue.

Revise

The Rubric Says   Details develop the characters, setting, and plot.

Writing Strategy   Use details to help the reader imagine the characters, setting, and plot.

The rubric reminds me to use details to develop the setting, characters, and plot. I'll add a few details in the beginning to help my reader picture me better. In this story, I'm a character playing a character!

I also want to make sure that all the details—including the dialogue—build interest and suspense. Then the reader will want to keep reading to find out what happens next.

[DRAFT]

long, August
It was a hot day. I was playing superhero with my little brother.

I was dressed up as Superkid.
I was pretending to take on the bad guy when Michael herd

something. He yelled, "What's that noise?"

I went on chasing the make-believe theif.

"I dont hear anything," I said.

added details

Apply

Read your draft. Find places where you can add details about the character, setting, and plot.

Revise

The Rubric Says	The writer uses strong verbs that make the story come to life and convey events precisely.
Writing Strategy	Change common verbs to exciting action verbs.

When I read the rubric again, I saw that strong verbs build suspense. I'll go through my draft and replace dull verbs with exciting verbs. For example, I can write *yelled* instead of *said*. See how much more interesting my story becomes when I use action verbs? Now I just have to make sure that my verbs agree with their subjects.

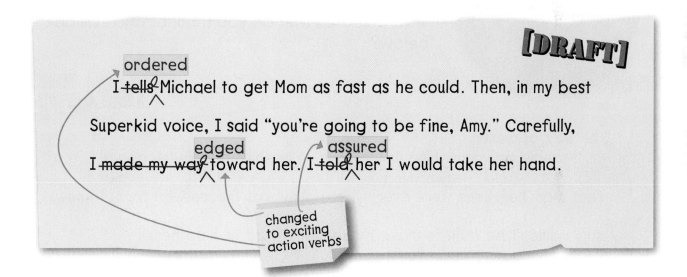

[DRAFT]

ordered

I ~~tells~~ Michael to get Mom as fast as he could. Then, in my best

Superkid voice, I said "you're going to be fine, Amy." Carefully,

edged   assured

I ~~made my way~~ toward her. I ~~told~~ her I would take her hand.

changed to exciting action verbs

Reflect

Look at Jack's verbs. How do they help to build suspense in this part of the story?

Apply

Look at your draft again. Replace dull or overused verbs with exciting ones. Make sure these verbs agree with their subjects.

Revise

The Rubric Says   Sentence beginnings are varied. Transition words connect ideas.

Writing Strategy   Use transition words to begin sentences.

Now it's time to check all my sentences. The rubric says I need to vary my sentence beginnings. By putting transition words at the beginning of a sentence, I do two things. One is that I vary the way my sentences begin, which helps to make them flow smoothly. The other thing is that I give the reader a little bit more information. What do you think of my revision below?

[DRAFT]

revised longer sentence

As we got closer,
   I saw what was making Amy scream. A beehive had fallen about five
      ∧   , and   swarming   so   that
feet from her. Bees were everywhere. Amy was frozen with fear. I knew
              ∧   ∧   ∧   ∧

she wouldn't be able to move by herself. I had to help her.

added transition

short sentence gets reader's attention

Apply

Check your draft again. Revise sentences to vary the rhythm and get your reader's attention.

| **The Rubric Says** | Quotation marks, apostrophes, and other punctuation marks are used correctly. |
| **Writing Strategy** | Check the punctuation. |

I'm ready to check my spelling, punctuation, and capitalization. I also need to check all the dialogue in my story. Each direct quotation should begin and end with quotation marks. A new paragraph shows that a new speaker is talking. I'll also check to make sure I've punctuated contractions correctly.

Writer's Term

Direct Quotations

Direct quotations give the exact words of someone speaking. Put quotation marks around a direct quotation. Also, indent the first line of each new speaker.

[DRAFT]

"I dont hear anything," I said. I went on chasing the make-believe

thief

~~theif~~.

indented for new speaker

"Stop running! Michael shouted. "i hear someone screaming."

Reflect

Look at the way Jack revised his sentences. What do you think of his revisions? Look at Jack's edits. Are they correct? How do quotation marks help you read the dialogue?

Apply   Conventions

Edit your draft carefully. Check that you have used quotation marks and apostrophes correctly.

For more practice using quotation marks and apostrophes, use the exercises on the next two pages.

Direct Quotations

Know the Rule

A **direct quotation** is a speaker's exact words. Use quotation marks at the beginning and end of the speaker's exact words. Use a comma to separate the speaker's exact words from the rest of the sentence. Begin a direct quotation with a capital letter and add end punctuation before the last quotation mark.

Examples:
The child shouted, **"W**ow**!"**
"I'm not surprised**,"** the man replied.

Practice the Rule

Number a sheet of paper from 1–10. Read each sentence. If the sentence has errors in punctuation, rewrite the sentence correctly. If the sentence uses punctuation correctly, write **Correct**.

1. Our teacher said, "Kids, we're going to visit an apiary."

2. What's an apiary asked Gina.

3. "An apiary is a place where a beekeeper keeps hives of bees" explained Mr. Frantz.

4. Mr. Frantz continued, "The beekeeper takes care of the bees and then harvests honey from each hive."

5. Ryan asked, But aren't bees dangerous? Won't we get stung?"

6. Mr. Frantz said, "No, we won't be touching any hives, and the bees are peaceful if we leave them alone.

7. "Beekeepers wear protective clothes when it's time to harvest the honey," Mr. Frantz said.

8. "Oh, I see" exclaimed Gina.

9. "That way the beekeeper can't get stung," she added.

10. A beekeeper's work is very interesting said Mr. Frantz.

Apostrophes

Know the Rule

A **possessive noun** shows ownership. Add an **apostrophe (')** and an *-s* to a singular noun to show ownership.

> **Example:**
> I hurried to **Ms. Garcia's** classroom.

Add an apostrophe after the *-s* of a plural noun to show ownership.

> **Example:**
> I found the **students'** books in her room.

Use an apostrophe and an *-s* if the plural noun doesn't end in an *-s*.

> **Example:**
> The **children's** room was a mess!

A **contraction** is made of two words put together, like *doesn't* (does not). An apostrophe takes the place of one or more letters.

> **Example:**
> The children **hadn't** (had not) cleaned up their art project.

Practice the Rule

Rewrite each sentence on a separate sheet of paper, adding apostrophes as needed. Sometimes two apostrophes are needed in one sentence.

1. Theres a nest of bees in Tonys backyard.
2. Tonys father saw it, but he hasnt disturbed it.
3. We arent allowed to go anywhere near it.
4. Theyve seen many bees swarming around.
5. Tonys mom is worried that well get stung.
6. I havent been stung by a bee, yet!
7. Im pretty sure that its painful, though.
8. For now, well just have to play in our backyard.
9. As far as we know, there isnt a bees nest at my house.
10. Weve looked all around, but we cant find one.

Publish

+Presentation

Publishing Strategy Publish my story as a big book to read to younger students.

Presentation Strategy Add illustrations that support and clarify the story elements.

My adventure story is done! Now it's time to publish it. There are many ways to publish a story. I think that younger students would really enjoy my adventure, so I think I'll publish it in a big book. A big book has the story's words printed very large. Each page has a picture that shows what is happening in the story. I need to be sure my writing is neat and my illustrations are clear. Before I draw the pictures and make the big book, I want to check my story one last time. Here's the checklist I will use.

My Final Checklist

Did I—

✔ use quotation marks for direct quotes?

✔ use apostrophes correctly?

✔ use illustrations to support my story?

✔ use neat handwriting or word processing?

✔ put my name on my story?

Apply

Use the checklist to prepare your final copy for publication.

Just Call Me Superkid
by Jack

It was a long, hot August day. I was playing superhero with my little brother. I was dressed up as Superkid, and I was pretending to take on the bad guy when Michael heard something. He yelled, "What's that noise?"

"I don't hear anything," I said. I went on chasing the make-believe thief.

"Stop running!" Michael shouted. "I hear someone screaming."

I listened, too. Sure enough, I heard someone. Then I saw little Amy Sisson standing in the road. Michael and I flew down the street to her to find out what was wrong.

As we got closer, I saw what was making Amy scream. A beehive had fallen about five feet from her, and bees were swarming everywhere. Amy was so frozen with fear that I knew she wouldn't be able to move by herself. I had to help her.

I was plenty scared of those bees, too, but I was five years older than Amy. More important, I felt like Superkid. I didn't get any closer to the bees, but I did tell Amy quietly in my most soothing voice that I could help her. I told her not to be afraid. Superkid was there.

I ordered Michael to get Mom as fast as he could. Then, in my best Superkid voice, I said, "You're going to be fine, Amy." Carefully I edged toward her. I assured her that I would take her hand. I said that we would walk slowly backward from the hive. I don't know how I made myself go to Amy, but I did. The first step was the hardest. Soon Mom was there, taking steps backward with us. Only five minutes later, we were far away from the buzzing bees, walking Amy to her front door.

As soon as Amy got inside, she cried, "Daddy! Daddy! Superkid saved me!" Well, I guess Amy was right.

Reflect

Use the rubric to check Jack's story. Which trait is strongest? Weakest? Be sure to use the 6-point rubric on pages 52–53 to score your own story.

What's a Play?

It's a piece of writing that tells a story that can be acted out.

What's in a Play?

Stage Directions
Stage directions are written instructions that tell the characters and stage crew what to do. Stage directions also help explain the characters, setting, and plot.

Story Elements
A play has characters, a setting, and a plot, just like a story. Most plays have at least two characters. The setting tells where and when the play takes place. The plot is the action of the play.

Dialogue
The story is told through dialogue. Dialogue is the conversation, or spoken lines, among characters. Spoken lines come after the name of the character that is speaking.

Problem
Like all good stories, a good play has a problem the characters must overcome or solve.

Why write a Play?

There are many reasons to write a play. Here are two important ones.

To Explore

Writing a play helps me explore and experience a specific time period. For example, I can write a play about the life of an important historical character or an exciting event I learned about in my social studies class.

To Entertain

When you put on a play, you get to work with other people. It's fun to write and act out a play with friends.

Linking Narrative Writing Traits to a Play

In this chapter, you will write a story that can be acted out. This type of narrative writing is called a play. Jack will guide you through the stages of the writing process: Prewrite, Draft, Revise, Edit, and Publish. In each stage, Jack will show you important writing strategies that are linked to the Narrative Writing Traits below.

Narrative Writing Traits

Ideas
- a topic that is just the right size, not too big or too small
- details and facts that develop the narrative

Organization
- a natural and logical sequence
- a strong beginning and a satisfying ending
- transitions that signal the sequence of events

Voice
- a voice and tone that are perfect for the writing
- dialogue that, when used, sounds just right for the characters

Word Choice
- concrete words and phrases that describe the characters and events

Sentence Fluency
- a variety of sentence lengths to make the story flow smoothly

Conventions
- no or few errors in spelling, grammar, punctuation, and capitalization

Before you write, read Lanie Song's play on the next three pages. Then use the play rubric on pages 78–79 to decide how well she did. (You might want to look back at What's in a Play? on page 72, too!)

A Short Trip to Tomorrow

by Lanie Song

CHARACTERS — characters

Maggie, sister, age 9
Jay, brother, age 11
Ellen, mother
Bob, father

SETTING: Seattle, Washington, April 1962 — setting

SCENE 1: *Family sitting around the kitchen table, just finishing dinner*

Ellen: Did you hear the news? The World's Fair just started! Maggie and I heard the announcement over the radio. President Kennedy opened it.

Bob: Is he in town?

Maggie: (*excitedly*) No, he announced it over the telephone. And guess what? This is the coolest! They used a sound from a faraway star to open the fair. The star is light years away! — dialogue

Jay: (*rolling his eyes, not impressed*) There you go again, Maggs, dreaming about outer space. Get real. — stage direction

Ellen: It's true, Jay. Your sister has it right. Scientists intercepted sound waves that came from a distant star. The sound began over 10,000 years ago!

Bob: I'd say that goes along with the space age theme of the fair.

Maggie: I'll say! There are all kinds of really neat things to do, like you can take a rocket trip through outer space, and…

Jay: (*interrupts Maggie*) Yeah, and you can wait in long lines with gazillions of other people. Sheesh! That's not for me.

Bob: (*rubs his chin, thinking*) Jay's probably right, there. Many people from all over the world will be coming to Seattle for the World's Fair. Still, it isn't every day it's in your own hometown. What do you think, Ellen? Should we take the kids and go?

Ellen and Maggie: Yes!!

Bob: What about it, Jay?

Jay: (*sighs and mumbles*) I guess so. But I don't have to like it!

Play MODEL

SCENE 2: *Family boards a monorail train car that rides high above the city's streets*

Maggie: This is so cool!

Ellen: It sure is! They built this train for the fair, you know, to transport people from the city's center.

Bob: I heard that the engineers designed it to carry 10,000 people to their destinations in an hour!

Jay: (*grumpily*) What did I tell you about the crowds and long lines?

Maggie: (*excitedly, with face pressed against window*) Hey! I can see Puget Sound! And the Cascade Mountains! I love being high in the sky!

stage direction

Ellen: We're here! Let's see the fair!

Bob: (*as family exits the monorail*) Now listen, kids. Stick together and keep track of each other. We don't want to spend any time in line at the lost children's booth! C'mon! Let's head for the Science Pavilion first.

Maggie: Sounds good to me! C'mon, Jay!

Jay: (*reluctantly follows*) Sheesh! I've never seen so many people in one place. Get a look at those lines!

SCENE 3: *After tour, family gathers outside pavilion*

Bob: Well, what did you make of that tour, kids?

Maggie: Oh, Dad, that was the coolest—an imaginary rocket ride! I saw Jupiter, Saturn, Neptune, and Pluto! We must have traveled millions of miles!

Ellen: And all we had to do was look up at the world's largest movie screen to take that journey.

Maggie: Whaddya think, Jay? Worth the wait in line?

Jay: (*staring up at a tall structure in the distance*) Maggs, quit buggin' me! It was just a dumb movie, not a real ride.

stage direction

Bob: Just imagine, Son. Ordinary people like us will travel in spaceships someday, much in the same way we travel by car today.

Maggie: You tell him, Dad! John Glenn just orbited Earth three times a couple of months ago! That's a first, but I don't think it will be the last!

Ellen: And don't forget President Kennedy said that we'd have a real "man on the moon" by the end of this decade.

Jay: (*still staring up in amazement*) Man, look at that Space Needle!

Maggie: (*follows Jay's gaze*) Wow! Doesn't the top look like a flying saucer?

Jay: (*still looking up, in awe*) It sure does!

Maggie: The Space Needle is the tallest building west of the Mississippi. It's as high as a 60-story building! And, did you know that it's the symbol of this fair?

Ellen: (*turns to speak to Bob*) Honey, at the top of the Needle is a restaurant. What do you say we take the kids there for lunch?

Bob: My thoughts, exactly, but there's probably a very long line. Do you think Jay will mind?

Jay: (*responds loudly as he overhears his parents*) Who cares? We have to go up there!

Bob: (*looks up at the Needle as he thinks out loud*) …heard that the restaurant spins slowly…makes a complete circle every hour or so…should get some great views from up there. (*then says loudly*) All right, Team Mercury, let's go!

SCENE 4: *Family sitting at a lunch table in the Space Needle's restaurant, far above the fairgrounds*

Jay: (*looking out the window at the action far below*) This really is cool, isn't it Dad?

Bob: Sure is, Jay. This really does feel like the future, doesn't it?

Maggie: It's exciting to think about what could happen in the future and what the world will be like then.

Jay: Well, I saw an exhibit sign for The World of Tomorrow. Let's go there next.

Ellen: (*smiling*) Jay, that's a great idea, but are you sure you won't mind the long line?

Jay: (*smiling back*) Mom, it's not every day the World's Fair comes to my hometown!

Play Rubric

Use this 6-point rubric to plan and score a play.

	6	**5**	**4**	
Ideas	Details are accurate and appropriate for the situation in the play. Dialogue and stage directions develop the characters, setting, and plot.	Details are accurate and appropriate. Most of the dialogue and stage directions develop the play.	Details are mostly accurate and appropriate. Some of the dialogue and stage directions develop the play.	
Organization	Events happen in logical sequence. The script has a clear beginning, middle, and end.	Most events happen in logical sequence. The script has a clear beginning, middle, and end.	Some events are out of sequence. The script does not have a clear beginning, middle, and end.	
Voice	The dialogue sounds natural and fits the characters.	Most of the dialogue sounds natural and fits the characters.	Dialogue sounds unrealistic or awkward in a few places.	
Word Choice	Concrete words and phrases describe the events precisely.	Concrete words and phrases describe most events precisely.	Concrete words and phrases describe most events.	
Sentence Fluency	A variety of sentence types helps the dialogue flow smoothly.	Most sentences help the dialogue flow smoothly.	Several sentences in a row share the same structure.	
Conventions	The writing contains no errors. All commas are used correctly.	A few errors are present but do not confuse the reader. Commas are used correctly.	Several errors confuse the reader. Some commas are used incorrectly.	

✛Presentation   Play format is easy to follow.

3	2	1	
Some details are accurate and appropriate. Little dialogue and too few stage directions develop the play.	Some details are not accurate or appropriate. Dialogue or stage directions are confusing or not related.	Details are not accurate or not related. Dialogue or stage directions are not included.	**Ideas**
Some events are out of sequence. The end may be incomplete.	Many events are out of sequence in the middle. The end is incomplete.	The writing is not organized as a script.	**Organization**
Dialogue sounds unrealistic or awkward in many places.	Dialogue does not fit the characters.	Characters are described but do not speak.	**Voice**
A few concrete words and phrases describe the events.	The words are repetitious, misused, or don't describe the events precisely.	Word choice is limited. Some words are wrong. The events are not described.	**Word Choice**
Many sentences share the same structure.	Sentences are poorly written. Flow is interrupted.	Sentences are incomplete or incorrect.	**Sentence Fluency**
Many errors confuse the reader. Commas are used incorrectly.	Serious errors stop the reader. Commas are missing.	The writing has not been edited.	**Conventions**

See Appendix B for 4-, 5-, and 6-point narrative rubrics.

Using the Play Rubric to Study the Model

Did you notice that the model on pages 75–77 points out some key elements of a play? As she wrote "A Short Trip to Tomorrow," Lanie Song used these elements to help her write her play. She also used the 6-point rubric on pages 78–79 to plan, draft, revise, and edit the writing. A rubric is a great tool to evaluate writing during the writing process.

Now let's use the same rubric to score the model. To do this, we'll focus on each trait separately, starting with Ideas. We'll use the top descriptor for each trait (column 6), along with examples from the model, to help us understand how the traits work together. How would you score Lanie on each trait?

Ideas

- **Details are accurate and appropriate for the situation in the play.**
- **Dialogue and stage directions develop the characters, setting, and plot.**

Most of the action in Lanie Song's play takes place at the 1962 World's Fair in Seattle, Washington. She includes many factual, interesting details that help bring this time period to life. You also learn about the time period through the dialogue, the conversations among the characters in the play. The scene changes and stage directions help explain the events, too.

SCENE 1: *Family sitting around the kitchen table, just finishing dinner*

Ellen: Did you hear the news? The World's Fair just started! Maggie and I heard the announcement over the radio. President Kennedy opened it.

Bob: Is he in town?

Maggie: (*excitedly*) No, he announced it over the telephone. And guess what? This is the coolest! They used a sound from a faraway star to open the fair. The star is light years away!

Jay: (*rolling his eyes, not impressed*) There you go again, Maggs, dreaming about outer space. Get real.

Organization

- Events happen in logical sequence.
- The script has a clear beginning, middle, and end.

The play opens as the family talks about the World's Fair coming to their hometown. In Scene 2, the family rides the monorail to the fair and decides to visit the Science Pavilion. In Scene 3, they decide to have lunch at the new Space Needle. I could really follow the action in each scene, and the order of events makes sense. I like the way the writer ties the ending to the beginning, too. In the end, Jay decides long lines aren't so bad after all.

Ellen: (*smiling*) Jay, that's a great idea, but are you sure you won't mind the long line?

Jay: (*smiling back*) Mom, it's not every day the World's Fair comes to my hometown!

Voice

- The dialogue sounds natural and fits the characters.

Maggie shows excitement about going to the fair, but Jay complains at first. I think their dialogue really shows their personalities by what they say and how they say it. All of their conversations sound like real people talking.

I also like the way the writer includes casual expressions, such as *yeah*, *gazillions*, and *sheesh*. She even has the characters interrupt one another, just like real people sometimes interrupt each other. This makes the dialogue sound very realistic.

Maggie: I'll say! There are all kinds of really neat things to do, like you can take a rocket trip through outer space, and...

Jay: (*interrupts Maggie*) Yeah, and you can wait in long lines with gazillions of other people. Sheesh! That's not for me.

Using the play Rubric to Study the Model

Word Choice

- Concrete words and phrases describe the events precisely.

Maggie and Jay are about my age and use words that I use. I noticed that their parents use more precise words. For example, Ellen uses the words *transport* and *city center*, and Bob uses *engineers, designed,* and *destinations.* Their words give clear, accurate information about the fair.

Maggie: This is so cool!

Ellen: It sure is! They built this train for the fair, you know, to transport people from the city's center.

Bob: I heard that the engineers designed it to carry 10,000 people to their destinations in an hour!

Jay: (*grumpily*) What did I tell you about the crowds and long lines?

Maggie: (*excitedly, with face pressed against window*) Hey! I can see Puget Sound! And the Cascade Mountains! I love being high in the sky!

Sentence Fluency

- A variety of sentence types helps the dialogue flow smoothly.

In the dialogue, some sentences make statements, others ask questions, and some show excitement, just like real conversations. I noticed that the sentences vary in length, too. They kept my interest and moved the play along at a good pace.

Bob: Well, what did you make of that tour, kids?

Maggie: Oh, Dad, that was the coolest—an imaginary rocket ride! I saw Jupiter, Saturn, Neptune, and Pluto! We must have traveled millions of miles!

Ellen: And all we had to do was look up at the world's largest movie screen to take that journey.

Conventions
- **The writing contains no errors.**
- **All commas are used correctly.**

It's clear to me that the writer edited her play carefully. Her spelling, punctuation, and capitalization are correct. I noticed that she placed commas where they are needed, too. I also noticed that Lanie used a word processor to prepare her final copy.

Bob: Just imagine, Son. Ordinary people like us will travel in spaceships someday, much in the same way we travel by car today.

Maggie: You tell him, Dad! John Glenn just orbited Earth three times a couple of months ago! That's a first, but I don't think it will be the last!

Ellen: And don't forget President Kennedy said that we'd have a real "man on the moon" by the end of this decade.

✚Presentation Play format is easy to follow.

My Turn!

Now it's my turn to write a play. I'll use the 6-point rubric on pages 78–79 and good writing strategies to help me. Follow along to see how I do it.

Prewrite

The Rubric Says   Details are accurate and appropriate for the situation in the play.

Writing Strategy   Choose a topic for the play. Then collect details that fit the story.

We are studying state history in social studies. So my teacher has asked us each to write a play about moving to Washington. I will need to do some research to find accurate details in order to make my play realistic. I can go to the library to find books and articles. I can also go to reliable websites on the Internet for pictures about my topic. I might even visit a travel agency for brochures that show places to visit. I'll remember to take good notes and keep track of my sources as I collect my ideas.

My Topic—
Moving to Tacoma, Washington

✔ Tacoma is the third-largest city in Washington.

✔ It's a port city that exports and imports goods.

✔ Native Americans call Mt. Rainier *Tacobet*, meaning "mother of the waters."

✔ The first steam train reached Tacoma in 1873.

✔ Tacoma became known as City of Destiny.

Apply

Get ready to write your play. Choose a topic you want to explore. Then list the details you know about it. Collect more details from books, the Internet, and other good sources. Be sure to take good notes and keep track of your sources.

The Rubric Says   Events happen in logical sequence.

Writing Strategy   Use a Story Map to plan a play.

A play is a special form of a story. It has the same parts—a setting, interesting characters, and a good plot. My teacher suggested using a Story Map. A Story Map will help me plan the events of the play in order.

Writer's Term

Story Map
A **Story Map** organizes the setting, characters, problem, action, and end of a story.

Story Map

Setting   Where Tucson, Arizona   **When** Present time

Characters Marissa, Ethan, Ms. Crane

Problem Marissa tells Ethan that she is moving away. She doesn't want to go and lose her friends.

Action Ethan wants to cheer up Marissa. He heads to the library to find out about Tacoma, Washington.

End Ethan tells Marissa what he learns and helps change her mind about moving.

Reflect

Look at Jack's Story Map. How will it help him write a play?

Apply

Plan your play. Use a Story Map to organize your ideas for the setting, characters, problem, action, and end.

Draft

Focus on Word Choice

The Rubric Says   Concrete words and phrases describe the events precisely.

Writing Strategy   Choose words and phrases to convey ideas precisely.

I think I'm ready to draft my play now. I can use my notes and Story Map to help me get started.

Choosing the right words is always important, but it's especially important when writing a play. Everything the characters say has to give precise information to the audience about the characters, the setting, and the plot.

> **Writer's Term**
>
> **Play Format**
> Write the speaker's name and a colon before each spoken line or set of lines. Place stage directions in parentheses. Notice that dialogue in a play is not enclosed in quotation marks. Lines that carry over to the next line are indented so that the speakers' names stand out.

Since I'm writing about the state of Washington, there may be some precise words I can use in my play, like *port* (a harbor where ships load and unload goods) or *salmon canneries* (processing plants for fish). These words tell about specific things that are found there, and they add factual information to my play.

As I write my draft, I'll use a word processor so that I can format the play. I'll also try to avoid making mistakes, but I know I can fix them later when I edit. Here's my draft.

[DRAFT]

Destiny, Here I Come!

SCENE 1: *Marissa's house*

Marissa: My life is ruined!

Ethan: Why? What happened?

Marissa: My mom just told me that we're moving. Oh, Ethan, I don't...
I won't...

Ethan: What? Moving? Where?

Marissa: Washington! We have to start packing. But I don't want to go!

Ethan: Which city are you moving to?

Marissa: Tacoma. I guess it's pretty big, but not as big as Tucson, my
mom said.

Ethan: Well it's no desert. Tucson's far from an ocean gets almost no rain and
hardly changes with the seasons. I hear it rains a lot in Washington, and
everything's green in the summer. I bet Tacoma's air smells like the sea.

Marissa: But Ethan I like it here!

precise words describe the topic

SCENE 2: *School library*

Ethan: Hi, Ms. Crane.

Ms. Crane: Hi, Ethan.

Ethan: I'd like to find out everything I can about Tacoma, Washington. My
friend Marissa is moving there.

Ms. Crane: Yes, she did mention moving when she returned her books. She
seemed pretty upset, and she didn't stay to visit like she usually does.
Let's see if we can find some facts about Tacoma that might make her
feel better.

Ethan: Wow! There are several books and articles right here.

Reflect

Read the beginning of Jack's
draft. How does it follow the
format of a play?

Apply

Use your notes and Story Map to
write your draft.

Revise

Focus on **Ideas**

The Rubric Says   Dialogue and stage directions develop the characters, setting, and plot.

Writing Strategy   Put details in the dialogue and stage directions.

The rubric reminds me how important the dialogue and stage directions are in a play. A play uses fewer words than a story to let the reader know when and where the action takes place, or who the characters are and what they are like. I need to add this information to Scene 1. I'll use my imagination and add interesting details.

Writer's Term

Dialogue and Stage Directions

Dialogue is what characters say to each other.

Stage Directions tell how characters look or what they do on stage.

[DRAFT]

SCENE 1: *Marissa's house*
       (sees Ethan and tries not to cry) ← added details in stage directions
Marissa: My life is ruined!
          ∧

Ethan: Why? What happened?
       (rubs her eyes with her sleeve)
Marissa: My mom just told me that we're moving. Oh, Ethan,
          ∧
       I don't... I won't...

                                            added details in dialogue

Ethan: What? Moving? Where?
          She starts a new job there next month.
Marissa: Washington! We have to start packing. But I don't
                  ∧
       want to go!

Apply

Read your draft. Look for places to add details to the dialogue and stage directions.

Revise

The Rubric Says   The script has a clear beginning, middle, and end.

Writing Strategy   Let the readers know what's happening right away.

I looked back at the rubric. The play should begin with as much information as possible so that the reader knows where the play takes place and learns something about the characters. It should also tell what the play is going to be about and the problem the characters are facing.

Writer's Term

Beginning
The **beginning** of a play grabs the reader's attention. It makes the reader eager for the play to unfold.

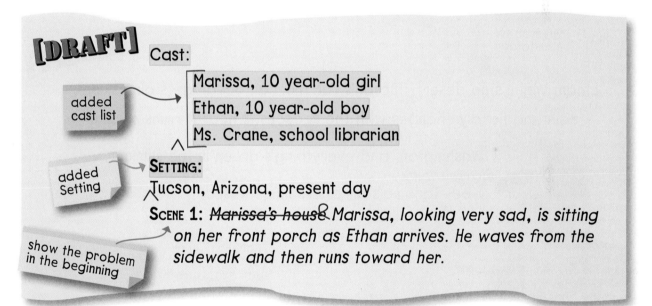

[DRAFT]

Cast:

added cast list →

Marissa, 10 year-old girl

Ethan, 10 year-old boy

Ms. Crane, school librarian

added Setting →

SETTING:

Tucson, Arizona, present day

SCENE 1: ~~Marissa's house~~ *Marissa, looking very sad, is sitting on her front porch as Ethan arrives. He waves from the sidewalk and then runs toward her.*

show the problem in the beginning →

Reflect

Look at Jack's revisions. How do they inform the reader?

Apply

Look at your draft again. Be sure to tell where the story takes place and list the characters. Also, make sure to present the problem in the beginning.

Revise

Focus on  Sentence Fluency

The Rubric Says	A variety of sentence types helps the dialogue flow smoothly.
Writing Strategy	Choose punctuation for effect.

As I read my draft aloud, I found a part that just didn't flow. The rubric reminds me to use a variety of sentence types. I'll use different types of sentences and punctuation to show emotion and help move the play along.

Writer's Term

Sentence Types

A **statement** gives information.

An **interrogative** sentence asks a question.

An **exclamatory** sentence shows strong feeling.

changed statement to an exclamation to add emotion

[DRAFT]

Ethan: Well it's no desert! Tucson's far from an ocean gets almost no rain and hardly changes with the seasons. I hear it rains a lot in Washington, and everything's green in the summer. Do you think I bet Tacoma's air smells like the sea?

changed statement to a question to add interest

Apply

Read your draft aloud. Be sure the dialogue is expressive and flows smoothly.

The Rubric Says   The writing contains no errors. All commas are used correctly.

Writing Strategy   Check to make sure commas are used correctly.

I'm finally ready to check my spelling, capitalization, and grammar. The rubric reminds me to check that I used commas correctly. I need to add commas in the part I just revised.

Writer's Term

Commas

Commas are used to separate items in a list of three or more items. The last comma goes before the the word **and** or the word **or**.

Commas are used after introductory words such as **Yes, No,** or **Well.** Place commas around a person's name when the person is being spoken to.

Ethan: Well, it's no desert! Tucson's far from an ocean, gets almost no rain, and hardly changes with the seasons. I hear it rains a lot in Washington, and everything's green in summer. Do you think the air smells like the sea?

added necessary commas

Marissa: But, Ethan, I like it here!

[DRAFT]

Reflect

Edit your draft carefully. Did you use commas correctly? Look at the changes Jack made to his sentences. Is his punctuation correct? Does it help you tell how the characters should speak?

Apply   *Conventions*

Look at your draft again. Be sure to tell where the story takes place and list the characters. Also make sure to present the problem in the beginning.

For more practice with commas, use the exercises on the next two pages.

Commas in a Series

Know the Rule

A series is a list of three or more words or phrases. Commas are used to separate the items in a series. The last comma in a series goes before the word *and* or the word *or*.

Example:
Pike Place Market in Seattle sells fish, produce, cheese, **and** herbs.

Practice the Rule

Number a sheet of paper from 1–10. Rewrite each sentence correctly, and insert commas where they belong.

1. The market buzzes with the activities of merchants shoppers and visitors.
2. Farmers come to sell their fresh berries greens herbs and vegetables.
3. Pike Place Market closes only for Thanksgiving Christmas and New Year's Day.
4. Diners can go there to eat breakfast lunch or dinner.
5. Fruits grown in Washington State include apples cherries plums and peaches.
6. Cheese is made using milk from a cow goat or sheep.
7. Fish found in Washington include salmon trout and sturgeon.
8. The fish are caught in lakes rivers and oceans.
9. Bakeries at the market sell pastries cheesecakes breads and muffins.
10. You can buy creamed honey spreads made from wildflowers huckleberries raspberries or cherries.

Commas After Introductory Words

Know the Rule

Use a **comma** to show a pause in a sentence. When a sentence begins with an **introductory word**, such as *Yes, No,* or *Well*, put a comma after that word. If a sentence includes someone's name and the sentence is spoken to that person, use one or two commas to separate the person's name from the rest of the sentence.

Examples:
Nick, have you ever been to Washington?
Yes, I've been to many beautiful places in Washington.

Practice the Rule

Number a sheet of paper from 1–10. Rewrite each sentence correctly, and insert commas where they belong.

1. Keri didn't you go hiking in Mt. Rainier National Park?
2. No my family and I went on trails in and around Mt. Olympus.
3. Rita you wouldn't believe the beautiful views along the way!
4. Well I would really like to go to the San Juan Islands someday.
5. Yes that would be a great place to go whale watching.
6. Rudi have you ever gone on a river cruise down the Columbia River?
7. No but I hope to some day.
8. Well I think Washington is the most beautiful place in the world.
9. For once Keri I agree with you.
10. I appreciate that Rudi!

Publish

+Presentation

Publishing Strategy Publish copies of my play for classmates to perform.

Presentation Strategy Use a computer to format the play.

My play is finished! I've decided that I would like my classmates to perform it. Maybe we'll even record our performance as a podcast or videotape it! I'll check the formatting to be sure that I put the speakers' names in dark print and indented the lines. I'll also make sure I used italics for the stage directions. Here's the checklist I used to prepare my final copy.

My Final Checklist

Did I—

✔ use commas and other punctuation correctly and effectively?

✔ edit and proofread carefully?

✔ include the title of the play and my name at the top?

✔ make a neat final copy in play format?

Apply

Use Jack's checklist to prepare your final copy. Ask your classmates to act out your play.

Destiny, Here I Come!
by Jack

CHARACTERS:

Marissa, ten-year-old girl

Ethan, ten-year-old boy

Ms. Crane, school librarian

SETTING: Tucson, Arizona, present day

SCENE 1: *Marissa, looking very sad, is sitting on her front porch as Ethan arrives. He waves from the sidewalk and then runs toward her.*

Marissa: (*sees Ethan and tries not to cry*) My life is ruined!

Ethan: Why? What happened?

Marissa: (*rubs her eyes with her sleeve*) My mom just told me that we're moving. Oh, Ethan, I don't... I won't...

Ethan: (*very surprised*) What? Moving? Where?

Marissa: Washington! She starts a new job there next month. We have to start packing. (*stomps her foot with each word*) But I don't want to go!

Ethan: Which city are you moving to?

Marissa: Tacoma. I guess it's pretty big, but not as big as Tucson, my mom said.

Ethan: Well, it's no desert! Tucson's far from an ocean, gets almost no rain, and hardly changes with the seasons. I hear it rains a lot in Washington, and everything's green in the summer. Do you think Tacoma's air smells like the sea?

Marissa: But, Ethan, I like it here! I don't want to lose all my friends! (*runs into the house, leaving Ethan standing alone on the porch*)

Ethan: (*thinks out loud*) I must find a way to help Marissa!

SCENE 2: *School library. Ethan heads straight for Ms. Crane's desk.*

Ethan: Hi, Ms. Crane. Can you help me?

Ms. Crane: Hi, Ethan. What can I do for you?

Ethan: I'd like to find out everything I can about Tacoma, Washington. My friend Marissa is moving there.

Ms. Crane: Yes, she mentioned that yesterday when she returned her books. She seemed pretty upset about it. Let's see if we can find some facts about Tacoma that might cheer her up.

(They use the library's computer to search for information on Tacoma.)

Ethan: Wow! There are several books and articles here.

(Both walk to shelves under the windows.)

Ms. Crane: Here's a book on Tacoma's railroad and coal-mining days and another on its early lumber and fishing industries.

Ethan: Thanks, Ms. Crane!

Ms. Crane: *(reaches for a travel magazine behind the checkout desk)* And here's a recent article about Tacoma titled "City of Destiny." Will these give you a good start?

Ethan: *(looks through the materials and smiles)* Absolutely! This is awesome! Thanks, Ms. Crane!

SCENE 3: *Marissa's house, after school the next day*

Ethan: *(knocks on front door, soft at first, then louder)* Marissa, are you home?

Marissa: It's you! You came back! I thought maybe when I left you on the porch you'd never... *(clears throat)* I'm just packing some of my stuff. It'll take me awhile, in case you wanted to go and do something.

Ethan: That's okay. I just came over to see how you were doing. Guess what? I've been busy, too.

Marissa: Doin' what?

Ethan: Well, first I want to say that I think you're very lucky!

Marissa: Why?

Ethan: Because Tacoma is a great place to live, that's why! But here's the best part. You will find your destiny!

Marissa: What are you talking about?

Ethan: I'm talking about Tacoma! It's called City of Destiny!

Marissa: What's destiny?

Ethan: Destiny means following your path, Marissa.

Marissa: *(her eyes light up a little)* Well, I guess I like that idea. But how do you know Tacoma's called City of Destiny?

Ethan: Oh, I found out some really cool things about the city.

Marissa: OK, Mr. Knows-a-Lot, what exactly did you find out that might change my mind about moving?

Ethan: Well, did you know that in the late 1800s the Northern Pacific Railway connected the Great Lakes to Puget Sound right there in Tacoma? That's when they started calling it City of Destiny.

Marissa: *(looks surprised and pleased)* Cool...

Ethan: A lot of new settlers headed out there then. The city began booming with industry. Sawmills, coal mines, lumberyards, and salmon canneries opened and hired a lot of people. Tacoma's an important port city. It still exports and imports many goods.

Marissa: *(looking more interested)* What else did you find out about Tacoma?

Ethan: Well, Tacoma got its name from its first settlers, Native Americans. Tacobet is their name for Mt. Rainier. It means "mother of the waters."

Marissa: Wow, maybe *your* destiny will bring you to Tacoma, Ethan! Thank you for all the great info! I guess moving won't be so bad after all. Can you stay for supper? I'll ask! *(she runs inside and calls out happily)* Mom! Ethan says I'm ready to follow my destiny!

Reflect

How well did Jack follow the play rubric? Use the rubric on pages 78–79 to score your own play, too.

Narrative test writing

Read the Writing Prompt

Every writing test starts with a writing prompt. Most writing prompts have three parts:

Setup This part of the writing prompt gives you the background information you need to get ready for writing.

Task This part of the writing prompt tells you exactly what you're supposed to write: a story about what happened in the castle.

Scoring Guide This part tells how your writing will be scored. To get the best score, you should include everything listed in this part.

Remember the rubrics you've been using in this book? When you take a writing test, you don't always have all the information that's on a rubric. But the scoring guide is a lot like a rubric. It lists everything you need to think about to write a good paper. Many scoring guides will include the six important traits of writing that are in all of the rubrics we've looked at:

 Ideas  Organization  Voice

 Word Choice  Sentence Fluency  Conventions

Suppose your family told you that you were moving to a new place. When you pulled up to your new home, this is what you saw.

Write a story about what happened over the next few months after you moved in.

Be sure your story
- includes interesting details to develop the plot and characters.
- grabs the audience's attention at the beginning.
- uses first-person point of view.
- uses exact words to describe the experience precisely.
- has a variety of sentence lengths.
- has correct grammar, spelling, and punctuation.

Writing Traits
in the Scoring Guide

The scoring guide in the prompt on page 99 has been made into this chart. Does it remind you of the rubrics you've used? Not all prompts include all of the writing traits, but this one does. Use them to do your best writing. Remember to work neatly and put your name on each page!

 • **Be sure your story includes interesting details to develop the plot and characters.**

 • **Be sure your story grabs the audience's attention at the beginning.**

 • **Be sure your voice connects with the audience. Use first-person point of view.**

 • **Be sure to use exact words to describe the experience precisely.**

 • **Be sure to vary your sentence lengths.**

 • **Be sure your story has correct grammar, spelling, and punctuation.**

Look at Marta Simmons' story on the next page. Did she follow the scoring guide?

My New HOME

by Marta Simmons

Do you ever imagine yourself living like royalty? I used to dream I was a princess in a castle. Life would be so perfect.

Then one day last year, it happened. We were moving, but I hadn't seen our new house yet. I just knew it would be bigger than our old apartment. Mom and Dad piled us all in the car and we headed off. After we had been driving for a while, Mom turned and said, "Close your eyes. It's just around the next corner." Then when she said to open our eyes, I couldn't believe what I saw.

It was a castle, like the kind you see in movies or read about in fairy tales with knights and princesses living in it. It had tall towers, a drawbridge, and a moat with alligators!

My family moved into the castle that day. We didn't need any of our stuff from our old house, since we started wearing clothes from long ago when the castle was built. Instead of going to school, we had a tutor to teach us in the castle.

After a few weeks, I began to get kind of bored. There were servants to do all the chores, and there were no kids my age.

Each day seemed to pass more and more slowly. Sometimes I spent hours counting the stones that made up the turret where I'm sure they used to keep misbehaving princesses. I'd pile old rugs on the floor trying to get a glimpse of what was over the wall that separated the courtyard from the rest of the neighborhood.

Our new home was so big that a game of hide-and-seek with my sisters lasted all day. I missed my friends and I missed my old room in my old apartment, even though I had shared it with my sisters.

Then one day, my parents called us all together. They said, "We decided we're not really castle people. We're moving back."

Well, you never saw a group of kids get ready so fast in your life. In minutes Jessie, Anna, Katie, and I were packed and ready to go. We drove back to our old building. It was just like when we left it.

Now, I can't wait to go back to school tomorrow. And I can't wait to sleep in my old room—sisters and all. Sometimes you really just need to get away from home to appreciate it.

Using the Scoring Guide to Study the Model

Now, let's use the scoring guide to check Marta's writing test, "My New Home." See if you can find examples from her writing to show how well she did on each part of the scoring guide.

- **The story includes interesting details to develop the plot and characters.**

The scoring guide says to use details to develop the story. Marta's details reveal her characters and the action.

After we had been driving for a while, Mom turned and said, "Close your eyes. It's just around the next corner." Then when she said to open our eyes, I couldn't believe what I saw.

- **The story grabs the audience's attention at the beginning.**

The scoring guide reminds you to keep the audience in mind as you write and be sure to get its attention. Marta starts her story with a question that grabs the audience's attention.

Do you ever imagine yourself living like royalty? I used to dream I was a princess in a castle. Life would be so perfect.

Voice

- **The story uses first-person point of view to connect with the audience.**

The scoring guide tells you to use first-person point of view. Marta puts herself in her story by using words like *I* and *my*. Also, notice how she speaks directly to the reader.

After a few weeks, I began to get kind of bored. There were servants to do all the chores, and there were no kids my age.

Word Choice

- **The story uses exact words to describe the experience precisely.**

Marta uses phrases like "counting the stones" and "misbehaving princesses" that really help the reader picture her and follow the events. Read what she wrote.

Each day seemed to pass more and more slowly. Sometimes I spent hours counting the stones that made up the turret where I'm sure they used to keep misbehaving princesses.

Using the Scoring Guide to Study the Model

• The story has a variety of sentence lengths.

The scoring guide reminds you to use a variety of sentence lengths. Marta uses both long and short sentences. They move the story along and keep the reader's interest.

Then one day, my parents called us all together. They said, "We decided we're not really castle people. We're moving back."

• The story has correct grammar, spelling, and punctuation.

Looking back at the scoring guide, you can see the reminder to check grammar and spelling. You should look for any mistakes that you often make, such as problems with commas. Marta seems to have caught all of the grammar and spelling mistakes. Her final copy doesn't have any errors.

Planning My Time

Before giving us a writing test prompt, my teacher tells us how much time we'll have to complete the test. I'll think about how much time I have. Then I'll divide the time up into the different parts of the writing process. I'll also make sure I give myself some time to study the writing prompt. Look at how I've divided my time into four steps.

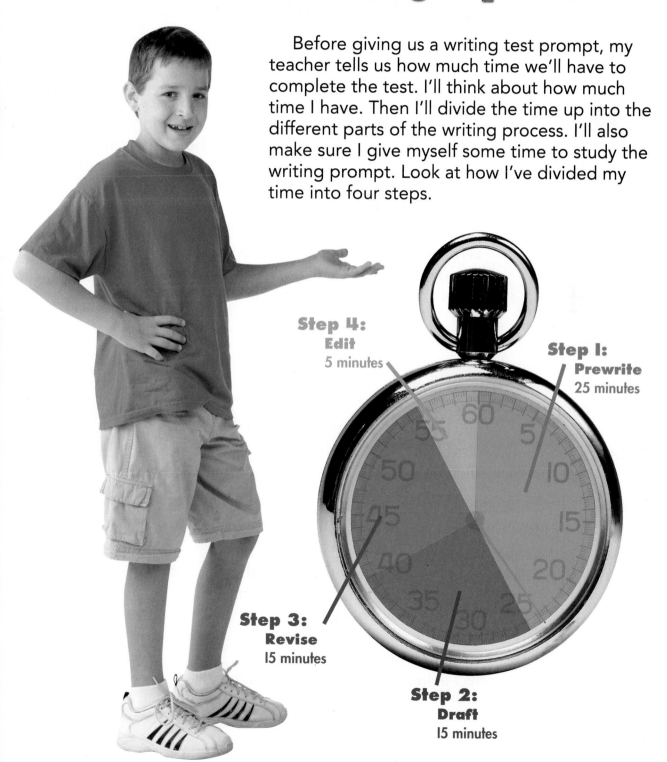

Step 4:
Edit
5 minutes

Step 1:
Prewrite
25 minutes

Step 3:
Revise
15 minutes

Step 2:
Draft
15 minutes

Prewrite

Focus on **Ideas**

Writing Strategy   Study the writing prompt to find out what to do.

Once I have my writing prompt, I study it and make sure I know exactly what I'm supposed to do. Usually a writing prompt has three parts. You should find and label the setup, task, and scoring guide on your prompt, just like I did below. Then you can circle key words that tell what kind of writing you need to do. I circled the picture of the clown. This is who I will be writing about. I also circled *Write a story* because it tells what kind of writing I'll be doing. Finally I circled *what happened* because I need to tell what the clown did.

My Writing Test Prompt

Setup — Suppose you arrived at school to find that your teacher wasn't there. Instead you saw this person in your classroom.

Task — (Write a story) about (what happened) at school during the next week with this person in your classroom.

Scoring Guide — Be sure your story
- includes interesting details to develop the plot and characters.
- grabs the audience's attention at the beginning.
- uses first-person point of view.
- uses exact words.
- has a variety of sentence lengths.
- has correct grammar, spelling, and punctuation.

Next, I'll think about how the scoring guide relates to the six writing traits I've studied in the rubrics. Not all of the traits will be included in every scoring guide, but I need to remember them all to write a good story.

Ideas

- **Be sure your story includes interesting details to develop the plot and characters.**

I want to make sure that my details reveal the action and my characters.

Organization

- **Be sure your story grabs the audience's attention at the beginning.**

I have to make a good first impression. I don't want the reader to think my story is boring!

Voice

- **Be sure your voice connects with the audience. Use first-person point of view.**

I am going to put myself in the story so my reader will know it's true.

Word Choice

- **Be sure to use exact words to describe the experience precisely.**

My descriptions need to be clear so I don't confuse my reader.

Sentence Fluency

- **Be sure to vary your sentence lengths.**

I will use a variety of sentence lengths and well-written dialogue so my story moves along at a good pace.

Conventions

- **Be sure your story has correct grammar, spelling, and punctuation.**

Whenever I write anything, I need to check grammar, spelling, and punctuation!

Prewrite

Focus on **Ideas**

Writing Strategy Respond to the task.

I've learned that writers always gather information before they begin writing. When you write to take a test, you can gather information from the writing prompt. Let's take another look at the task in the writing prompt, since this is the part of the prompt that explains what I'm supposed to write. Remember, you won't have much time when writing for a test! That's why it's really important to think about how you'll respond before you begin to write.

I know that I have to write a story. I need to tell what happened at school when a clown was in my classroom. I think jotting down some notes will help, but I have to do it quickly!

Task — Write a story about what happened at school during the next week with this person in your classroom.

Notes

- The clown trips people with his big feet.
- The clown takes over the class.
- The clown gets us in trouble.

Apply

Before you start writing, think about how you'll respond to the task in your writing prompt. Then you can jot down some notes to help you gather information.

Prewrite

Writing Strategy Choose a graphic organizer.

I don't have a lot of time, so I need to start organizing my ideas. First I need to pick the right organizer for my writing. I'm writing a story, so a Story Map is a good prewriting tool. The Story Map will help me get the basics of my story down, like when and where it takes place and what happens. Some of the information comes right out of the setup and task in my writing prompt.

Setting Where in school
         When last week

Characters circus clown, my class

Problem A circus clown takes over the class.

Plot Events The circus clown keeps getting us in trouble.
          People trip on his big feet.
          We have to show him how to act in school.
          He honks his nose when we get the right answers.

Ending The circus clown learns how to behave in school.

Reflect

Look at the Story Map. Will Jack be in the story? Are the events in order?

Apply

Choose the best graphic organizer for the assignment. Fill it with important details such as characters, setting, and plot.

Prewrite

Focus on **Organization**

Writing Strategy Check the graphic organizer against the scoring guide.

In a test, you don't always get much time to revise. Prewriting is more important than ever! So before I write, I'll check my Story Map against the scoring guide in the writing prompt.

Setting **Where** in school

When last week

Characters circus clown, my class

Problem A circus clown takes over the class.

Plot Events The circus clown keeps getting us in trouble.

People trip on his big feet.

We have to show him how to act in school.

He honks his nose when we get the right answers.

Ending The circus clown learns how to behave in school.

Ideas

- Be sure your story includes interesting details to develop the plot and characters.

That's in the Characters and Plot Events parts of my Story Map.

Organization

- Be sure your story grabs the audience's attention at the beginning.

This isn't in my Story Map, but that's okay. I'll try a few different ways to write my beginning and choose the best one.

Voice

- Be sure your voice connects with the audience and uses first-person point of view.

I need to remember to use a first-person voice all the way through.

Word Choice

- Be sure to use exact words to describe the experience precisely.

I need to make sure I use exact words to clearly describe each event in my Story Map.

Sentence Fluency

- Be sure to vary your sentence lengths.

I will remember to vary the sentences to keep the story moving.

Conventions

- Be sure your story has correct grammar, spelling, and punctuation.

I need to check grammar, spelling, and punctuation when I edit my draft.

Reflect

Does Jack's Story Map follow the scoring guide? In which ways?

Apply

Before you begin writing, be sure you understand what to do.

Draft

Focus on **Ideas**

Writing Strategy Use interesting details.

My story needs to include details about the characters, setting, and plot. Details will help the reader understand the story better and hold the reader's attention. Look at the details I include about our substitute teacher.

[DRAFT]

The Substitute

details about setting

A big surprise was waiting for us last Monday morning. Our teacher had told us she would be out all week, so we weren't surprised to find a substitute teacher when we got to school. We were surprised at the kind of sub we had, though.

details about events

Mr. Foot introduced himself to the class. We couldn't beleive it he was a clown! He was bald on top. He wore baggy pants.

details about character

[DRAFT]

We started doing math. Each time one kid answered a math problem right, Mr. Foot honked his nose. It made a beep sound. We didn't know what to make of Mr. Foot. At first we tried to act cool, like nothing special was going on. But then Mr. Foot looked sad, so we started giggling at the funny things he did. Once, as we were walking down the hall, he stuck out his big shoes and tripped the librarian. (she didn't get hurt.) We all started laughing and she told the principal that our class was out of control.

We had a class meeting at resess. We decided that we would teach Mr. Foot how to act in school. When he pulled out a frog, we ignored it and handed him a piece of chalk.

We stopped laughing at his nose honking, so he stopped doing it. And we told him that the librarian did not like his joke. By the end of the week Mr. Foot had learned his lesson. And we couldn't wait for things to get back to normal when the teacher came back.

details about character

Reflect

Read the draft. Which details help you picture the character Mr. Foot?

Apply

Details about characters, setting, and plot help the reader understand the story better. Interesting details will hold the reader's attention.

Revise

Focus on Organization

Writing Strategy   Get the reader's attention at the beginning.

Every story needs a good beginning, middle, and end. I can use the information from my Story Map to write all three sections. Looking at the scoring guide, I see that it's very important to get the audience's attention at the beginning. Starting the story with a question can get the reader's attention right away.

[DRAFT]

Did you ever wish something really amazing would happen? ◄ *grab the reader's attention*
∧ A big surprise was waiting for us last Monday morning. Our

teacher had told us she would be out all week, so we weren't

surprised to find a substitute teacher when we got to school. We

were surprised at the kind of sub we had, though.

Apply

Questions are a good way to get a reader's attention. Try to use a question at the beginning of your story.

Writing Strategy   Use first-person point of view.

    I'll read my draft again to make sure I used the first-person point of view. By using the personal pronouns *I*, *me*, *my*, *we*, *us*, and *our*, I make the readers feel as if they are part of my story. These are the same pronouns that I use when I talk to people. They make my writing voice sound like me and connect with my readers all the way through.

[DRAFT]

    By the end of the week Mr. Foot had learned his lesson. And we couldn't wait for things to get back to normal when ~~the~~ our teacher came back.

> changed to first-person point of view

Reflect

Look at Jack's change. Why did he change *the* to *our*?

Apply

Use first-person point of view to tell your story to the reader.

Revise

Writing Strategy   Choose words and phrases to convey ideas precisely.

Okay, I'll read my paper again. Is there anything I need to make clearer? The rubrics in this unit had a lot of tips on making my writing clear, so I know several strategies I could use. The scoring guide says to use exact words to describe each event. I'll look for vague words to replace with precise words to give my audience a clearer picture of the events.

[DRAFT]

We started doing math. Each time one kid answered a math

It sounded like a bicycle horn.

problem right, Mr. Foot honked his nose. ~~It made a beep sound.~~

We didn't know what to make of Mr. Foot.

used precise words

Apply

Read your draft. Replace dull words with vivid ones to create a clear picture for the reader.

Writing Strategy Check the grammar, spelling, capitalization, and punctuation.

The scoring guide says to use correct grammar and spelling. I also need to check my capitalization and punctuation. When I planned my time, I left plenty of time to check for these kinds of errors.

The Substitute
by Jack

Did you ever wish something really amazing would happen? A big surprise was waiting for us last Monday morning. Our teacher had told us she would be out all week, so we weren't surprised to find a substitute teacher when we got to school. We were surprised at the kind of sub we had, though.

Mr. Foot introduced himself to the class. We couldn't ~~beleive~~ believe it ⊙ he was a clown! He was bald on top with orange hair that stuck out over his ears. He wore baggy pants with purple and green polka dots. He kept pulling ~~handkercheifs~~ handkerchiefs and flowers out of his pockets.

Apply

Every time you write for a test, you need to check your grammar, spelling, capitalization, and punctuation.

[FINAL DRAFT]

We started doing math. Each time one kid answered a math problem right, Mr. Foot honked his nose. It sounded like a bicycle horn. We didn't know what to make of Mr. Foot. At first we tried to act cool, like nothing special was going on. But then Mr. Foot looked sad, so we started giggling at the funny things he did. Once, as we were walking down the hall, he stuck out his big shoes and tripped the librarian. (she didn't get hurt.) We all started laughing, and she told the principal that our class was out of control. Would we all get in trouble?

recess

We had a class meeting at resess. We decided that we would teach Mr. Foot how to act in school. When he pulled out a frog, we ignored it and handed him a piece of chalk.

We stopped laughing at his nose honking, so he stopped doing it. And we told him that the librarian did not like his joke. By the end of the week, Mr. Foot had learned his lesson. And we couldn't wait for things to get back to normal when our teacher came back.

Reflect

How do proofreading marks help a writer keep an eye on the clock?

We're finished! That wasn't so bad! Remember these important tips when you write for a test.

TEST TIPS

1. **Study the writing prompt before you start to write.** Most writing prompts have three parts: the setup, the task, and the scoring guide. The parts probably won't be labeled. You have to figure them out for yourself!

2. **Make sure you understand the task before you start to write.**
   - Read all three parts of the writing prompt carefully.
   - Circle key words in the task part of the writing prompt that tell what kind of writing you need to do. The task might also identify your audience.
   - Make sure you know how you'll be graded.
   - Say the assignment in your own words to yourself.

3. **Keep an eye on the clock.** Decide how much time you will spend on each part of the writing process and try to stick to your schedule. Don't spend so much time on prewriting that you don't have enough time left to write.

4. **Reread your writing. Compare it to the scoring guide at least twice.** Remember the rubrics you have used all year? A scoring guide on a writing test is like a rubric. It can help you keep what's important in mind.

5. **Plan, plan, plan!** You don't get much time to revise during a test, so planning is more important than ever.

6. **Write neatly.** Remember: If the people who score your test can't read your writing, it doesn't matter how good your essay is!

Informative/ Explanatory writing explains a topic or gives facts.

Hi, my name is Alika. I'm learning all about informative/explanatory writing, and I really like it! One of my favorite things to do is to observe nature along the Hawaiian coast. I also love the Hawaiian culture—especially the great food! My writing skills are getting better. Now I can do a better job of reporting about the sea animals, landforms, and interesting culture around me.

IN THIS UNIT

- **Compare-and-Contrast Essay**
- **Research Report**
- **How-To Essay**
- SCIENCE CONNECTION ▶ **Summary**
- **Writing for a Test**

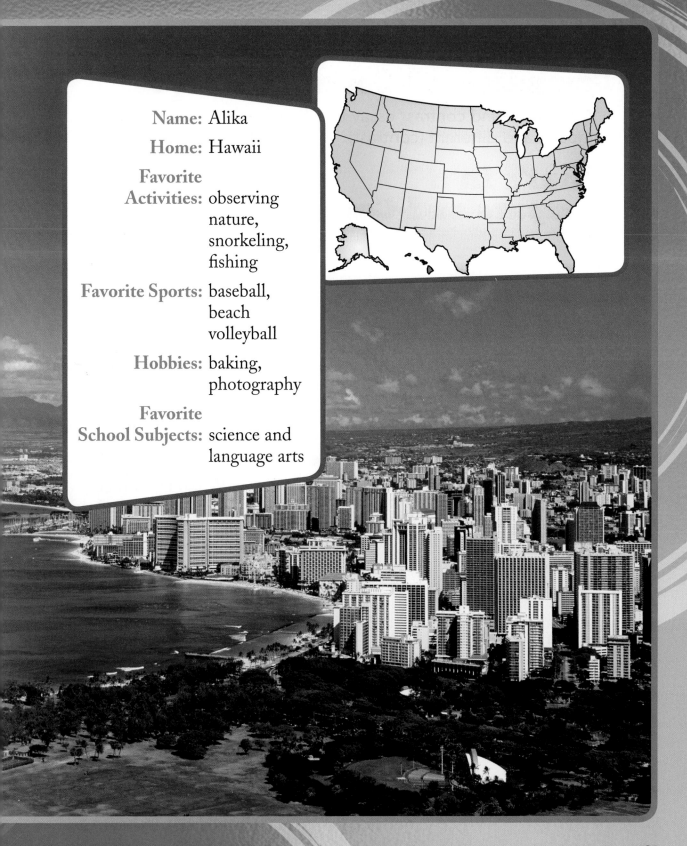

Name: Alika

Home: Hawaii

Favorite Activities: observing nature, snorkeling, fishing

Favorite Sports: baseball, beach volleyball

Hobbies: baking, photography

Favorite School Subjects: science and language arts

What's a Compare-and-Contrast Essay?

A compare-and contrast essay tells how two or more things are alike (compare) and different (contrast).

What's in a Compare-and-Contrast Essay?

Two (or more) Topics
A topic is what I'm writing about. A compare-and-contrast essay usually has at least two topics. I could compare and contrast my pet bird and my pet dog.

Comparisons
When I compare two things, I tell the ways that they are alike or similar.

Contrasts
When I contrast two things, I tell how they are different.

Why write a Compare-and-Contrast Essay?

There are lots of reasons for writing a compare-and-contrast essay. Here are two good reasons.

To Inform

I can explain something that's new to my reader by comparing and contrasting it with something that's familiar to the reader. I might teach my classmates about seasons in Alaska by comparing and contrasting them with seasons in Hawaii.

To Evaluate

If I compare and contrast two things fairly and without bias, my reader can decide which one he or she thinks is better.

Linking Informative/Explanatory Writing Traits to a Compare-and-Contrast Essay

In this chapter, you will write about how two things are the same and different. This type of informative/explanatory writing is called a compare-and-contrast essay. Alika will guide you through the stages of the writing process: Prewrite, Draft, Revise, Edit, and Publish. In each stage, Alika will show you important writing strategies that are linked to the Informative/Explanatory Writing Traits below.

Informative/Explanatory Writing Traits

Ideas
- clear topic and main ideas
- details, information, and examples that answer the reader's questions about the topic

Organization
- a strong introduction, body, and conclusion
- well-organized paragraphs
- transitions that connect ideas

Voice
- a voice and tone that are appropriate for the purpose and audience

Word Choice
- precise words
- domain-specific vocabulary that is used correctly and explained as necessary

Sentence Fluency
- clear, direct sentences that flow smoothly

Conventions
- no or few errors in grammar, usage, mechanics, and spelling

Before you write, read Taisha Moore's compare-and-contrast essay on the next page. Then use the compare-and-contrast essay rubric on pages 126–127 to decide how well she did. (You might want to look back at What's in a Compare-and-Contrast Essay? on page 122, too!)

As Different as Day and Night

Compare-and-
MODEL
Contrast Essay

by Taisha Moore

two topics

Which two objects in the sky are as different as day and night? One answer to this question is "the sun and the moon." The sun is a bright daytime light. The moon is a beautiful and changing light in the night sky.

The sun and the moon are both bright objects, but the sun is a star. Earth and the other planets in the solar system revolve around the sun. All life on Earth depends on the sun. Plants need the sun to grow, and animals and people need the sun's heat and light. Unlike the sun, the moon is a satellite. It revolves around Earth. Life on Earth does not depend on the moon, but the moon affects many things on Earth, including the tides.

comparison

Both the sun and the moon seem to change or to move in the sky. The sun seems to rise and set. The moon appears in different places at different times of the year and even at different times of the night.

The moon has a 29-day cycle. Phases of the moon make its circular shape look different at different times of the month. It sometimes looks like a thin crescent, half of a moon, or a full moon. We see only the part of the moon that is lit by sunlight. The sun doesn't have a cycle.

contrast

The moon and the sun also differ in how far away they are from Earth. About one quarter of a million miles away, the moon is Earth's closest neighbor in space. That is one reason we see it so easily. On the other hand, the sun is 93 million miles away. Only its brightness makes it easy to see.

There is no life on either the sun or the moon. The sun has a boiling, busy, bubbling surface. The center of the sun can get as hot as 27 million degrees Fahrenheit. The moon, on the other hand, has no activity. It has no air, no clouds, and no water.

The sun provides our daytime light, and the moon sometimes lights up the darkness. We sometimes use the sun as our symbol for "day" and the moon as our symbol for "night."

Compare-and-Contrast Essay Rubric

Use this 6-point rubric to plan and score a compare-and-contrast essay.

	6	5	4
Ideas	Two topics for comparison are clear. Good examples clearly compare and contrast the topics.	Two topics for comparison are clear. Most examples clearly compare and contrast the topics.	Two topics for comparison are present. The examples do not compare equally.
Organization	The essay is organized by similarities and differences. A strong lead gets the reader's attention.	Similarities and differences are organized. The lead could be stronger.	Most of the time similarities and differences are organized. The lead is not strong.
Voice	The writer's voice sounds knowledgeable. It is clear that the writer wants to inform the reader.	The writer's voice sounds knowledgeable and informative most of the time.	The writer's voice sounds knowledgeable and informative some of the time.
Word Choice	Domain-specific vocabulary is used correctly. It is clearly defined or explained.	Domain-specific vocabulary is used. One or two words are not defined or explained.	Domain-specific vocabulary is used correctly. Many words are not explained or they are not explained well.
Sentence Fluency	Sentences vary in length and type. Effective transitions create a smooth flow.	Most sentences vary in length and type. One or two transitions are needed to improve the flow.	Many sentences share the same length and type. More or better transitions would improve the flow.
Conventions	All homophones are correct. The meaning is clear.	Some homophones are incorrect, but they do not interfere with meaning.	There are a few errors with homophones, but the reader can figure out the meaning.

✛ Presentation   Each paragraph is indented.

3	2	1	
The topics for comparison are clear, but examples are unbalanced and/or vague.	The topics are not stated clearly. Examples are misleading or missing.	The topics are not clear. Examples seem to be unrelated.	**Ideas**
Similarities and differences are not well organized. The lead is very weak.	Similarities and differences are not clear or organized. The lead is weak or absent.	The essay is not organized. The writing is very difficult to understand.	**Organization**
The writer's voice sounds inconsistent, insecure, or vague. The reader feels confused.	The writer's voice is weak and may not be appropriate.	The writer's voice is very weak or absent. The reader cannot tell what the writer knows.	**Voice**
Some domain-specific vocabulary is used incorrectly. Explanations are poor or incomplete.	Domain-specific vocabulary is used incorrectly. Explanations are missing.	Domain-specific vocabulary is not used.	**Word Choice**
Sentences share the same length and type. Transitions are not used.	Several sentences are incomplete. Transitions are confusing or incorrect.	Sentences are incomplete or incorrect. The essay is difficult to read.	**Sentence Fluency**
Noticeable errors with homophones confuse the reader.	Many errors with homophones make it hard to read and understand the text.	The writing contains many errors. It is very difficult to read.	**Conventions**

See Appendix B for 4-, 5-, and 6-point informative/explanatory rubrics.

Using the Rubric to Study the Model

Did you notice that the model on page 125 points out some key elements of a compare-and-contrast essay? As she wrote "As Different as Day and Night," Taisha Moore used these elements to help her compare and contrast the moon and the sun. She also used the 6-point rubric on pages 126–127 to plan, draft, revise, and edit the writing. A rubric is a great tool to evaluate writing during the writing process.

Now let's use the same rubric to score the model. To do this, we'll focus on each trait separately, starting with Ideas. We'll use the top descriptor for each trait (column 6), along with examples from the model, to help us understand how the traits work together. How would you score Taisha on each trait?

- **Two topics for comparison are clear.**
- **Good examples clearly compare and contrast the topics.**

Taisha makes the topics clear in the first two sentences of her essay. She compares and contrasts the sun and the moon. She uses good, clear examples in each paragraph. In the following paragraph, Taisha talks about differences in distance.

The moon and the sun also differ in how far away they are from Earth. About one quarter of a million miles away, the moon is Earth's closest neighbor in space. That is one reason we see it so easily. On the other hand, the sun is 93 million miles away. Only its brightness makes it easy to see.

Organization

- The essay is organized by similarities and differences.
- A strong lead gets the reader's attention.

The similarities and differences are well organized. Each paragraph compares and contrasts different features of the sun and moon. Taisha's lead—the first sentence—asks an interesting question. It got my attention right away.

Which two objects in the sky are as different as day and night?

Voice

- The writer's voice sounds knowledgeable.
- It is clear that the writer wants to inform the reader.

Taisha's voice sounds knowledgeable about her topic. She gives facts about the similarities and differences of the sun and the moon. It is clear that her purpose is to inform the reader. In this paragraph, Taisha gives information about the light of the sun and the moon.

The sun and the moon are both bright objects, but the sun is a star. Earth and the other planets in the solar system revolve around the sun. All life on Earth depends on the sun. Plants need the sun to grow, and animals and people need the sun's heat and light. Unlike the sun, the moon is a satellite. It revolves around Earth. Life on Earth does not depend on the moon, but the moon affects many things on Earth, including the tides.

Compare-and-Contrast Essay

Using the Rubric to Study the Model

Word Choice

- Domain-specific vocabulary is used correctly.
- It is clearly defined or explained.

Taisha uses content-related words to explain the similarities and differences of the sun and the moon. In this paragraph, Taisha clearly defines and explains the phases of the moon.

The moon has a 29-day cycle. Phases of the moon make its circular shape look different at different times of the month. It sometimes looks like a thin crescent, half of a moon, or a full moon. We see only the part of the moon that is lit by sunlight. The sun doesn't have a cycle.

Sentence Fluency

- Sentences vary in length and type.
- Effective transitions create a smooth flow.

The writer uses a variety of sentences in her essay. Some are short, simple sentences. Some are longer and complex. Taisha also uses transitions effectively. *Both, on the other hand, unlike,* and *but* create a good flow in the essay.

The center of the sun can get as hot as 27 million degrees Fahrenheit. The moon, on the other hand, has no activity. It has no air, no clouds, and no water.

Conventions
- All homophones are correct.
- The meaning is clear.

Taisha uses homophones correctly. In this example, she does not confuse *its* (belonging to *it*) with *it's* (the contraction for *it is*). By using words correctly, Taisha makes her meaning clear to the reader.

On the other hand, the sun is 93 million miles away. Only its brightness makes it easy to see.

✚ Presentation   Each paragraph is indented.

My Turn!

Now I'm going to write my own compare-and-contrast essay! Follow along to see how I use good writing strategies. I will use the model and the rubric to help me, too.

Prewrite

Focus on **Ideas**

The Rubric Says Two topics for comparison are clear. Good examples clearly compare and contrast the topics.

Writing Strategy Choose two things to compare and contrast. Make notes about both things.

When my teacher asked us to write a compare-and-contrast essay, I decided to compare sharks and whales. Sharks are really interesting fish, and whales are the biggest creatures in the ocean. I've already read a lot about both of them. My teacher said to use at least two sources to find out new information and verify what I know about sharks and whales. I listed everything I learned during my research.

What I Know About Sharks and Whales

Sharks	Whales
• are fish	• make sounds—humpbacks "sing"
• breathe through gills	• are mammals
• 6 inches to about 40 feet long	• have great eyesight, great hearing
• do not make sounds	• have lungs and blowholes
• very good hearing and vision	• can be 10 feet to 100 feet long
• excellent sense of smell	• hardly any sense of smell
	• huge!

Apply

Brainstorm a list of topics that you would like to compare and contrast. Select the pair that you think will be the most interesting. Jot down some notes.

The Rubric Says   The essay is organized by similarities and differences.

Writing Strategy   Make an Attribute Chart to show similarities and differences.

The rubric reminds me that I need to organize my ideas. For example, sharks breathe underwater, but whales have to come up for air. How sharks and whales breathe is an attribute. I took the ideas on my list and made an Attribute Chart.

Writer's Term

Attribute Chart
An **attribute** (at•ruh•byoot) is a quality of something. An **Attribute Chart** organizes information about how two things are alike or different.

Attribute Chart

Shark	Attribute	Whale
fish	kind of animal	mammal
underwater with gills	how it breathes	above water with lungs and blowhole
6 inches to 40 feet	its length	10 to 100 feet
none	sounds it makes	many sounds
great vision and hearing	hearing and vision	great vision and hearing
excellent	sense of smell	poor

Reflect

Look at the notes and the Attribute Chart. How will the attributes in the chart help with writing a good compare-and-contrast essay?

Apply

Look at your notes on the topics that you chose to compare and contrast. What attributes do the two topics have in common? How are they different? Use your notes to make an Attribute Chart.

Draft

Focus on **Ideas**

The Rubric Says   Two topics for comparison are clear.

Writing Strategy   Name both topics and treat them the same.

Now I'm ready to write. I'll use my Attribute Chart to write a draft. I need to remember that a compare-and-contrast essay shows both differences and similarities.

The rubric reminds me that both topics need to be clearly stated. I should treat both topics equally, too. That means neither topic should get more attention or have more examples than the other. For example, if I talk about how whales and sharks are different, I should be sure to say as much about whales as I do about sharks.

As I'm writing, I'll do the best I can with grammar and spelling, but I won't worry about mistakes. I'll fix them later. Here is part of my draft.

[DRAFT]

Whales and Sharks

I am going to compare and contrast sharks and whales. ← *two topics*

A tiny shark is only six inches long! Its called a dwarf shark.

The smallest whale is about ten feet long.

comparison

Whales and sharks are alike in many ways. They are usually

both very large. Whales are larger than sharks. Whales and

sharks both have excellent hearing and vision. However, sharks

have a terrific sense of smell. Whales have almost no sense of

smell at all.

contrast

Whales and sharks have other differences, to. A big

difference is that sharks are fish. They breathe underwater

through gills. Whales are mammals, so they have lungs. They

have to rise to the surface of the water to breathe through

blowholes.

Reflect

Read the draft. Are both topics given equal attention?

Apply

Write a draft of a compare-and-contrast essay. Remember to state both topics clearly. Also, be sure to treat both topics equally.

Revise

Focus on Organization

The Rubric Says	A strong lead gets the reader's attention.
Writing Strategy	Begin with a compare-and-contrast lead that gets the reader's attention.

After I wrote my first draft, I checked it against the rubric. The rubric tells me that I need to think about my audience. I want to get the reader interested in my topics right away. That means I have to start with a great compare-and-contrast sentence, or lead!

Writer's Term

Lead

A **lead** is the first sentence of a piece of writing. A good lead grabs the reader's attention and makes him or her want to read more. A lead can be a question or a surprising statement.

Question Lead: Do you know which of the five senses is the shark's best and the whale's worst?

Surprise Lead: Not everyone knows that a shark can be six inches long or that a whale can sing!

[DRAFT]

Have you ever heard of a six-inch shark or a ten-foot whale? I am going to compare and contrast sharks and whales. A tiny shark is only six inches long! Its called a dwarf shark. The smallest whale is about ten feet long.

added catchy lead

Apply

Read your draft. Look for places to add interesting examples to your compare-and-contrast essay. Add these examples to your draft.

The Rubric Says   The writer's voice sounds knowledgeable. It is clear that the writer wants to inform the reader.

Writing Strategy   Share my knowledge and enthusiasm about the topics.

The rubric reminds me to sound knowledgeable about the topics and to inform the reader. I should think about the purpose of my essay as I revise. I should also think about my audience. I want to inform and engage the reader. I want to sound like an expert on the topics so that the reader will believe the information. If I share my enthusiasm for the topics, then the reader will be interested, too. I'll add some details to share more of my knowledge, and I'll look for places to express my excitement about the topics.

[DRAFT]

Another difference is in the sounds that whales and sharks make while they swim. ~~Sharks are silent. Whales make noise.~~ Sharks swim silently, while whales communicate with whistles, barks, and screams. The humpback whale even sings!

shared knowledge

showed interest

Reflect

Look at the revisions. How does Alika show his knowledge and interest in the topics?

Apply

Read your draft again. Look for places where you can show your knowledge and enthusiasm about the topics.

Revise

Focus on Word Choice

The Rubric Says   Domain-specific vocabulary is used correctly. It is clearly defined or explained.

Writing Strategy   Explain words that readers might not know.

I read my draft again. There are precise words that I have to use to explain the similarities and differences between sharks and whales. The rubric reminds me that domain-specific vocabulary, or words about my topics, need to be used correctly. I won't assume that my readers know what the words mean. I will provide an explanation or definition for the ones I use in my essay.

[DRAFT]

Whales and sharks have other differences, to. A big difference is that sharks are fish. They breathe underwater through gills. Whales are mammals, so they have lungs. They have to rise to the surface of the water to breathe ~~through blowholes.~~ They breathe through one or two nostrils at the top of their head called blowholes.

defined vocabulary word

Apply

Use precise words about each topic in your essay. Be sure to define or explain what they mean.

Edit

The Rubric Says   All homophones are correct. The meaning is clear.

Writing Strategy   Make sure that homophones are used correctly.

Now I need to check for errors. I always check spelling, punctuation, and capitalization. I'll also make sure that I've used every homophone correctly. Here's the end of my draft.

> **Writer's Term** ___
>
> **Homophones**
> **Homophones** are words that sound the same but have different spellings and meanings.

[DRAFT]

Both whales and sharks are fascinating ~~aminals~~. ~~Its~~ not   *animals*   *It's*

surprising that ~~their~~ the subjects of poems, stories, and   *they're*

compare-and-contrast essays!

corrected homophones

Reflect

Look at the edits. Are all spelling, punctuation, and capitalization problems fixed? Are homophones used correctly?

Apply

Conventions

Edit your draft for spelling, punctuation, and capitalization. Make sure that you have used every homophone correctly.

For more practice identifying and using homophones correctly, use the exercises on the next two pages.

Homophones

Know the Rule

Homophones are words that sound alike but have different spellings and meanings.

Your is a possessive pronoun that means "belonging to you."
You're is a contraction made from the words "you are."

Their is a possessive pronoun that means "belonging to them."
There is an adverb that means "in that place." **They're** is a contraction made from the words "they are."

Its is a possessive pronoun that means "belonging to it." **It's** is a contraction made from the words "it is" or "it has."

Two is a number. **Too** means "also" or "more than enough."
To often means "towards."

Practice the Rule

Number a piece of paper from 1–10. Write the word in parentheses that completes each sentence correctly.

1. My class went (two/too/to) a natural history museum.
2. We went to a whale exhibit (their/there/they're).
3. We learned that a whale isn't a fish; (its/it's) a mammal.
4. A whale has a blowhole on the top of (its/it's) head.
5. Whales use (their/there/they're) blowholes to breathe air.
6. A whale's flipper is a little like (your/you're) hand.
7. We found that there are (two/too/to) kinds of whales.
8. The whale that (your/you're) looking at is a baleen whale.
9. Large amounts of seawater go into (their/there/they're) mouths.
10. The baleen hangs (their/there/they're) like a loose fringe curtain.

More Homophones

Know the Rule

Homophones are frequently confused because they sound alike. Remember, though, that they are spelled differently. When you use homophones in your writing, be sure to check the spelling. The spell checker on a computer cannot tell which homophone you meant to use.

Practice the Rule

Number a piece of paper from 1–10. Read each sentence. If the sentence uses the wrong homophone, write the correct one. If the sentence uses the correct homophone, write **Correct**.

1. Whales swim differently than fish due.
2. Fish move there tails from side to side.
3. Whales move their tails up and down.
4. A whale's tale must be very strong.
5. They're largest muscles are in their tails.
6. They are able too travel great distances.
7. They are known for there long-distance migrations.
8. Whales travel from cool waters two warm waters.
9. The gray whale travels up to 14,000 miles round trip.
10. Its one of the longest migrations of any mammal.

Publish

+Presentation

Publishing Strategy   Display my essay on the classroom bulletin board.

Presentation Strategy   Indent every paragraph.

I finished my essay! Some of my classmates asked to read my paper. There are many ways to publish a compare-and-contrast essay. I could post it on our school's website or put it with other classmates' essays in a book. I decided that I am going to put it on the class bulletin board. To make sure my essay is easy to read, I may decide to use a computer. I'll need to remember to indent the first line of each new paragraph to clearly separate them. On the computer, I can use the spell checker, but I need to be sure to check the spelling of homophones because the spell checker will not catch them. Here's my final checklist.

My Final Checklist

Did I—

✔ use homophones correctly?

✔ use neat handwriting or word processing?

✔ indent every paragraph?

✔ check for spelling, grammar, and punctuation?

Apply

Make a checklist to review your own compare-and-contrast essay. Be sure to check your essay carefully one last time before publishing it. Then make a final copy to post on your classroom bulletin board.

Whales and Sharks
by Alika

Have you ever heard of a six-inch shark or a ten-foot whale? The smallest shark is only six inches long! It's called a dwarf shark. The smallest whale is about ten feet long.

Whales and sharks are alike in many ways. They are usually both very large. However, whales are larger than sharks. Sharks can grow to 40 feet long, but whales can grow to 100 feet long. Whales and sharks both have excellent hearing and vision. However, sharks have a terrific sense of smell, while whales have almost no sense of smell at all.

Whales and sharks have other differences, too. A big difference is that sharks are fish. They breathe underwater through gills. Whales are mammals, so they have lungs. They have to rise to the surface of the water to breathe. They breathe through one or two nostrils at the top of their head called blowholes.

Another difference is in the sounds that whales and sharks make while they swim. Sharks swim silently, while whales communicate with whistles, barks, and screams. The humpback whale even sings!

Both whales and sharks are fascinating animals. It's not surprising that they're the subjects of poems, stories, and compare-and-contrast essays!

Reflect

Use the rubric to check Alika's paper. Are all the traits of a good compare-and-contrast essay there? How does your essay compare against the rubric?

What's a Research Report?

A research report is a piece of writing that gives facts and details about a topic.

What's in a Research Report?

Introduction
In the introduction, I tell the audience what my topic is and why it is interesting. I get the attention of my readers and make them curious to find out more.

Body
The body is the longest part of my report. I develop the idea I presented in the introduction. The body is where I add plenty of facts and details. If I'm writing about sand dunes, I might tell how dunes are formed, what they look like, and how high they get.

Conclusion
My conclusion summarizes the most important information about my topic.

Why write a Research Report?

There are many reasons to write a research report. Here are three reasons.

To Inform

People in many different careers make research reports to provide information. Police make research reports to tell how an investigation is going. People in business make research reports about training programs for new workers.

To Entertain

Many people enjoy learning about topics that interest them. Nonfiction writers may publish research reports in magazines, newspapers, and books.

To Change

Research reports are often used to support a certain viewpoint when people want to convince others to make changes. Research reports that show how certain animals are becoming extinct have led to the Endangered Species Act.

Linking Informative/Explanatory Writing Traits to a Research Report

In this chapter, you will write to share what you have learned about a topic. This type of informative/explanatory writing is called a research report. Alika will guide you through the stages of the writing process: Prewrite, Draft, Revise, Edit, and Publish. In each stage, Alika will show you important writing strategies that are linked to the Informative/Explanatory Writing Traits below.

Informative/Explanatory Writing Traits

- a clear topic and main ideas
- details, information, and examples that answer the reader's questions about the topic

- a strong introduction, body, and conclusion
- well-organized paragraphs
- transitions that connect ideas

- a voice and tone that are appropriate for the purpose and audience

- precise words
- domain-specific vocabulary that is used correctly and explained as necessary

- clear, direct sentences that flow smoothly

- no or few errors in grammar, usage, mechanics, and spelling

Before you write, read Jason Yang's research report on the next page. Then use the research report rubric on pages 148–149 to decide how well he did. (You might want to look back at What's in a Research Report? on page 144, too!)

Fixing the Leaning Tower of Pisa

by Jason Yang

introduction

Pisa is a city in Italy. This city has become famous for its leaning bell tower, an architectural mistake. In fact, the bell tower is known as the Leaning Tower of Pisa. It began to lean soon after it was built 800 years ago.

body paragraphs

The Leaning Tower of Pisa is a very special place. Made of white marble with 207 columns, the tower is very beautiful. It is also very heavy. Most of the walls are nine to ten feet thick. With its thick walls and marble, the tower weighs about 16,000 tons.

Many attempts have been made to straighten the tower. The south side of the tower leans, so the most common solution has been to put weights on the north side. This has never worked. People also tried putting concrete around the base of the tower. Then they attached cables to support the tower. At one time, 80 tons of concrete were poured into the foundation, but that solution didn't work either. People have also suggested putting huge weights against the tower to hold it upright.

In 1990 the tower was leaning so much that it had to be closed. A committee was formed to solve the problem.

Finally an attempt to save the Leaning Tower of Pisa worked. It seemed to be an unlikely plan at first. It involved moving sand. Led by a chief engineer named Dr. Paolo Heiniger, work crews removed almost 80 tons of soil from under the tower. They took away the soft sand that had caused the tower to lean in the first place. As they did, they slowly moved the south side of the tower toward the north.

conclusion

Today the tower still leans. The top is still more than 15 feet out over the base. Nevertheless, this is less than the 17 feet of "lean" in 1990. It is also a big enough improvement to reopen the tower. Besides, people didn't really want the tower to stop leaning. They just didn't want it to fall.

Research Report Rubric

Use this 6-point rubric to plan and score a research report.

	6	5	4
Ideas	The report focuses on one topic. All details and facts are related and accurate.	The report focuses on one topic. Most of the details and facts are related.	The report focuses on one topic. Some of the information is vague or not related to the topic.
Organization	The report has a strong introduction, body, and conclusion. The conclusion sums up the report in a memorable way.	The report has an introduction, body, and conclusion. The conclusion sums up the report.	The report has an introduction, body, and conclusion. The introduction and conclusion are not strong.
Voice	The writer's voice sounds knowledgeable. It is clear the writer cares about the topic.	The writer's voice sounds knowledgeable and informative most of the time.	The writer's voice sounds knowledgeable some of the time. The writer seems to care about the topic.
Word Choice	Precise words are used correctly and explained clearly.	Precise words are used correctly and explained most of the time.	Many of the writer's words are precise and correctly used. Some are not explained.
Sentence Fluency	The writing flows because sentence lengths and types vary.	Most sentences vary in length and type.	Some sentences are the same length and type. More variety would make the writing flow better.
Conventions	All capitalization and titles are correct. The report is easy to read.	There are a few errors in capitalization or titles, but they do not interfere with meaning.	Minor errors in capitalization and titles are noticeable and distracting.

✛ Presentation The report is prepared on the computer with a limited number of clear fonts.

3	2	1	
The report does not focus on one topic. Some details and facts may be inaccurate.	The focus is vague. Information and details are very general and not based on facts.	The topic is not clear. Many details and facts are not related to the topic.	**Ideas**
The report has an introduction, body, and conclusion. The conclusion does not sum up the report.	The introduction and body are weak or incomplete. The conclusion does not sum up the report.	The report does not have an introduction, body, or conclusion.	**Organization**
The writer's voice is inconsistent and vague at times. The reader is confused.	The writer's voice may be inappropriate for the purpose and audience. The voice is hard to identify.	The writer's voice is very weak or absent.	**Voice**
Some of the words are too general. Their meaning is sometimes unclear to the reader.	Some words are repetitive or unrelated. Their meaning is not explained.	Many words are too general and incorrectly used.	**Word Choice**
Many sentences are the same in length and type. They do not flow well together.	Sentences are too brief or too wordy. Reading is choppy and awkward.	Sentences are incomplete or incorrect. The report is difficult to read.	**Sentence Fluency**
Frequent errors in capitalization, titles, and other conventions confuse the reader.	Many errors in capitalization and titles make the text difficult to read and understand. The writer shows lack of control over conventions.	The writing contains many errors in capitalization and titles. It is very difficult to read.	**Conventions**

See Appendix B for 4-, 5-, and 6-point informative/explanatory rubrics.

Research Report
Using the Rubric to Study the Model

Did you notice that the model on page 147 points out some key elements of a research report? As he wrote "Fixing the Leaning Tower of Pisa," Jason Yang used these elements to help him tell what he learned about the famous tower in Pisa, Italy. He also used the 6-point rubric on pages 148–149 to plan, draft, revise, and edit the writing. A rubric is a great tool to evaluate writing during the writing process.

Now let's use the same rubric to score the model. To do this, we'll focus on each trait separately, starting with Ideas. We'll use the top descriptor for each trait (column 6), along with examples from the model, to help us understand how the traits work together. How would you score Jason on each trait?

Ideas

- **The report focuses on one topic.**
- **All details and facts are related and accurate.**

I really enjoyed reading this report. Jason tells us about the Leaning Tower of Pisa and shares interesting facts about it. He gives a lot of details to help the reader understand his topic. This is a good example of a paragraph with some of those important facts.

The Leaning Tower of Pisa is a very special place. Made of white marble with 207 columns, the tower is very beautiful. It is also very heavy. Most of the walls are nine to ten feet thick. With its thick walls and marble, the tower weighs about 16,000 tons.

 **Organization**

- The report has a strong introduction, body, and conclusion.
- The conclusion sums up the report in a memorable way.

Jason's introduction caught my attention right away, and I wanted to keep reading. I really like the conclusion, too. The Leaning Tower of Pisa, "an architectural mistake," is one place I'd like to visit someday!

Today the tower still leans. The top is still more than 15 feet out over the base. Nevertheless, this is less than the 17 feet of "lean" in 1990. It is also a big enough improvement to reopen the tower. Besides, people didn't really want the tower to stop leaning. They just didn't want it to fall.

 **Voice**

- The writer's voice sounds knowledgeable.
- It is clear the writer cares about the topic.

I learned a lot about the Leaning Tower of Pisa from this report. Jason sounds knowledgeable. It's clear he had carefully researched the topic. Here is a good example—the writer explains how people tried to fix the tower.

Finally an attempt to save the Leaning Tower of Pisa worked. It seemed to be an unlikely plan at first. It involved moving sand. Led by a chief engineer named Dr. Paolo Heiniger, work crews removed almost 80 tons of soil from under the tower. They took away the soft sand that had caused the tower to lean in the first place. As they did, they slowly moved the south side of the tower toward the north.

Using the Research Report Rubric to Study the Model

Word Choice

• Precise words are used correctly and explained clearly.

In this report, Jason uses appositives to add more information about the nouns in his sentences. In the sentence below, *an architectural mistake* is an appositive that provides more information about the tower.

This city has become famous for its leaning bell tower, an architectural mistake.

Sentence Fluency

• The writing flows because sentence lengths and types vary.

The writer used a variety of sentence lengths and types. Here is an example of how the writer used both simple and compound sentences to give the text rhythm and flow.

Many attempts have been made to straighten the tower. The south side of the tower leans, so the most common solution has been to put weights on the north side. This has never worked.

Conventions
- All capitalization and titles are correct.
- The report is easy to read.

Jason did a good job editing his paper. He capitalized the first word of every sentence, all the proper nouns, and the one abbreviation of a person's title.

Led by a chief engineer named Dr. Paolo Heiniger, work crews removed almost 80 tons of soil from under the tower. They took away the soft sand that had caused the tower to lean in the first place.

✛Presentation The report is prepared on the computer with a limited number of clear fonts.

My Turn!

Now it's my turn to write a research report! I'll use the rubric and good writing strategies to help me. Follow along to see how I do it.

Prewrite

Focus on **Ideas**

The Rubric Says   The report focuses on one topic.

Writing Strategy   Narrow a topic and take notes.

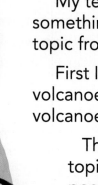

My teacher asked us to write a research report on something about volcanoes. We had to narrow the topic from volcanoes in general to something specific.

First I skimmed an encyclopedia article about volcanoes to narrow my topic. One thing about volcanoes that interests me most is living near one.

Then I found a book that told more about my topic. As I read the book, I took notes on what people keep in mind if they live near a volcano.

My Book Notes on Living Near Volcanoes

escape plans	emergency supplies	dangers
routes to take	flashlight	blasts
higher land	radio	ash
away from wind	batteries	lava
place to meet	food and water	
	can opener	
	first-aid kit	

Apply

Do some research and narrow your topic. Then make a list of important things to remember about your topic.

The Rubric Says   The report has a strong introduction, body, and conclusion.

Writing Strategy   Use a Web to organize the notes.

I know from the rubric that every main idea needs information to back it up. I'll use a Web to organize my report. I can put the topic in the center. The categories from my notes will go in the next set of circles. Then the details for each category will go in smaller circles connected to the categories.

Writer's Term

Web

A **Web** organizes information about one main topic. The main topic goes in the center. Related details go in outside circles connected to the center.

Web

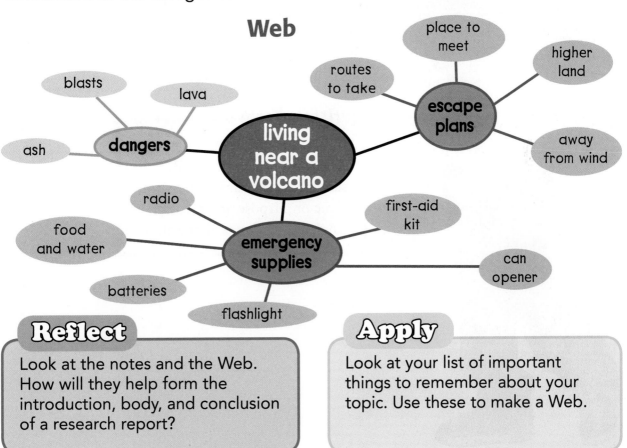

Reflect

Look at the notes and the Web. How will they help form the introduction, body, and conclusion of a research report?

Apply

Look at your list of important things to remember about your topic. Use these to make a Web.

Draft

Focus on **Organization**

The Rubric Says	The report has a strong introduction, body, and conclusion. The conclusion sums up the report in a memorable way.
Writing Strategy	Use my graphic organizer to plan my paragraphs.

It's time to write my first draft. I know from the rubric that my report should have an introduction, body, and conclusion. I'll use my Web to organize my paragraphs. The introduction and conclusion will both be about the information in the center of the Web—living near a volcano. The dark orange, blue, and purple circles will be the paragraph topics in the body of the report. The lighter colored circles will be the details for each paragraph topic.

> ### Writer's Term
> **Paragraph**
> A **paragraph** is a group of sentences that share a common topic or purpose and focus on a single main idea or thought.

[DRAFT]

In the Shadow of a Volcano

introduction

Living near a volcano can be crazy. People who live near a

volcano learn to live near danger by being ready to act quickly.

They must also be prepared in other ways.

The danger from an erupting volcano is real. When authorities

tell people to leave their homes, residents move fast.

main idea

body paragraphs

Those who live near a volcano have their emergency items

ready. people keep a Flashlight and extra batteries handy. they

have a radio that runs on batteries, too. They keep Canned Food

and Bottled Water on hand. a first-aid kit and a can opener that is

not electric can save lifes.

related detail

related detail

Reflect

Read the beginning of Alika's draft. Is the topic clear? Which facts and details are included?

Apply

Use your Web to write a draft of your research report. Be sure the main topic is clear. Give each category its own paragraph and include all the details.

Revise

The Rubric Says The writer's voice sounds knowledgeable. It is clear the writer cares about the topic.

Writing Strategy Use a formal tone and plenty of facts.

The rubric tells me to sound knowledgeable about my topic. I should think about my purpose and audience for this report. My purpose is to inform the reader, and the audience will be my teacher and classmates. I need to sound like an expert so they will believe the facts in my report. By using plenty of facts, I will show them what I know. By using a formal tone, I will sound like an authority on the topic.

Writer's Term

Formal Tone

A **formal tone** is the way you would sound if you talked to an adult or to people you don't know very well. It is respectful and polite. When speaking or writing with a formal tone, you use complete sentences and avoid casual language.

[DRAFT]

used formal tone

Living near a volcano can be ~~crazy~~. ^risky People who live near a

volcano learn to live near danger by being ready to act quickly.

They must also be prepared in other ways.

Apply

Read your draft. Think about your purpose and audience. Remember to use a formal tone and add plenty of facts.

Focus on Word Choice

The Rubric Says Precise words are used correctly and explained clearly.

Writing Strategy Use appositives to explain nouns the reader may not know.

When using words that are specific to my topic, I can do a favor for the reader by providing more detail about the words. An appositive is one way to do this for nouns. I checked my report. My second paragraph has a word that I should explain. Take a look at how I revised that sentence.

Writer's Term
Appositives
An **appositive** is a word or phrase that follows a noun and helps identify or describe it.

[DRAFT]

added appositive

, the officials in control,

The danger from an erupting volcano is real. When authorities ∧

tell people to leave their homes, residents move fast.

Reflect
Look at the revision. How does adding the appositive help the reader?

Apply
Read your draft again. Be sure that your report has appositives where needed.

Revise

Focus on Sentence Fluency

The Rubric Says   The writing flows because sentence lengths and types vary.

Writing Strategy   Write both simple and compound sentences.

The rubric reminds me to use a mix of sentence lengths and types. By using a variety of simple and compound sentences, I'll give my text rhythm and flow. I should read my draft out loud and listen for places where short sentences could be combined to make longer ones. I can join sentences using the words *and*, *or*, or *but*.

I read my draft out loud and listened for places where sentences could be combined. I found two short, related sentences in this paragraph. I combined them by using the word *and*.

[DRAFT]

Having an escape plan is important for people who live near a

volcano. They decide on a route to take if they have to leave their homes. **, and**

~~T~~hey make sure everyone knows the plan.

combined sentences

Apply

Check your draft. Look for places to combine sentences with *and*, *or*, or *but*.

The Rubric Says	All capitalization and titles are correct.
Writing Strategy	Use capital letters correctly.

When I proofread, I always check spelling and punctuation. This time I'm going to pay special attention to capitalization. I want to be sure I've started every sentence with a capital letter. I'm also going to check that I've capitalized all proper nouns, all important words in titles, and all abbreviations of personal titles. Finally, I have to make sure that I have not used any capital letters that are unnecessary.

---

have a radio that runs on batteries, too. They keep ~~C~~anned ~~F~~ood

and ~~B~~ottled ~~W~~ater on hand. ~~a~~ first-aid kit and a can opener that is

not electric can save ~~lifes.~~ lives

[DRAFT]

Reflect

Look at the edits. Are all the spelling, capitalization, and punctuation mistakes fixed?

Apply   Conventions

Edit your draft for spelling and punctuation. Make sure that all capital letters and titles are correct.

For more practice with capitalization and titles, use the exercises on the next two pages.

Capitalization

Know the Rule

Use a **capital letter** for

- the first word in every sentence.
- all proper nouns.
- the first word, the last word, and all important words in titles.
- abbreviations of personal titles.

Practice the Rule

Number a piece of paper from 1–12. Write each sentence using the correct capitalization. If a sentence is correct, write **Correct**.

1. have you read any books by ms. Margaret Poynter?
2. I got one of her books from the springfield public library.
3. The book is called *volcanoes: The fiery mountains*.
4. I learned about a park in hawaii where you can sometimes see a volcano in action.
5. Like japan, Hawaii has volcanic mountains.
6. volcanoes create many landforms.
7. There is an odd mountain in wyoming called devil's tower.
8. This is a famous landmark in north America.
9. Devil's Tower is made from old lava.
10. This mountain was in the film *Close encounters of the third Kind*.
11. Have you heard of the volcano that erupted in washington?
12. This mountain erupted on may 18, 1980.

Titles

Know the Rule

Underline **book titles** and **movie titles** when you write them by hand. Put them in italics when you use a computer. Use quotation marks around the **titles of songs, poems**, and **stories**. Capitalize the first word, last word, and all the important words of any title. Always capitalize *is*, *are*, *was*, and *were* in titles. Do not capitalize *a*, *an*, *the*, *and*, *to*, *on*, *or*, *of*, or *with* unless that word is the first word or the last word in the title.

Practice the Rule

Number a piece of paper from 1–10. Rewrite each title. Use correct punctuation and capitalization.

Type	Title
1. Book	great volcanoes
2. Poem	mr. volcano
3. Song	lava flows
4. Movie	the eruption of mount vesuvius
5. Short Story	the story of volcanoes
6. Book	Living near a volcano
7. Poem	ash on the land
8. Book	exploring Pompeii
9. Movie	The Iceland volcano
10. Short Story	One day in summer

Publish

+Presentation

Publishing Strategy	Publish the report on the school's website.
Presentation Strategy	Make good design decisions on the computer.

My research report is finished! If I publish my report on my school's website, other people will be able to read it. Anything going up on the school's website has to be neat and readable. I will use the computer to make neat margins and spacing on the page. I will also choose two clear, readable fonts for the report and the title.

Before I publish, I'll read my report one more time. Here is my final checklist.

My Final Checklist

Did I—

✔ follow capitalization rules?

✔ punctuate titles correctly?

✔ make neat margins and use regular spacing?

✔ choose two clear fonts?

✔ put my name on the report?

Apply

Make a checklist to check your own research report one last time before you publish it. Then publish your research report.

In the Shadow of a Volcano
by Alika

Living near a volcano can be risky. People who live near a volcano learn to live near danger by being ready to act quickly. They must also be prepared in other ways.

The danger from an erupting volcano is real. When authorities, the officials in control, tell people to leave their homes, residents move fast. Some blasts travel many miles. Volcanoes can send out ash, which can harm people. Lava flowing from an erupting volcano is also dangerous.

Those who live near a volcano have their emergency items ready. People keep a flashlight and extra batteries handy. They have a radio that runs on batteries, too. They keep canned food and bottled water on hand. A first-aid kit and a can opener that is not electric can save lives.

Having an escape plan is important for people who live near a volcano. They decide on a route to take if they have to leave their homes, and they make sure everyone knows the plan. They always head toward higher ground because lava and mud flow downhill. Also, they try to stay downwind. The wind can carry objects and harmful gas. The plan includes a place for everyone to meet later.

People who live on or near active volcanoes usually adjust to their dangerous neighbors. In the book *Volcanoes and Earthquakes*, Jon Erickson says that people learn to treat volcanoes "as though they were just a normal part of their lives."

Reflect

Use the rubric to check Alika's report. Are the traits of a good research report there? How does your report compare against the rubric?

What's a How-To Essay?

A how-to essay explains how to do or make something.

What's in a How-To Essay?

Materials
These are the things I will need to do my project. I might explain how to make a birdhouse. My materials for that project would be pieces of wood, a saw, a ruler, a pencil, and a hammer and nails.

Steps
Steps tell what you have to do to complete the task. To explain my project, I have to tell you the steps in order.

Why write a How-To Essay?

People write how-to essays for a lot of different reasons. Here are two important ones.

To Inform

Sometimes I want to share what I know how to do with others. I can write the instructions in a how-to essay.

People have written how-to essays on many topics, from studying for a test to coaching a basketball team. If you want to know how to do something, you can probably find a how-to essay in a book or on the Internet.

To Entertain

My readers may want the instructions in a how-to essay for entertainment. I may write a how-to essay about origami so readers can enjoy making paper animals and flowers. I may write a how-to essay about building a birdhouse. The reader may build one in order to enjoy watching birds from the window.

Linking Informative/Explanatory Writing Traits to a How-To Essay

In this chapter, you will write to explain how to do something. This type of informative/explanatory writing is called a how-to essay. Alika will guide you through the stages of the writing process: Prewrite, Draft, Revise, Edit, and Publish. In each stage, Alika will show you important writing strategies that are linked to the Informative/Explanatory Writing Traits below.

Informative/Explanatory Writing Traits

Ideas
- clear topic and main ideas
- details, information, and examples that answer the reader's questions about the topic

Organization
- a strong introduction, body, and conclusion
- well-organized paragraphs
- transitions that connect ideas

Voice
- a voice and tone that are appropriate for the purpose and audience

Word Choice
- precise words
- domain-specific vocabulary that is used correctly and explained as necessary

Sentence Fluency
- clear, direct sentences that flow smoothly

Conventions
- no or few errors in grammar, usage, mechanics, and spelling

Before you write, read Carlos Ortiz's how-to essay on the next page. Then use the how-to essay rubric on pages 170–171 to decide how well he did. (You might want to look back at What's in a How-To Essay? on page 166, too!)

Doing Research for a Town History Report

How-To MODEL Essay

by Carlos Ortiz

What was your town like when it was brand-new? Many towns have an interesting history. Research your town's history and write a report that tells about the "early days."

A good place to begin your report is with the founding of the town. Before you start your research, you should make a list of questions you want to answer. Here are some important questions: Where is the town located? When was the town built? Who were the first people who lived there? Why did they think this was a good place to start a community? What were their plans for the future?

There are many places to look for this information. Start by visiting the town hall or the library. Some towns also have a local history museum. Town records and old newspapers are great sources of information.

step

materials

After you have collected a lot of facts about the early days of your town, you can look for pictures to put in your report. Maps and photographs can show how the town has grown and how buildings have changed.

step

materials

While you do your research, make sure to write down the sources for all your facts and stories. A good research report ends with a list of all the sources the writer used.

Don't start writing your report just yet, though! The next step is likely to be the most fun. Seek out the "living memory" of your town. A town's "living memory" is the oldest members of the community. They have seen a lot during their own lifetimes. They might even remember stories told by their parents or grandparents. Maybe some of their ancestors helped settle the town.

final step

Finally, it's time to write your report. By this time you should be quite an expert on your town's early days.

How-To Essay Rubric

Use this 6-point rubric to plan and score a how-to essay.

	6	5	4	
Ideas	The essay tells how to do or make something. All details are related to the process.	The essay tells how to do or make something. Most of the details are related to the process.	The essay tells how to do or make something. One or two details seem unrelated to the process.	
Organization	All the steps are labeled and in the right order. Appropriate transitions guide the reader by linking the sentences.	Most of the steps are labeled and in the right order. Most transitions guide the reader by linking the sentences.	Some steps may be out of order. Some transitions guide the reader by linking the sentences.	
Voice	The writer's voice sounds natural and informative. It is clear that the writer cares about the topic.	The writer's voice sounds natural and informative most of the time. The writer cares about the topic.	The writer sounds too formal or is not informative in places. The reader cannot always tell that the writer cares about the topic.	
Word Choice	The writer uses precise language (specific nouns and strong verbs) that help the reader "see" the process.	More specific nouns or stronger verbs are needed to help the reader "see" the process.	Some verbs and nouns are specific and used appropriately. A few may be vague, but they are not distracting.	
Sentence Fluency	Sentence beginnings are varied and helpful to the reader.	Sentence beginnings are mostly varied and helpful to the reader.	A few sentence beginnings are repetitive.	
Conventions	All pronouns are used correctly.	Most pronouns are used correctly. Errors do not distract the reader.	A few pronouns are used incorrectly, but the errors do not interfere with meaning.	

✚ Presentation   All paragraphs are indented.

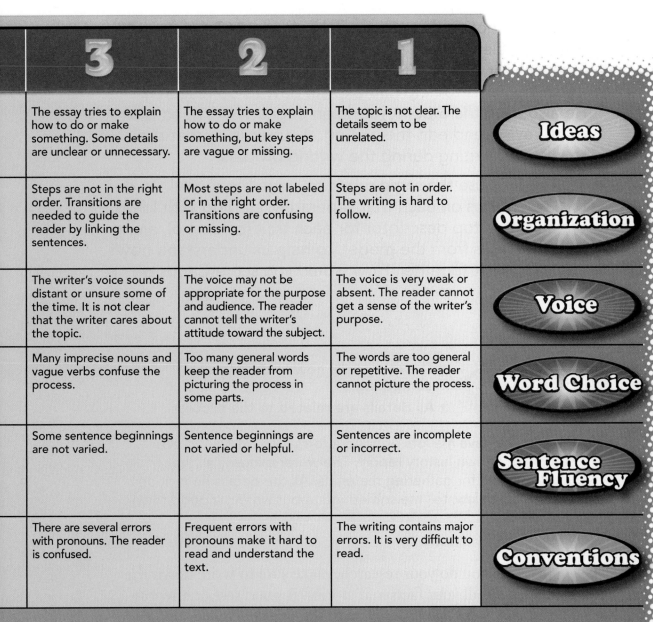

3	2	1	
The essay tries to explain how to do or make something. Some details are unclear or unnecessary.	The essay tries to explain how to do or make something, but key steps are vague or missing.	The topic is not clear. The details seem to be unrelated.	Ideas
Steps are not in the right order. Transitions are needed to guide the reader by linking the sentences.	Most steps are not labeled or in the right order. Transitions are confusing or missing.	Steps are not in order. The writing is hard to follow.	Organization
The writer's voice sounds distant or unsure some of the time. It is not clear that the writer cares about the topic.	The voice may not be appropriate for the purpose and audience. The reader cannot tell the writer's attitude toward the subject.	The voice is very weak or absent. The reader cannot get a sense of the writer's purpose.	Voice
Many imprecise nouns and vague verbs confuse the process.	Too many general words keep the reader from picturing the process in some parts.	The words are too general or repetitive. The reader cannot picture the process.	Word Choice
Some sentence beginnings are not varied.	Sentence beginnings are not varied or helpful.	Sentences are incomplete or incorrect.	Sentence Fluency
There are several errors with pronouns. The reader is confused.	Frequent errors with pronouns make it hard to read and understand the text.	The writing contains major errors. It is very difficult to read.	Conventions

See Appendix B for 4-, 5-, and 6-point informative/explanatory rubrics.

How-To Essay
Using the Rubric to Study the Model

Did you notice that the model on page 169 points out some key elements of a how-to essay? As he wrote "Doing Research for a Town History Report," Carlos Ortiz used these elements to help him explain how to do research. He also used the 6-point rubric on pages 170–171 to plan, draft, revise, and edit the writing. A rubric is a great tool to evaluate writing during the writing process.

Now let's use the same rubric to score the model. To do this, we'll focus on each trait separately, starting with Ideas. We'll use the top descriptor for each trait (column 6), along with examples from the model, to help us understand how the traits work together. How would you score Carlos on each trait?

- **The essay tells how to do or make something.**
- **All details are related to the process.**

This essay gave me lots of good information on how to do research for a town history report. The writer explains all the important steps for gathering materials. All the details he includes, like the ones below, tell me something about writing a good town history report.

> While you do your research, make sure to write down the sources for all your facts and stories. A good research report ends with a list of all the sources the writer used.

Organization

- All the steps are labeled and in the right order.
- Appropriate transitions guide the reader by linking the sentences.

Carlos writes all the steps in order. His essay is easy to follow because he makes sure the reader knows what to do first to research a town. In this example, he tells the reader to begin by visiting the town hall or the library.

There are many places to look for this information. Start by visiting the town hall or the library. Some towns also have a local history museum. Town records and old newspapers are great sources of information.

After you have collected a lot of facts about the early days of your town, you can look for pictures to put in your report.

Voice

- The writer's voice sounds natural and informative.
- It is clear that the writer cares about the topic.

I can tell that Carlos cares about learning his town's history. His voice sounds natural all the way through, and he sounds like an expert on writing research reports. The introduction is a good example. He seems to be talking directly to me.

What was your town like when it was brand-new? Many towns have an interesting history. Research your town's history and write a report that tells about the "early days."

Using the Rubric to Study the Model
How-To Essay

Word Choice

• The writer uses precise language (specific nouns and strong verbs) that help the reader "see" the process.

Reading the essay, I could picture the different steps in researching a town history report. In this paragraph, *collected* is a strong verb that paints a clearer picture than if Carlos had used a weak verb like *got*. The words *maps and photographs* are specific and tell what kinds of pictures he means.

After you have collected a lot of facts about the early days of your town, you can look for pictures to put in your report. Maps and photographs can show how the town has grown and how buildings have changed.

Sentence Fluency

• Sentence beginnings are varied and helpful to the reader.

The writer helped me follow the steps by giving helpful information at the beginning of the sentences. Here's a good example. Notice how the words at the beginning of the sentences help the reader follow along.

A good place to begin your report is with the founding of the town. Before you start your research, you should make a list of questions you want to answer. Here are some important questions: Where is the town located? When was the town built? Who were the first people who lived there?

Conventions • All pronouns are used correctly.

Every word in the essay is spelled correctly. All the sentences begin with a capital letter and end with the correct punctuation. When Carlos uses a pronoun in place of a noun, he uses it correctly.

A town's "living memory" is the oldest members of the community. They have seen a lot during their own lifetimes. They might even remember stories told by their parents or grandparents.

✛Presentation All paragraphs are indented.

My Turn!

Now it's my turn to write a how-to essay! I'll use the rubric and good writing strategies to help me. Read along to see how I do this.

Prewrite

Focus on **Ideas**

The Rubric Says   The essay tells how to do or make something.

Writing Strategy   Choose something to do or make. Make a list of all the important steps.

My teacher asked us to think of something we can do or make. I thought about the chocolate brownies my Grandma taught me to make. I decided my essay would explain how to make these great brownies! I'm sure lots of the kids in my class would like to try making them. To get started, I should make a list of all the important steps.

Important Steps for Making Brownies

- Melt butter, semisweet chocolate, and milk chocolate chips.
- Use a saucepan.
- Put in eggs and vanilla (beat the eggs).
- Add brown sugar and honey.
- Add flour and salt.
- Put in the macadamia nuts.
- Spread the batter in a baking pan, and bake for 30 minutes.
- You need a square baking pan.
- Put a little butter and parchment paper in the bottom of the pan.
- Cool brownies before you cut them into squares.

Apply

Brainstorm a list of things that you like to do or make. Pick one that you think would be interesting to write about in a how-to essay. Then make a list of all the important steps.

The Rubric Says   All the steps are labeled and in the right order.

Writing Strategy   Make an outline to list the steps from first to last.

The rubric says that my steps need to be in order. I can use an outline to put my list of steps for making brownies in order, from first to last.

Outline

I. **Introduction**
   I make chocolate brownies that taste like Hawaii to me.

II. **Body**
   A. Butter and line the bottom of a square baking pan with parchment paper.
   B. Melt butter, semisweet chocolate, and milk chocolate chips together in a saucepan.
   C. Add brown sugar and honey.
   D. Put in beaten eggs and vanilla.
   E. Add flour, salt, and nuts.
   F. Spread the batter in a baking pan and bake for 30 minutes.

III. **Conclusion**
   Let the brownies cool, and then cut them into squares and eat them.

Writer's Term

Outline
An **outline** is a writing plan that lists the main ideas next to roman numerals. It lists the details next to letters.

Reflect
Look at the notes and the outline. How do they help organize the information?

Apply
Look at the list of important steps that you made. Use an outline to organize your steps. Put them in order, from first step to last step.

Draft

The Rubric Says The writer's voice sounds natural and informative. It is clear that the writer cares about the topic.

Writing Strategy Use a friendly, natural voice so that the reader can picture the process.

Now it's time to write the first draft of my how-to essay. I'll use my outline to keep the steps in my essay organized. I know from the rubric that I need to use a voice that sounds natural and informative. I'll keep my writing voice sounding friendly and natural by "talking" to my reader directly. I will also include useful information so I sound like an expert on the topic.

I always do my best with spelling and grammar, but I won't worry about mistakes right now. I'll get a chance to fix them later. The beginning of my draft is on the next page.

[DRAFT]

used a friendly, natural voice

Fantastic Chocolate Macadamia Nut Brownies

These fantastic Chocolate Macadamia Nut Brownies that I make taste like Hawaii to me. Try making some and see if you agree!

sentences guide the reader

Start by brushing a little butter inside of a square baking pan. After you do that, it's important to cover the bottom of the pan with a piece of parchment paper.

put steps in correct order

Now it's time to make the batter. Melt half a stick of butter, three ounces of semisweet chocolate, and three-fourths cup of milk chocolate chips in a large saucepan. Set the heat low. and keep stirring so that nothing burns.

While the butter and chocolate melt together, remove the pan from the stove. Add half a cup of brown sugar and two tablespoons of honey to the pan.

Reflect

Read the first part of Alika's draft. What does the writer do to make his voice friendly and informative?

Apply

Use your outline to write a draft of your how-to essay. Imagine that you are talking to a person so that your voice sounds natural and friendly.

Revise

Focus on Ideas

The Rubric Says   All details are related to the process.

Writing Strategy   Take out details that are not related to the process.

The rubric says that all of the details in my essay should relate to the process. After reading my first draft again, I saw that in the middle of my draft, I had included information about macadamia nuts that doesn't relate to making brownies. I'll have to take it out of my essay. If I leave it in, it could distract readers from the directions.

Finally stir in two-thirds cup of chopped macadamia nuts.

~~I don't chop the nuts too much because I love a big, crunchy~~

~~piece of nut in every bite of brownie!~~

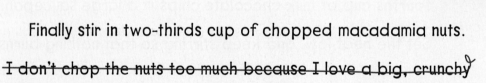

deleted unnecessary information

[DRAFT]

Reflect

Look at the revision. Why is the information deleted?

Apply

Read your draft again. Look for details that are not related to the process and take them out.

The Rubric Says	The writer uses precise language (specific nouns and strong verbs) that help the reader "see" the process.
Writing Strategy	Use words that help readers picture the process.

I know from the rubric that I should use specific nouns and strong verbs. Precise words help the reader understand the process. A word like *batter* instead of *brownies* is more helpful for the beginning of the process. A word like *spread* gives a better picture of how to put the batter in the pan.

[DRAFT]

added specific words

spread   Bake

When the batter is completely mixed, put it in the pan. Heat

the brownies for about 30 minutes.

Reflect

Look at the revisions. How do they help the reader picture the process?

Apply

Read your draft. Make sure that the reader can picture the process. Use specific nouns and strong verbs.

Revise

Focus on  **Sentence Fluency**

The Rubric Says   Sentence beginnings are varied and helpful to the reader.

Writing Strategy   Make sure sentence beginnings guide the reader.

It's important that the reader is able follow the steps of my essay. I can guide the reader by placing helpful information at the beginning of the sentences. Words like *now* and *first* show the order of the steps. They are easier to spot if I put them at the beginning of the sentences. Also, they make my writing sound smooth.

added helpful word

[DRAFT]

First

Now it's time to make the batter. Melt half a stick of butter,

three ounces of semisweet chocolate, and three-fourths cup

of milk chocolate chips in a large saucepan. Set the heat low

and keep stirring so that nothing burns.

fixed punctuation

Apply

Read your draft. Make sure your sentences guide the reader through the process.

The Rubric Says All pronouns are used correctly.

Writing Strategy Check that all pronouns are used correctly.

The rubric tells me that I need to check my essay for errors. I'm going to check spelling, punctuation, and capitalization first. Then I'm going to make sure that I've used all the pronouns correctly.

Writer's Term

Pronouns
A **pronoun** can replace a noun naming a person, place, or thing. Pronouns include **I, me, you, we, us, he, she, it, they,** and **them**.

corrected pronoun

set the pan of brownies on the kitchen counter to cool. When

                                    them   peel
the brownies are cold, cut it into squares (Don't forget to peel

the parchment paper off the bottoms!)

[DRAFT]

Reflect
Look at the edits. Are all pronouns used correctly?

Apply Conventions
Edit your draft for spelling, punctuation, and capitalization. Check that you have used all pronouns correctly.

For more practice using pronouns correctly, use the exercises on the next two pages.

Subject and Object Pronouns

Know the Rule

A **pronoun** is a word that can take the place of one or more nouns in a sentence. A **subject pronoun** takes the place of one or more nouns in the subject of a sentence.

Use the pronouns *I, we, he, she,* and *they* as subjects in sentences.

An **object pronoun** follows action verbs or prepositions, such as *to, at, for, of,* and *with.*

Use the pronouns *me, us, him, her,* and *them* as objects in sentences. The pronoun *you* is used as a subject or an object. The pronoun *it* can be a subject or an object.

Practice the Rule

Number a sheet of paper from 1–8. Write a pronoun that can take the place of the underlined word or words in each sentence.

1. <u>My friend Paulo and I</u> live in a small town on the island of Maui.
2. Every Saturday morning, <u>Paulo and I</u> run over to the bakery owned by Mr. and Mrs. Lee.
3. <u>The Lees</u> make the best fresh bread and pastries on Maui!
4. Mrs. Lee uses family recipes, and <u>Mrs. Lee</u> bakes a mango bread that is delicious.
5. <u>Mango bread</u> is made using fresh mangoes and macadamia nuts.
6. Mr. Lee runs the bakery shop, and <u>Mr. Lee</u> always has a loaf of mango bread waiting for me on Saturdays.
7. Paulo always buys papaya muffins and takes <u>the papaya muffins</u> home to his mother.
8. Sometimes Paulo eats one of <u>the papaya muffins</u> before he gets home. They're so good!

Pronoun Antecedents

Know the Rule

A **pronoun** must match the noun it replaces. A singular pronoun must be used in place of a singular noun. A plural pronoun must be used in place of a plural noun.
> **Examples:**
> Mr. Singh teaches music. **He** also plays the piano.
> The students think Mr. Singh is great! **They** all love music.

Practice the Rule

Number a sheet of paper from 1–10. Write the correct pronoun to complete each sentence.

1. My sister loves to bake. _____ decided to take a baking class.
2. The teacher, Tim, is a pastry chef. _____ works at a fancy restaurant.
3. My sister brought home apple tarts from class. _____ were delicious!
4. Next the class made a pineapple cake. My sister said _____ had three layers.
5. My brother and I were hoping to taste a piece, but _____ didn't get to try it.
6. I hope my sister makes cookies sometime. _____ are easy to make.
7. I like walnuts in my cookies, but my sister is allergic to _____.
8. Oatmeal cookies are good with raisins in _____.
9. A cherry pie would be good, too. _____ is my favorite dessert.
10. Maybe I should eat a piece of fruit. _____ would be better for me!

Publish

+Presentation

Publishing Strategy   Publish the essay in a class how-to book.

Presentation Strategy   Indent every paragraph.

I've completed my how-to essay! Now I have to decide how to publish it. I chose the topic of making brownies because I thought kids in my class would like to try making their own. Other kids want to share their how-to essays, too. We decided to put all our essays together in a class how-to book. The book will go in the class library.

I want to be sure my classmates can follow the directions, so I will indent each paragraph. This makes it easy to see where a new step or idea starts. Also, I'll put a little extra space between the paragraphs so the reader can easily find his or her place after looking away. Before I publish my how-to essay, I'm going to check it over one last time. Here's the final checklist I'll use.

My Final Checklist

Did I—

✔ proofread carefully for capitalization, punctuation, and grammar?

✔ use pronouns correctly?

✔ indent every paragraph?

✔ put an extra space between paragraphs?

Apply

Use this checklist to publish your own how-to essay. Be sure to check your essay one last time before publishing it.

Fantastic Chocolate Macadamia Nut Brownies
by Alika

These Fantastic Chocolate Macadamia Nut Brownies that I make taste like Hawaii to me. Try making some, and see if you agree!

Before you make the brownie batter, you have to heat the oven to 350 degrees. Then brush a little butter inside of an eight-inch square baking pan. After you do that, cover the bottom of the pan with a piece of parchment paper.

Now it's time to make the batter. First melt half a stick of butter, three ounces of semisweet chocolate, and three-fourths cup of milk chocolate chips in a large saucepan. Set the heat low and keep stirring so that nothing burns.

After the butter and chocolate melt together, remove the pan from the stove. Then add half a cup of brown sugar and two tablespoons of honey to the pan. Mix everything well so that there aren't any lumps! Once that is done, let the mixture cool for a few minutes.

While you are waiting for the chocolate mixture to cool, beat two eggs with one teaspoon of vanilla extract. Then add the eggs to the chocolate. (If you don't let the chocolate cool down first, the heat will turn the eggs into scrambled eggs!)

Now sift one cup flour along with half a teaspoon of salt into the chocolate. Mix it all together gently. Finally stir in two-thirds cup of chopped macadamia nuts.

When the batter is completely mixed, spread it in the pan. Bake the brownies for about 30 minutes.

Set the pan of brownies on the kitchen counter to cool. When the brownies are cold, cut them into squares. (Don't forget to peel the parchment paper off the bottoms!) Enjoy your Fantastic Chocolate Macadamia Nut Brownies with a glass of milk or a scoop of ice cream.

Reflect

Use the rubric to check Alika's essay. Are the traits of a good how-to essay there? Check your own how-to essay with the rubric, too.

What's a Summary?

A summary is a shorter piece of writing that tells the main points of a longer piece of writing.

What's in a Summary?

Main Ideas
A summary should explain the main ideas of an original piece of writing. The purpose of a good summary is to help the reader understand and remember the main ideas.

Supporting Details
A summary should include important details from the original piece. All details should support the main ideas.

Organization
Summaries should state the most important point first so the reader knows what the summary explains.

Length
Because a summary is shorter than the original piece of writing, the writer has to be careful not to use too many extra words.

Why write a Summary?

There are many reasons to write a summary. In fact, you will probably write summaries in most of your classes. Here are three important reasons to write them.

To Inform
Summaries are a great way to share information. I can write a summary to inform others about a book or an article I've read, a speech that I've heard, or a movie I've seen.

To Understand
Summarizing is a good way to make sure I understand someone else's ideas. If I can pick out all the main ideas, then I know I understand what the author is trying to get across.

To Research
Summarizing could be really useful when I'm doing research. When I'm starting a project, I read a lot of different reference materials before I focus on my topic. If I write a summary of each reference article, I can keep track of things.

Linking Informative/Explanatory Writing Traits to a Summary

In this chapter, you will briefly tell about an article you have read. This type of informative/explanatory writing is called a summary. Alika will guide you through the stages of the writing process: Prewrite, Draft, Revise, Edit, and Publish. In each stage, Alika will show you important writing strategies that are linked to the Informative/Explanatory Writing Traits below.

Informative/Explanatory Writing Traits

- clear topic and main ideas
- details, information, and examples that answer the reader's questions about the topic

- a strong introduction, body, and conclusion
- well-organized paragraphs
- transitions that connect ideas

- a voice and tone that are appropriate for the purpose and audience

- precise words
- domain-specific vocabulary that is used correctly and explained as necessary

- clear, direct sentences that flow smoothly

- no or few errors in grammar, usage, mechanics, and spelling

Before you write, read Mitchell Martino's summary of an article about photosynthesis. Then use the summary rubric on pages 194–195 to decide how well he did. (You might want to look back at What's in a Summary? on page 188, too!)

What Is Photosynthesis?

by Leah Flora
Summary by Mitchell Martino

main ideas

All living things need food to live and grow. People do this by eating food. Plants do this by making their own food in a process called photosynthesis.

organization

Plants need three things to make food—energy, carbon dioxide, and water. Plants get energy from the sunlight, carbon dioxide from the air, and water from the soil. With these three ingredients, plants can perform photosynthesis, which means "putting together with light." *Photo* means "light" and *synthesis* means "putting together."

supporting details

All the action happens in the leaves of green plants. Plants are green because of chlorophyll. The green chlorophyll is inside structures called chloroplasts. The chloroplasts collect energy from sunlight. (That's the "light" part of *photosynthesis*.) Carbon dioxide enters the underside of leaves through tiny holes called stomata, and water from the roots moves up the plant through tubes called xylem. With energy from sunlight, the chloroplasts combine the carbon dioxide and water. (That's the "putting together" part.) As a result, plants create sugars, or food, as well as give off oxygen during the process of photosynthesis.

We need plants to survive. Plants store some of the food they make, and that's how fruits, such as apples, and vegetables, such as carrots, give our own bodies energy. Because plants also give off oxygen, we have fresh air to breathe. Life on this planet would not be possible without plants.

one-page length

What Is Photosynthesis?

by Leah Flora

Food for Thought

Does a plant eat? You might be thinking, "That's silly. Of course plants don't eat food!" Not so fast! You may be surprised to learn that plants convert light, gas, and water to make their own food.

You Are What You Eat

No doubt you've heard this old saying, and it still holds true. People and many other animals, including fish and birds, consume parts of plants, like the roots, the stems, the flowers, and the leaves. They also eat the seeds, fruits, and vegetables that are produced by plants every day.

It's no secret that our bodies depend on plants. We need them in order to breathe and remain healthy. Many green plants contain the nutrients we use in vitamins and medicines.

Photo Op

In order to be food for us, plants first produce food for themselves. The process of making their food is called *photosynthesis* (foh • toh • **sin** • thih • sis). *Photo* means "light" and *synthesis* means "putting together."

Using three things—energy from sunlight, carbon dioxide from the air, and water from the soil—plants manufacture their own food.

A Little Sunlight, Please

Plants' food manufacturing process takes place in the leaves of green plants in special cell structures called *chloroplasts*. This part of the plant cell contains *chlorophyll* molecules that are called *photoreceptors*. These light-sensitive molecules absorb the sun's energy as sunlight shines on the surface of the leaves. Chlorophyll gives leaves their green color.

Breath of Fresh Air

On the underside of leaves are tiny openings called *stomata*. Carbon dioxide, an invisible gas, is a *byproduct* of human and animal respiration. The carbon dioxide we exhale into the air is taken in through the stomata on plant leaves.

CO_2 by Any Other Name

To complete the cycle, plants take up rainwater and the nutrients in the soil through their roots. The water travels upward through tubes

called *xylem* to reach the leaves. Even the tallest trees pull water to their leaves against gravity! When the water reaches the leaves, those efficient chloroplasts "put together" the water and carbon dioxide (CO_2). This process forms sugars, which are the food for the plant. Tubes called *phloem* carry and store the sugars inside the plant.

Thank a Plant

It's good that plants and people share the planet! Both plants and people benefit from the process of photosynthesis. Not only do plants make food (sugars) for their own use, but through their leaves they release the oxygen we breathe. Plants also produce something else that is important to our survival—fruits, grains, and vegetables! So, the next time you take a bite from a juicy apple, munch a carrot stick, or dream under the shade of an oak tree, remember to thank a plant!

Summary Rubric

Use this 6-point rubric to plan and score a summary.

	6	5	4
Ideas	The topic is clear. Only main ideas and supporting details are included.	The topic is clear. Most main ideas are supported.	The topic is clear. Some details do not support the main ideas.
Organization	The main points are given in logical order. The summary is easy to follow.	Most main points are given in a logical order. Most of the summary is easy to follow.	A few main points are in logical order. The summary is not easy to follow in places.
Voice	The tone is consistent and appropriate for the purpose and the audience.	The tone is consistent and appropriate most of the time.	The tone is appropriate in the beginning, but it fades.
Word Choice	Domain-specific vocabulary is used and explained. Strong verbs help the reader understand the topic.	Domain-specific words are used and explained. Most of the verbs are strong and helpful.	Several domain-specific words may be used incorrectly or need explanations. Most of the verbs are strong and helpful.
Sentence Fluency	Sentences are clear and direct.	Most sentences are clear and direct.	A few sentences are not clear.
Conventions	The writing contains no errors. There are no double negatives. Verbs are correct.	A few errors are present but do not confuse the reader. There are no double negatives.	Several errors confuse the reader. Double negatives or incorrect verbs stop the reader.

+ Presentation The summary is neat and legible.

3	2	1	
The topic may not be clear. Many details do not support the topic.	The topic is not clear. Details do not support the topic.	The topic is not given. Details are not provided.	**Ideas**
Some main points are not in order, making the summary difficult to follow.	Main points are not in order, confusing the reader.	The writing is not organized as a summary.	**Organization**
The tone is somewhat formal, but uses casual language in some places.	The voice and tone are too informal for the purpose and audience.	The voice is absent. The reader does not know the writer's purpose.	**Voice**
Domain-specific words are not used. Many verbs are weak.	Domain-specific vocabulary may be used incorrectly. Verbs are very weak.	Many words are not specific and used incorrectly.	**Word Choice**
Some sentences are too long, causing the reader to have to reread.	Many sentences are awkward to read or are too long, confusing the reader.	Sentences are incomplete or incorrect.	**Sentence Fluency**
Many errors get in the way of meaning. Double negatives are used. Some verbs are incorrect.	Serious errors stop the reader. Double negatives are used. Some verbs are incorrect.	The writing has not been edited.	**Conventions**

See Appendix B for 4-, 5-, and 6-point informative/explanatory rubrics.

Using the Rubric to Study the Model

Did you notice that the model on page 191 points out some key elements of a summary? As he wrote, Mitchell used these elements to help him summarize how plants make food and how plants are food for us. He also used the 6-point rubric on pages 194–195 to plan, draft, revise, and edit the writing. A rubric is a great tool to evaluate writing during the writing process.

Now let's use the same rubric to score the model. To do this, we'll focus on each trait separately, starting with Ideas. We'll use the top descriptor for each trait (column 6), along with examples from the model, to help us understand how the traits work.

Ideas

- **The topic is clear.**
- **Only main ideas and supporting details are included.**

I think Mitchell does a good job of summarizing the article. The article is about how plants make their own food through the process of photosynthesis. Even though the summary is shorter, it includes the main ideas in the article.

I also noticed that the article included information that we use nutrients from plants in vitamins and medicines. These details would not have fit Mitchell's main points, so he left them out.

With these three ingredients, plants can perform photosynthesis, which means "putting together with light." *Photo* means "light" and *synthesis* means "putting together."

Organization

- The main points are given in logical order.
- The summary is easy to follow.

Mitchell organizes his main points logically. His summary is very easy to follow. We're studying the parts of plants in science class. The summary really helped me understand how green plants make food for themselves and for us.

The chloroplasts collect energy from sunlight. (That's the "light" part of *photosynthesis*.) Carbon dioxide enters the underside of leaves through tiny holes called stomata, and water from the roots moves up the plant through tubes called xylem.

Voice

- The tone is consistent and appropriate for the purpose and the audience.

I know that Mitchell read the article carefully because he definitely sounds knowledgeable. I think he wants the reader to know that his information is accurate. He sounds enthusiastic about sharing what he's learned, but he uses a formal tone.

All living things need food to live and grow. People do this by eating food. Plants do this by making their own food in process called photosynthesis.

Using the Summary Rubric to Study the Model

Word Choice

- Domain-specific vocabulary is used and explained.
- Strong verbs help the reader understand the topic.

I noticed that Mitchell uses and explains many of the words from the article in his summary. If I hadn't read Ms. Flora's article, I would need these words to understand photosynthesis. Mitchell uses strong verbs, such as *perform, combine, create,* and *photosynthesize.* They really help me understand the process.

As a result, plants create sugars, or food, as well as give off oxygen during the process of photosynthesis.

Sentence Fluency

- Sentences are clear and direct.

Mitchell's sentences are clear and focused all the way through the summary. They support his purpose for writing. The sentences in the introduction state the topic and prepare the reader to learn about photosynthesis. The sentences in the body of the summary explain the process. The sentences in the conclusion tell how plants help us.

Because plants also give off oxygen, we have fresh air to breathe. Life on this planet would not be possible without plants.

Conventions
- The writing contains no errors.
- There are no double negatives.
- Verbs are correct.

I didn't notice any errors in the summary. All subjects and verbs agree, too. I'm sure that Mitchell used a dictionary to check the spelling and usage of unfamiliar words. In this example, the word *chloroplasts* is plural, so he was careful to use a plural verb, *combine*.

With energy from sunlight, the chloroplasts combine the carbon dioxide and water.

⁺Presentation The summary is neat and legible.

My Turn!

Now it's my turn to write a summary. I'll use the rubric and good writing strategies to help me. Read on to see how I do it.

Prewrite

The Rubric Says   The topic is clear. Only main ideas and supporting details are included.

Writing Strategy   Read an article and take notes about the main points.

My teacher asked us to read an article and write a summary of it. I chose an article on simple machines because we studied them in science. As I read, I found the main points in the article. On page 202, you will see the notes I took as I read.

Machines Work

by J. Johar-Newton

Machines Make Life Easier

Beep! Beep! Beep! Your alarm clock sounds and you reach to turn it off. As you stretch your arms and roll out of bed, you wonder what's for breakfast. Scrambled eggs? Cereal? You walk out to the kitchen and hear coffee percolating and toast popping out of the toaster. As you sit down at the table, you wonder: What would my day be like without machines? No alarm clock to wake me up. No stove or microwave to heat up food. No toast. Without machines, you would have to do a lot more work just to make it through breakfast!

Simple Machines

The machines you used this morning are complex with multiple parts working together, and they made work easier for you. But what is work? In science, work is the result of applying a force over a distance to move an object. A force is a push or a pull. Most simple machines reduce the amount of force needed to move an object. That makes work easier for you!

In this article, you will learn about one of the six types of simple machines: levers. There are three classes of levers.

Levers: A Class Act

The lever is an inflexible bar that moves on a fixed point called a fulcrum. Take, for example, a paint can with a tightly sealed lid. You can try to pry off the lid with your fingers, but you would need a great deal of force. Using a screwdriver as a lever can make the work of removing the lid easier.

First-Class Levers

In a first-class lever such as this, the fulcrum, where the screwdriver touches the rim of the can, is between the input and the output forces. As you apply an input force by pushing on one end of the lever, the lever pivots on the fulcrum. The other end of the lever moves in the opposite direction,

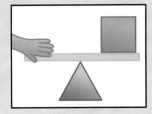

First-class lever

and the output force pops off the lid. The distance your hand moves is longer than the distance the lid moves. The work of getting the lid off was made easier. You put in a smaller amount of force over a longer distance and got a greater amount of force over a smaller distance. Seesaws, claw hammers, and crowbars are other examples of first-class levers.

Second-Class Levers

One type of second-class lever is a nutcracker. In second-class levers, the fulcrum—where the two handles, or levers, are joined—is at one end. The

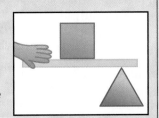

Second-class lever

input force is at the other end, where your hand is, with the output force in between. As you squeeze your hand inward, the levers turn around the fulcrum. The levers move in the same inward direction and exert an output force that cracks the nut's hard shell. The work of cracking the nut was made easier. You put in a smaller amount of force over a longer distance and got a greater amount of force over a smaller distance in return. Wheelbarrows and staplers are other examples of second-class levers.

Third-Class Levers

In a third-class lever, such as a baseball bat, the fulcrum, or pivot point, is at one end—in this case, your elbow. Your forearm becomes

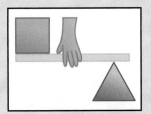

Third-class lever

part of the lever. The output force is at the other end, the end of the bat. The input force is in between, where your hands supply the force to swing the bat. As in a second-class lever, the input and output forces act in the same direction. In a third-class lever, however, a greater input force is needed over a smaller distance. In return, you get a smaller output force applied over a longer distance. The output force also acts with a greater speed, which is helpful when hitting a moving target. Tennis rackets, golf clubs, and fishing rods are other examples of third-class levers.

Natural Levers

Natural levers can be found inside our bodies. Our elbows, arms, knees, and jaw help us move objects every day.

As part of the family of simple machines, levers help us by making work and play easier. Look around you. What levers do you see? What levers have you used today?

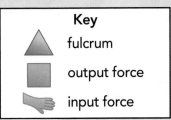

Key

△ fulcrum

▢ output force

✋ input force

To summarize the article "Machines Work," I first need to find the author's main points. Then I'll choose only the details that support them. Here are my notes. Did you pick out the same big ideas?

Notes on "Machines Work"

✔ Machines help us do work.

✔ Work happens when a force (push or pull) moves something over a distance.

✔ Simple machines are simple. Can reduce force you exert. Makes work easier.

✔ There are 6 simple machines. One is the lever. It's a bar that pivots on a fulcrum, fixed point.

   ✔ First-class lever needs a small force over a long distance to get a large force over a short distance. Input force and output force are in opposite directions. Examples include screwdrivers used to open lids, seesaws, claw hammers, crowbars.

✔ Second-class lever needs a small force over a long distance to get a large force over a short distance. Input and output forces are in same direction. Examples include nutcrackers, wheelbarrows, and staplers.

✔ Third-class lever needs a large force over a short distance to get a small force over a long distance. Input and output forces are in same direction. You gain speed. Examples include baseball bats, tennis rackets, golf clubs, and fishing rods.

Apply

Choose an article about a science topic that interests you. Read the article and take notes on the main points.

The Rubric Says   The main points are given in logical order.

Writing Strategy   Use a Five-Column Chart to organize the main points.

I need to organize my notes in a clear way so that I can put them in a logical order in my summary. This way my summary will be easy to follow. I'll use a Five-Column Chart to categorize ideas about levers. Each heading identifies a main point about levers. Each row gives details about a different class of lever. You can see my Five-Column Chart below.

Writer's Term

Five-Column Chart

A **Five-Column Chart** organizes information in specific categories. A main point is written in each heading, with important details in each column.

Five-Column Chart

Type of Lever and Examples	Placement of Fulcrum and Forces	Direction of Forces	Input Force/ Distance	Output Force/ Distance
First-class levers: screwdriver used to take off paint can lid, seesaw, claw hammer used to pry nails	Fulcrum between input and output forces	Opposite	Small/Long	Great/Short
Second-class levers: nutcracker, wheelbarrow, stapler	Fulcrum on one end, output force, input force	Same	Small/Long	Great/Short
Third-class levers: baseball bat, tennis racket, golf club, fishing rod	Fulcrum on one end, input force, output force	Same	Great/Short	Small/Long Output force is fast!

Reflect

How will Alika's Five-Column Chart help him write a summary?

Apply

Look at your notes. Organize them in a Five-Column Chart.

Draft

Focus on Word Choice

The Rubric Says   Domain-specific vocabulary is used and explained. Strong verbs help the reader understand the topic.

Writing Strategy   Use precise words and strong verbs.

I will need to use and explain some of the words from the article. For example, I will definitely use *lever* and *fulcrum*. I'll also choose strong verbs to help explain how simple machines work. One strong verb is clearer than using several vague, or unclear, words. I will keep this in mind while drafting, but I will focus on getting my ideas down first.

After I write down all of the important ideas, I will go back to the summary and revise with a focus on wording. As I draft, I will do my best not to make spelling, grammar, punctuation, or capitalization errors, but I know that I'll have a chance to fix them later when I edit.

Machines Work    [DRAFT]

Machines help us every day. Some machines are very complex; others are more simple. In science terms, work is the result of applying a force over a distance to move an object, which makes the work of moving the object much easier. Simple machines are tools that help make our work easier.

Proofreading Marks

⏋ Indent	ℓ Take out something
☰ Make a capital	⊙ Add a period
/ Make a small letter	⌗ New paragraph
∧ Add something	ⓢⓟ Spelling error

[DRAFT]

One of the six simple machines is called a lever. A lever is an inflexible bar that pivots on a fixed point called a fulcrum. The position of the fulcrum, the input force, and the output force determine whether the lever is a first-, second-, or third-class lever. Each lever has its own advantages.

A first-class lever, such as a seesaw, has the fulcrum located between the input and output forces. My cousin fell off a seesaw and broke her wrist. A smaller input force is applied over a longer distance, resulting in a greater output force applied over a shorter distance. The input and the output forces act in opposite directions. When you use a screwdriver to pry off a paint can lid, you are using a first-class lever to make work easier. Seesaws, claw hammers, and crowbars are examples of first-class levers.

precise words

strong verbs

precise words

Reflect

Read the beginning of Alika's draft. Did he choose precise words that help the reader understand the topic?

Apply

Use your notes and chart to draft your summary. Choose precise words and strong verbs to explain the main points.

Revise

Focus on Ideas

The Rubric Says   Only main ideas and supporting details are included.

Writing Strategy   Make sure all details support the main ideas.

The rubric reminds me to check my draft to make sure all my details support my ideas. I noticed that in my paragraph about first-class levers, I used *seesaw* as an example in both the first and last sentences.

I also deleted the sentence about my cousin because this detail does not support the main idea.

Writer's Term

Supporting Details
Supporting details provide important information the reader needs to understand the main ideas.

[DRAFT]

A first-class lever, ~~such as a seesaw,~~ has the fulcrum located between the input and output forces. ~~My cousin fell off a seesaw and broke her wrist.~~ A smaller input force is applied over a longer distance, resulting in a greater output force applied over a shorter distance. The input and the output forces act in opposite directions. When you use a screwdriver to pry off a paint can lid, you are using a first-class lever to make work easier. Seesaws, claw hammers, and crowbars are examples of first-class levers.

removed repetitive detail

removed non-supporting detail

Apply

Read your draft carefully. Make sure your details are important and support your ideas.

Revise

The Rubric Says   The main points are given in logical order.

Writing Strategy   Put the most important idea first.

The author's most important point needs to be stated at the beginning of my summary. I read my introduction again and decided that the first two sentences didn't really state the main idea. So I crossed them out and moved the last sentence in the paragraph to the beginning. Do you think my revision improves my introduction?

Simple machines are tools that help make our work easier. **[DRAFT]**

~~Machines help us every day. Some machines are very complex; others are more simple.~~ In science terms, work is the result of applying a force over a distance to move an object, which makes the work of moving the object much easier.

put most important idea first

Reflect

Did Alika improve the order of ideas in the introduction? In what way?

Apply

Make sure that your summary begins with the most important idea and that other important ideas follow logically.

Revise

Focus on Sentence Fluency

The Rubric Says   Sentences are clear and direct.

Writing Strategy   Write clear sentences.

I know from the rubric that my sentences need to be clear and direct. When I read my draft again, I noticed that the beginning of my paragraph about second-class levers was long and confusing. I revised it by breaking it into two sentences. Do you think I improved my writing?

[DRAFT]

A second-class lever has the fulcrum on one end, the input

and ←

force on the other, the output force in between, and the forces

in this kind of lever act in the same direction.

revised long, confusing sentence

Apply

Check your draft for long or confusing sentences and clarify them.

The Rubric Says	The writing contains no errors. There are no double negatives. Verbs are correct.
Writing Strategy	Check for double negatives. Make sure verbs are used correctly.

This is my chance to correct any mistakes I made while writing my draft. First I checked my spelling, capitalization, and punctuation to make sure my writing is correct. Then I reread my draft to look for double negatives and verb errors. I found some! Here are my edits.

Writer's Term

Negatives
A **negative** is a word that means "no" or "not." Do not use two negatives in the same sentence.

[DRAFT]

used correct verb

Each class of levers function to make our work easier. We
   s
may not think about them very much, but levers help us every

day. We can't ~~hardly~~ work or play without their help.

corrected double negative

Reflect

How do Alika's edits make the writing easier to understand?

Apply

Conventions

Edit your writing carefully. Be on the lookout for errors you make easily. Be sure you have not used double negatives.

For more practice in fixing double negatives and subject-verb errors, use the exercises on the next two pages.

Negatives

Know the Rule

A **negative** is a word that means "no" or "not." The words *no, not, nothing, none, never, nowhere,* and *nobody* are negatives. The word *not* is found in contractions such as *don't* or *wasn't*. Do not use two negatives, called a double negative, in the same sentence.

Practice the Rule

Number a separate sheet of paper from 1–10. Correctly rewrite the sentences that have double negatives. If the sentence is correct, write **Correct**.

1. Who can work or play without no simple machines?
2. We couldn't barely move the log a few inches without a lever.
3. There were no simple machines nowhere to help move the heavy boxes.
4. By using a smaller force over a longer distance, a lever can make work easier for you.
5. That rusty wheelbarrow can't barely hold the weight.
6. After smashing his thumb, he won't use no hammer to crack open a walnut.
7. She didn't mention no scissors as an example of a first-class lever.
8. Everyone agreed that a golf club is a third-class lever.
9. The lid hardly didn't budge until she applied an input force.
10. He told the men never to move no heavy loads without using a lever.

Action Verbs and Linking Verbs

Know the Rule

An **action verb** tells what the subject of a sentence does. (*Waves crashed on the beach.*) A **linking verb** links the subject with words that tell what the subject is or is like. (*The waves were powerful.*) Linking verbs include *am, is, are, was, were, become,* and *seem.* Hint: Look for the linking verbs in contractions, too.

Practice the Rule

Number a separate sheet of paper from 1–10. Write the verb in each sentence and tell whether it is an action verb or a linking verb.

1. A force is a push or a pull.
2. The lever pivots around the fulcrum.
3. That's not a lever! It's an inclined plane.
4. Each simple machine functions in a helpful way.
5. The hammer pries the rusty nail from the board.
6. He used his arm as a lever.
7. Machines with many parts are not simple machines.
8. The Jaws of Life opened the car door.
9. Is a pair of pliers a first-class lever?
10. The children sped toward the seesaw.

Publish

+Presentation

Publishing Strategy   Post the summary to the class website.

Presentation Strategy   Use a clear font and indent paragraphs.

My teacher is posting all of our summaries to a class website for the whole class to read. When I type my summary on the computer, I can use the word-processing features to make a neat copy. If I use a clear font and indent each paragraph, my summary will be easy to read. I made a final checklist to help me prepare my final copy.

My Final Checklist

Did I—

✔ check the spelling, punctuation, and capitalization?

✔ make sure my summary contains no double negatives?

✔ look to see that all verbs are used correctly?

✔ use a clear font and indent all paragraphs?

Apply

Use this checklist to prepare your final copy. Then publish your summary.

Machines Work
by J. Johar-Newton
Summary by Alika

Simple machines are tools that help make our work easier. In science terms, work is the result of applying a force over a distance to move an object. A force is a push or a pull. A simple machine can reduce the amount of force needed to move an object, which makes the work of moving the object much easier.

One of the six simple machines is called a lever. A lever is an inflexible bar that pivots on a fixed point called a fulcrum. The position of the fulcrum, the input force, and the output force determine whether the lever is a first-, second-, or third-class lever. Each lever has its own advantages.

A first-class lever has the fulcrum located between the input and output forces. A smaller input force is applied over a longer distance, resulting in a greater output force applied over a shorter distance. The forces push and pull in opposite directions. When you use a screwdriver to pry off a paint can lid, you are using a first-class lever to make work easier. Seesaws, claw hammers, and crowbars are examples of first-class levers.

A second-class lever has the fulcrum on one end, the input force on the other, and the output force in between. The forces in this kind of lever act in the same direction. As in the first-class lever, a smaller input force is applied over a longer distance, and a greater output force is applied over a shorter distance. Wheelbarrows and staplers are examples of second-class levers.

A third-class lever has the fulcrum on one end, the output force on the other, and the input force in between. The forces act in the same direction, but the input force is greater than the output force. In third-class levers, the input force acts over a shorter distance than the output force. What the output force lacks in strength it gains in speed, and that's what you need to drive a ball. Tennis rackets, golf clubs, and fishing rods are examples of third-class levers.

Each class of levers functions to make our work easier. We may not think about them very much, but levers help us every day. Even parts of our bodies act as natural levers. We can't work or play without their help.

Reflect

Use the rubric to score Alika's summary and your own.

Informative/ Explanatory test writing

Read the Writing Prompt

As you begin a writing test, the first thing you'll read is the writing prompt. Look for three helpful parts in the writing prompt.

Setup This part of the writing prompt gives you the background information you need to get ready for writing.

Task This part of the writing prompt tells you exactly what you're supposed to write: a report about the history of a topic that you know about.

Scoring Guide This section tells how your writing will be scored. To do well on the test, you should include everything on the list.

You've used rubrics for each expository piece you've written using this book. When you take a writing test, you don't always have all the information that a rubric gives you. That's okay. The scoring guide is a lot like a rubric. It lists everything you need to think about to write a good paper. Many scoring guides will include the six important traits of writing that are in the rubrics we've looked at:

People enjoy learning more about a topic that interests them. This topic might be something from sports, nature, or anything!

Write a report about the history of a topic that you know about.

Be sure your report

• provides interesting information related to the topic.

• has a clear introduction, body, and conclusion.

• uses a voice that sounds knowledgeable.

• uses precise words.

• has a variety of clear, direct sentences.

• has correct grammar, spelling, capitalization, and punctuation.

Writing Traits in the Scoring Guide

The scoring guide in the prompt on page 215 has been made into this chart. Does it remind you of the rubrics you've used? Not all prompts include all of the writing traits, but this one does. Use them to do your best writing. Remember to work neatly and put your name on each page.

 **Ideas**
- Be sure your report provides interesting information related to the topic.

 **Organization**
- Be sure your report has a clear introduction, body, and conclusion.

 **Voice**
- Be sure your report uses a voice that sounds knowledgeable.

 **Word Choice**
- Be sure your report uses precise words.

 **Sentence Fluency**
- Be sure your report has a variety of clear, direct sentences.

 **Conventions**
- Be sure your report has correct grammar, spelling, capitalization, and punctuation.

Let's look at the report by Leilani Bishop on the next page. Did she follow the scoring guide?

Mighty Ships of the U.S. Navy

Writing Prompt MODEL Response

by Leilani Bishop

The United States Navy has built many mighty ships. These ships have protected the United States for hundreds of years. As times changed, the ships did, too. When each vessel was built, it was the best and most modern battleship that could be made.

Work began on the first ships in 1794. These ships were called frigates. They protected American ships from pirates and attack by other countries. These ships had big cannons on board and could fight other warships. They were also fast and could get away if they were attacked by bigger ships. One of the frigates was built in Boston, Massachusetts. Its name is the USS *Constitution*, but most people know it as "Old Ironsides." The *Constitution* was used as a warship for more than 60 years. Then for about 40 years it was used to train sailors. Finally, around 1900, it went back to Boston. The *Constitution* is now a museum where people can learn about early warships.

America's warships kept getting bigger and better. Steam engines replaced sails in the late 1800s. Submarines became an important part of the Navy after 1914 and the start of World War I. When planes needed a safe place to land at sea, the Navy built aircraft carriers. Aircraft carriers helped America win World War II in the 1940s.

Aircraft carriers are truly mighty ships. Each carrier is like a floating city with a runway area for launching and landing planes. They use nuclear energy for power. About 3,200 crew members can live on one aircraft carrier. Their jobs might be on the flight deck or in the post office, a television or radio station, stores, a hospital, or a library. The USS *George H. W. Bush* is the most modern aircraft carrier in the Navy today. It is 1,092 feet long. That's more than three football fields put end-to-end!

From frigate to huge aircraft carrier, time has seen many changes in America's warships. Yet one thing has not changed. The mighty ships of the United States Navy will keep on keeping America safe.

Using the Scoring Guide to Study the Model

Let's use the scoring guide to check Leilani's writing test. We'll look for examples from her writing to show how well she did on each part of the scoring guide.

 **Ideas**
- **The report provides interesting information related to the topic.**

Leilani's report provides a lot of interesting information about the history of America's ships. In the body of her report, Leilani stays focused on the topic and tells about the history of Navy ships. A good example can be seen in the opening sentences of the body of her report.

> Work began on the first ships in 1794. These ships were called frigates. They protected American ships from pirates and attack by other countries.

 **Organization**
- **The report has a clear introduction, body, and conclusion.**

The report is well organized. The writer introduces the topic in the first paragraph, follows with interesting details in the body of the report, and wraps up with some concluding thoughts. Here's how she introduced her topic.

> The United States Navy has built many mighty ships. These ships have protected the United States for hundreds of years. As times changed, the ships did, too. When each vessel was built, it was the best and most modern battleship that could be made.

Voice • **The writer's voice sounds knowledgeable.**

Leilani uses lots of facts in her report. Here is a good example. In the first body paragraph, she tells the reader about the most famous of the frigates: the USS *Constitution*. She sounds like an expert on the subject.

One of the frigates was built in Boston, Massachusetts. Its name is the USS *Constitution*, but most people know it as "Old Ironsides." The *Constitution* was used as a warship for more than 60 years. Then for about 40 years it was used to train sailors.

Word Choice • **The report uses precise words.**

Leilani uses precise words in her report. In this part of the report, precise words like *sails*, *steam engines*, and *submarines* help the reader understand how ships have evolved.

America's warships kept getting bigger and better. Steam engines replaced sails in the late 1800s. Submarines became an important part of the Navy after 1914 and the start of World War I. When planes needed a safe place to land at sea, the Navy built aircraft carriers. Aircraft carriers helped America win World War II in the 1940s.

Using the Scoring Guide to Study the Model

- **The report has a variety of clear, direct sentences.**

The scoring guide says to include a variety of well-written sentences. This will make your writing more interesting and keep your reader's attention. In this example, notice how Leilani varies her sentences to keep the report moving along.

> Aircraft carriers are truly mighty ships. Each carrier is like a floating city with a runway area for launching and landing planes. They use nuclear energy for power. About 3,200 crew members can live on one aircraft carrier. Their jobs might be on the flight deck or in the post office, a television or radio station, stores, a hospital, or a library.

- **The report has correct grammar, spelling, capitalization, and punctuation.**

Usually the scoring guide will remind you to check your grammar, spelling, capitalization, and punctuation. Look for mistakes you made and correct them. Watch especially for mistakes that you make often, such as using pronouns or homophones incorrectly. Leilani has done a good job in her report. Her final draft doesn't have any errors.

Planning My Time

Before giving us the writing prompt, my teacher usually tells us how much time we have to complete the test. That gives me the chance to plan how to use the time. Since I know how much time I have, I can divide it into the different parts of the writing process. In my plan, I'll be sure to give myself some time to study the writing prompt. Here's how I've divided my time into four steps.

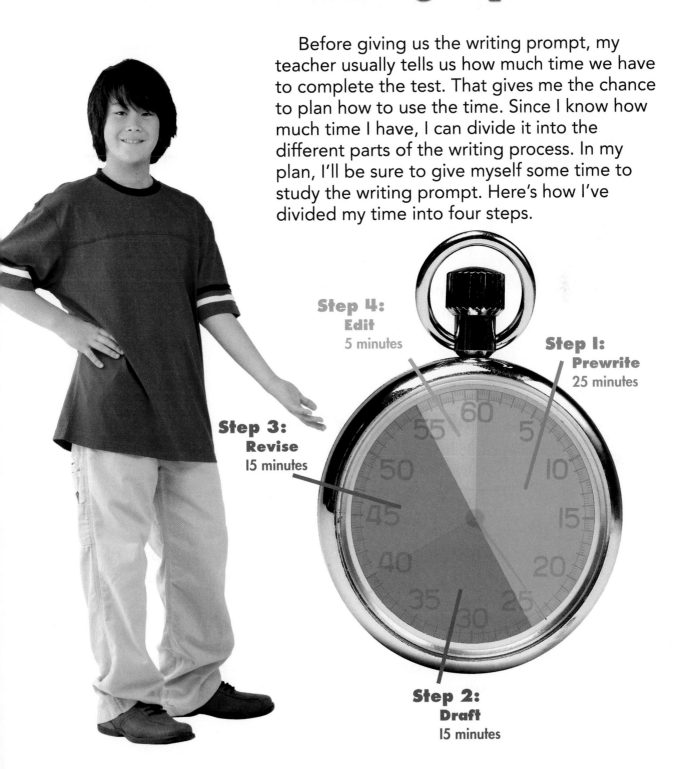

Step 4:
Edit
5 minutes

Step 1:
Prewrite
25 minutes

Step 3:
Revise
15 minutes

Step 2:
Draft
15 minutes

Prewrite

Focus on **Ideas**

Writing Strategy Study the writing prompt to know what to do.

When my teacher gives us the writing prompt, I study it to be sure I know exactly what I'm supposed to do. I find each of the parts and label them: the setup, the task, and the scoring guide. Then I circle key words in the writing prompt that tell what kind of writing to do. You should do the same thing when you take a writing test.

I circled **Write a report** because this tells what kind of writing I'll be doing. I also circled **a place you know** because that is the topic of my report—what I'll be writing about.

My Writing Test Prompt

Setup — Most people have places that they like. These places can be near where you live, in another state, or anywhere!

Task — (Write a report) about (a place you know.)

Scoring Guide — Be sure
- your report provides interesting information related to the topic.
- your report has a clear introduction, body, and conclusion.
- your voice sounds knowledgeable.
- you use precise words.
- your report has a variety of clear, direct sentences.
- your report has correct grammar, spelling, capitalization, and punctuation.

I've studied the writing prompt. Next I'll think about how the scoring guide relates to the six writing traits I've studied in the rubrics. Not all of the traits are included in every scoring guide. Even so, I need to remember them all to write a good report.

Ideas
- **Be sure your report provides interesting information related to one topic.**

I'll make sure that all of my facts are related to my topic.

Organization
- **Be sure your report has a clear introduction, body, and conclusion.**

I'll use a graphic organizer to organize my report. That way I'll know that my report is complete.

Voice
- **Be sure your voice sounds knowledgeable.**

By including facts, I can sound like an expert on the subject.

Word Choice
- **Be sure you use precise words.**

When I begin drafting my report, using words that convey my ideas precisely will make my writing easy to read and understand.

Sentence Fluency
- **Be sure your report has a variety of clear, direct sentences.**

Including a variety of sentences will make my writing more interesting. It will also keep the reader's attention.

Conventions
- **Be sure your report has correct grammar, spelling, capitalization, and punctuation.**

Carefully proofreading my writing is an important step. I'll do this after I write my first draft.

Prewrite

Focus on **Ideas**

Writing Strategy Respond to the writing task.

I've learned that writers first gather information to help them write. This is a key step when writing a report. It's even more important when you are writing for a test and don't have much time.

I'll start by looking again at the task in the writing prompt. The task explains what I'm supposed to write about. It tells me that I need to write a report about a place I know. So first I'll make a list of places to write about. Then I'll decide which place I have the most information about.

Task — [(Write a report) about (a place you know.)]

Places I Could Write About

- the Grand Canyon, Arizona
- Pearl Harbor, Oahu, Hawaii
- Washington, D.C.
- Shipwreck Beach, Oahu, Hawaii

Apply

Before you write, take time to think about how you'll respond to the task part of the prompt.
To gather information, jot down notes or make a short list.

Prewrite

Writing Strategy   Choose a graphic organizer.

I need to start organizing my ideas. I've decided to write my report about Pearl Harbor since I know the most about it. A good graphic organizer for a report is a Web. It will help me organize my information around the main topic.

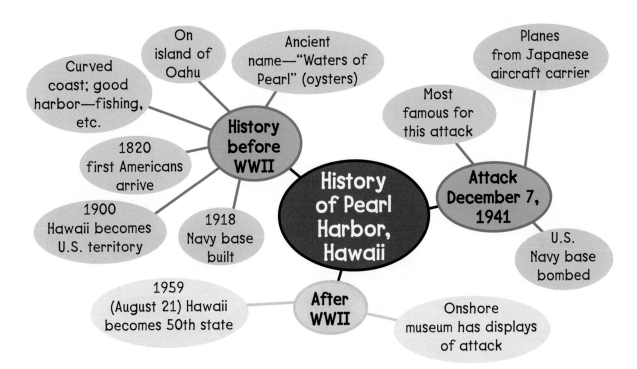

Reflect

Look at the graphic organizer. Does it include enough details to write a good report?

Apply

Choose the best graphic organizer for the assignment and include important details in it. Use your organizer as you begin to write.

Prewrite

Focus on Organization

Writing Strategy Check my graphic organizer against the scoring guide.

When you are writing for a test, you don't have much time to revise. So prewriting is more important than ever! Before I start drafting, I'll check my Web against the scoring guide in the writing prompt. Then I'll know for sure that I'm writing about the assigned topic.

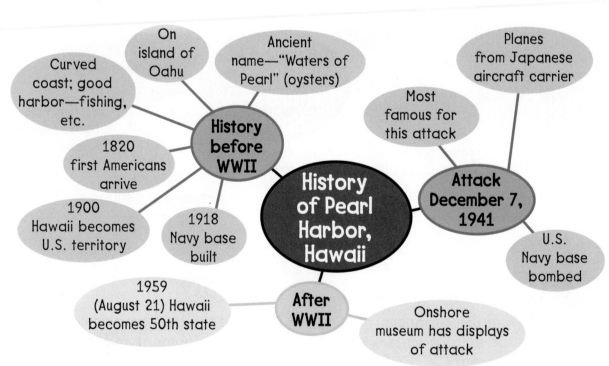

On island of Oahu

Ancient name—"Waters of Pearl" (oysters)

Curved coast; good harbor—fishing, etc.

1820 first Americans arrive

1900 Hawaii becomes U.S. territory

1918 Navy base built

History before WWII

Planes from Japanese aircraft carrier

Most famous for this attack

Attack December 7, 1941

U.S. Navy base bombed

History of Pearl Harbor, Hawaii

1959 (August 21) Hawaii becomes 50th state

After WWII

Onshore museum has displays of attack

Ideas

- Be sure your report provides interesting information related to the topic.

The topic and the information about it are all included in my Web.

Organization

- Be sure your report has a clear introduction, body, and conclusion.

I'll use the Web to write a clear introduction, body, and conclusion. The introduction and conclusion will focus on the information in the center circle. The body paragraph topics will be the words in the darker blue, green, and yellow circles.

Voice

- Be sure your report uses a voice that sounds knowledgeable.

There are facts in my notes and Web. I will use them to help me sound like an expert.

Word Choice

- Be sure your report uses precise words.

I'll use precise words to convey my ideas. This will make my writing easy to read and understand.

Sentence Fluency

- Be sure your report has a variety of clear, direct sentences.

I want to keep my reader's attention. I'll be sure to write a variety of sentences that are clear and interesting.

Conventions

- Be sure your report has correct grammar, spelling, capitalization, and punctuation.

I need to check my grammar, spelling, capitalization, and punctuation when I edit my draft.

Reflect

Why is it important to use a graphic organizer to get started?

Apply

Before you begin to write, be sure you understand what to do.

Draft

Focus on **Ideas**

Writing Strategy   Begin with a topic sentence.

Now it's time to start drafting. The scoring guide tells me to provide interesting information related to my topic. I'll begin my report with a topic sentence. This will be the most important part of the introduction. As I write the rest of my report, I'll stay focused on the topic so I won't confuse my readers.

[DRAFT]

Pearl Harbor, Hawaii

Pearl Harbor is a place with a lot of history. Most people only think of World War II when they hear "Pearl Harbor." A visit to Pearl Harbor, though, will show their are many interesting things about this place.

topic sentence

Planes from a Japanese aircraft carrier flew over Hawaii and bombed the United States Navy base at Pearl Harbor. After that, they were at war. People will always remember Pearl Harbor.

Pearl Harbor is not just a battle in World War II. Its also a beautiful place with an interesting history. Pearl Harbor is on the island of Oahu in Hawaii. The Ancient People of Hawaii named Pearl Harbor. The coast is curved. That makes the harbor a terrific place to go fishing, swimming, and sailing. The first Americans to live in Hawaii arrived in 1820. In 1900, Hawaii became a territory of the United States. In 1918, the navy base was built in Pearl Harbor. In 1959, Hawaii became the 50th state.

Pearl Harbor is famous for the terrible battle that took place there in 1941. A museum displays what the attack was like.

Reflect

Read the draft. Does the introduction include a good topic sentence? Does the writer stick to the topic?

Apply

A good topic sentence is the most important part of the introduction to your report. As you write the body of your report, stay focused on the topic so the reader will be able to follow your ideas easily.

Revise

Focus on Organization

Writing Strategy   Sum up my report in the conclusion.

I've written my draft. Now it's time to read my draft and make revisions. I know that the conclusion should relate to the introduction but sum up the report a little differently. The conclusion is the last thing readers will read and remember, so it has to be good!

[DRAFT]

Pearl Harbor, Hawaii, is a great place to visit. It

~~Pearl Harbor~~ is famous for the terrible battle that took place

Today Pearl Harbor is a place with a long
history and beautiful scenery.

their in 1941. A museum displays what the attack was like.

used pronoun

summed up report

Apply

Read your draft. Check to be sure your conclusion sums up the information in your report.

Revise

Writing Strategy   Use facts to sound knowledgeable.

The scoring guide tells me to be sure my voice sounds knowledgeable. I need to sound like an expert on my topic. One way to do that is to use facts. Notice how I added a date, which is a fact, to my draft.

added a fact

[DRAFT]

On December 7, 1941,

˄Planes from a Japanese aircraft carrier flew over Hawaii and

bombed the United States Navy base at Pearl Harbor.

Reflect

Look at the revision. How does the added fact make the writer sound more knowledgeable about the topic?

Apply

Read your draft. Look for places to add facts to sound like an expert on your topic.

Revise

Focus on Word Choice

Writing Strategy Choose words and phrases to convey ideas precisely.

The scoring guide reminds me to use precise language in my report. This will make my report easy to read and understand. I'll read my draft again. I want to be sure that all my ideas make sense.

[DRAFT]

the United States and Japan

base at Pearl Harbor. After that, ~~they~~

used precise language

for this reason.

were at war. People will always remember Pearl Harbor.

Reflect

Look at the revisions. Do the changes help the reader understand this part of the report?

Apply

Use precise language in your report. Revise any parts that may be unclear to the reader.

Writing Strategy   Check the grammar, spelling, capitalization, and punctuation.

The scoring guide reminds me to check my grammar, spelling, capitalization, and punctuation. It's a good thing that I planned how to use my time. Now I have plenty of time to check for errors. I'll carefully read my draft once more.

Pearl Harbor, Hawaii
by Alika

Pearl Harbor is a place with a lot of history. Most people

only think of World War II when they hear "Pearl Harbor." A visit

to Pearl Harbor, though, will show ~~their~~ there ^ are many interesting

things about this place.
On December 7, 1941,
^ Planes from a Japanese aircraft carrier flew over Hawaii

and bombed the United States Navy base at Pearl Harbor. After
the United States and Japan
that, ~~they~~ ^ were at war. People will always remember Pearl
    for this reason.
Harbor ^

Apply

Be sure to check your grammar, spelling, capitalization, and punctuation.

[FINAL DRAFT]

Pearl Harbor is not just a battle in World War II. ~~Its~~ It's also a

beautiful place with an interesting history. Pearl Harbor is on the

island of Oahu in Hawaii. The Ancient People of Hawaii named

They called it "Waters of Pearl"

because the bottom of the harbor   Since the coast is

was covered by oysters, and   curved, the harbor is

pearls come from oysters.   protected from big waves.

Pearl Harbor. ~~The coast is curved.~~ That makes the harbor a

terrific place to go fishing, swimming, and sailing. The first

Americans to live in Hawaii arrived in 1820. In 1900, Hawaii

became a territory of the United States. ~~In 1918,~~ the navy base

                                    It wasn't until

eighteen years later   August 21, 1959, that

was built in Pearl Harbor. ~~In 1959~~ Hawaii became the 50th state.

Pearl Harbor, Hawaii, is a great place to visit. It

~~Pearl Harbor~~ is famous for the terrible battle that took place

                        Today Pearl Harbor is a place with a long

                        history and beautiful scenery.

there in 1941. A museum displays what the attack was like.

Reflect

Check the report against the scoring guide. Did the writer include everything he will be graded on?

Can you believe it? We're finished! We used the writing prompt and scoring guide to write an interesting report. Remember these important tips when you write for a test.

TEST TIPS

1. **Study the writing prompt before you begin to write.** Remember that most writing prompts have three parts: the setup, the task, and the scoring guide. They won't be labeled. You'll have to figure them out for yourself.

2. **Make sure you understand the task before you begin to write.**
   - Read the three parts of the writing prompt. Then label them.
   - Circle key words in the task. These tell you what kind of writing you need to do. The task might also identify your audience.
   - Read the scoring guide. Make sure you know how you'll be graded.
   - Say the assignment in your own words to yourself.

3. **Plan your time. Then keep an eye on the clock.** Decide how much time you'll spend on each part of the writing process. Stick to your plan as closely as possible. You want to have plenty of time to revise and edit your draft.

4. **Use the scoring guide to check your draft.** The scoring guide is a valuable tool. Like the rubrics you've used on other papers, it reminds you of what is important. Reread your draft at least twice. Make sure that it does what the scoring guide says it should do.

5. **Plan your report well because you won't have much time for revising.** Make notes and use a graphic organizer before you write a draft.

6. **Write neatly.** Remember: The people who score your test must be able to read it!

Opinion writing

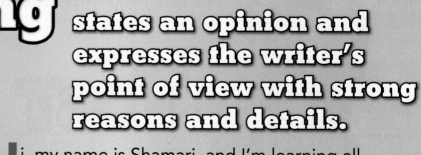

states an opinion and expresses the writer's point of view with strong reasons and details.

Hi, my name is Shamari, and I'm learning all about opinion writing. Opinion writing expresses the writer's point of view. For example, I love drawing pictures and visiting art museums. When I see art that I like, I write about it to tell others why they would love it, too. Learning more about opinion writing will help me do this well.

IN THIS UNIT

- **Opinion Essay**
- **Editorial**
- **Friendly Letter**
- LITERATURE CONNECTION ▷ **Response to Literature**
- **Writing for a Test**

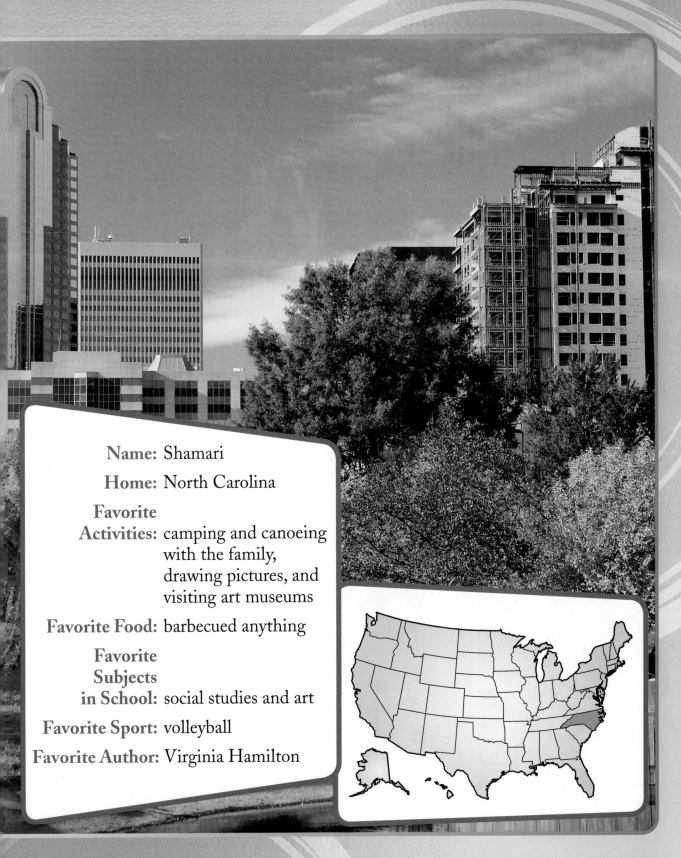

Name: Shamari

Home: North Carolina

Favorite
Activities: camping and canoeing
with the family,
drawing pictures, and
visiting art museums

Favorite Food: barbecued anything

Favorite
Subjects
in School: social studies and art

Favorite Sport: volleyball

Favorite Author: Virginia Hamilton

What's an Opinion Essay?

An opinion essay states my opinion and has reasons and details to support my point of view.

What's in an Opinion Essay?

Opinion
That's what I think about my topic. I can't prove that my opinion is right, but I can explain it and support it with reasons and information. For instance, I think my class should take a trip to the university art museum. It's full of beautiful paintings and sculptures!

Reasons
Reasons tell why I believe in my opinion. To help the audience understand my point of view, my reasons need to be backed up by accurate facts and details.

Introduction
The first paragraph of my essay will be my introduction. I'll get my reader interested in my topic and state my opinion.

Conclusion
That's my last paragraph. In my conclusion, I'll restate my opinion and sum up my reasons for supporting it.

Why write an Opinion Essay?

The main reason to write an opinion essay is to convince someone to believe or do something. Different people have different kinds of reasons for writing an opinion essay.

To Express an Opinion
I might write an opinion essay to members of the parent-teacher organization to ask them to consider my point of view about sponsoring a class trip.

A librarian might post an opinion essay for people who visit the library. He or she may provide facts and details to invite them to meet an author.

An applicant to a special program sometimes writes an opinion essay using clearly organized reasons to present himself or herself as the best candidate.

Linking Opinion Writing Traits to an Opinion Essay

In this chapter, you will try to convince your audience to agree with your opinion. This type of writing is called an opinion essay. Shamari will guide you through the stages of the writing process: Prewrite, Draft, Revise, Edit, and Publish. In each stage, Shamari will show you important writing strategies that are linked to the Opinion Writing Traits below.

Opinion Writing Traits

- a clear opinion
- strong reasons that are supported by facts and details

- a clear, logical organization
- an introduction, body, and conclusion
- transitions that connect opinions and reasons

- a voice and tone that are appropriate for the audience and purpose

- fair and balanced language
- specific words and phrases

- a variety of sentence patterns that make the writing flow

- no or few errors in spelling, grammar, punctuation, and capitalization

Before you write, read Bob West's opinion essay on the next page. Then use the opinion essay rubric on pages 242–243 to decide how well he did. (You might want to look back at What's in an Opinion Essay? on page 238, too!)

HELP KEEP OUR TOWN CLEAN!

Opinion
MODEL
Essay

by Bob West

introduction

The annual spring cleanup will take place next Saturday. We will pick up litter in our town's parks and public places. We also need to pick up the trash along the highway. Everyone in town should plan to help out.

opinion

reasons

The main reason for needing so many people is that the town has a huge amount of litter. Paper, bags, and bottles need to be picked up along the roads. The public boat landing needs to be cleaned up. The litter around Swan Pond is destroying the beauty of the woods and water. The small parks department cannot do all of this work. To do a good job, many people are needed. Teams of four people will be assigned to small sections of highways, parks, and other sites. The cleanup committee is hoping to have a hundred cleanup teams. If we all help, the town won't have to raise extra money for cleanup.

transition words

Another reason everyone should join in is to build community spirit. Teams of people who work together will get to know each other. They will feel needed in their town. Some people will become more aware of the litter problem. Once they know about it, they will discourage littering. They may want to talk about the problem with others. Our town will become a clean place. People who have worked hard to clean up won't want to see litter in their beautiful town again.

We should all gladly help out next Saturday. We have a huge litter problem, and it is up to us to solve it. The people who do the work will also benefit by building community spirit. As Mayor Willis has said, "When we take care of our town, we take care of ourselves."

conclusion

Opinion Essay Rubric

Use this 6-point rubric to plan and score an opinion essay.

	6	**5**	**4**	
Ideas	The writer's opinion is clear. The ideas are supported by plenty of strong details.	The writer's opinion is clear. The essay has some strong details.	The writer's opinion is clear. Strong details are needed.	
Organization	The reasons are organized in a clear order that supports the writer's purpose. Transition words make the essay easy to follow.	One or two reasons may be out of order. The writer uses some transition words.	Some reasons are not organized in a clear way. The writer uses some transition words.	
Voice	The writer's voice sounds sincere and has a serious tone that matches the writer's purpose. It connects with the reader.	The writer's voice sounds sincere and has a serious tone most of the time. It mostly connects with the reader.	The writer has a voice, but it may not always sound sincere or connect with the reader.	
Word Choice	The writer's language is fair and balanced. No loaded words or phrases are used.	The writer's language is fair almost all the time. One or two loaded words should be replaced.	The writer's language is fair most of the time. The writer uses some loaded words.	
Sentence Fluency	A variety of sentence patterns makes the essay flow.	Most sentence patterns are varied. Most of the essay flows naturally.	Some variety in sentence beginnings and structure adds interest.	
Conventions	Adverbs are used correctly. The meaning is clear.	Most adverbs are used correctly. The meaning is clear.	Some minor errors with adverbs exist, but they do not distract the reader.	

✛ Presentation   White space and text are balanced. The pages are numbered.

3	2	1	
The writer's opinion is not clear enough. Details are too few in number or weak.	The writer provides a general opinion. Only one or two details are provided.	The writer's opinion is not provided. The details are missing.	**Ideas**
Several reasons are out of order. More or better transition words are needed.	The reasons are not organized. Transition words are missing.	There is no clear organization. Transition words are not used.	**Organization**
The writer's voice sounds sincere only some of the time. It sometimes does not connect with the reader.	The voice is inconsistent and may be inappropriate for the purpose and audience. The reader is confused or distracted.	The voice is very weak or absent. The writer does not sound sincere or connect with the reader.	**Voice**
Much of the language is biased. Several loaded words are used.	Most of the words are emotional and biased. Some may offend the reader.	Word choice does not seem thought out. Words are biased and poorly used.	**Word Choice**
Few sentence patterns are present. The sentences do not flow naturally.	Sentence beginnings, length, and structure are not varied. The writing is choppy and awkward.	Sentences are incomplete or incorrect. The essay is very difficult to read.	**Sentence Fluency**
Several errors in the use of adverbs confuse the reader.	Many serious errors impair readability and meaning. Adverbs are vague, confusing, or missing.	The writing contains many major errors in the use of adverbs. It is very difficult to read.	**Conventions**

See Appendix B for 4-, 5-, and 6-point opinion rubrics.

Opinion Essay
Using the Rubric to Study the Model

Did you notice that the model on page 241 points out some key elements of an opinion essay? As he wrote "Help Keep Our Town Clean!" Bob West used these elements to help him convince others to agree with his opinion. He also used the 6-point rubric on pages 242–243 to plan, draft, revise, and edit the writing. A rubric is a great tool to evaluate writing during the writing process.

Now let's use the same rubric to score the model. To do this, we'll focus on each trait separately, starting with Ideas. We'll use the top descriptor for each trait (column 6), along with examples from the model, to help us understand how the traits work together. How would you score Bob on each trait?

- **The writer's opinion is clear.**
- **The ideas are supported by plenty of strong details.**

Bob does a good job of clearly stating his opinion in the essay's introduction: Everyone in town should help out with the spring cleanup. Then Bob presents strong details that support his reasons that people should get involved in the annual cleanup.

The main reason for needing so many people is that the town has a huge amount of litter. Paper, bags, and bottles need to be picked up along the roads. The public boat landing needs to be cleaned up. The litter around Swan Pond is destroying the beauty of the woods and water. The small parks department cannot do all of this work. To do a good job, many people are needed.

Organization

- The reasons are organized in a clear order that supports the writer's purpose.
- Transition words make the essay easy to follow.

In the body of the essay, Bob presents two important reasons for his opinion. He starts with his main reason and uses *Another reason* to begin the next paragraph. The essay is easy to follow.

The main reason for needing so many people is that the town has a huge amount of litter.

Another reason everyone should join in is to build community spirit.

Voice

- The writer's voice sounds sincere and has a serious tone that matches the writer's purpose.
- It connects with the reader.

Bob makes it clear that he's sincere about his opinion. He gives plenty of details that support his point of view. In his conclusion, he uses the word *we* to connect with the reader. This made me feel like part of the same community as Bob.

We should all gladly help out next Saturday. We have a huge litter problem, and it is up to us to solve it.

Using the Rubric to Study the Model

Opinion Essay

Word Choice

- **The writer's language is fair and balanced.**
- **No loaded words or phrases are used.**

Words like *litterbug* and *slob* are examples of loaded words, or words with extra meanings. Bob doesn't use loaded words. Instead, he just explains how the cleanup can help people.

> Some people will become more aware of the litter problem. Once they know about it, they will discourage littering. They may want to talk about the problem with others.

Sentence Fluency

- **A variety of sentence patterns makes the essay flow.**

Bob uses a variety of long and short, simple and complex sentences throughout his essay. This made his essay flow and helped me to follow his thinking.

> The small parks department cannot do all of this work. To do a good job, many people are needed. Teams of four people will be assigned to small sections of highways, parks, and other sites. The cleanup committee is hoping to have a hundred cleanup teams. If we all help, the town won't have to raise extra money for cleanup.

Conventions

- **Adverbs are used correctly.**
- **The meaning is clear.**

I read through the essay again. I had no trouble catching Bob's meaning. Bob also uses adverbs correctly. In these sentences, the adverbs *hard* and *gladly* describe verbs.

People who have worked hard to clean up won't want to see litter in their beautiful town again.

We should all gladly help out next Saturday.

✛ Presentation

White space and text are balanced. The pages are numbered.

My Turn!

Now it's my turn to write an opinion essay. Follow along to see how I use the rubric and good writing strategies to help me.

Prewrite

Focus on **Ideas**

The Rubric Says The writer's opinion is clear. The ideas are supported by plenty of strong details.

Writing Strategy Decide on an opinion. List reasons for the opinion.

My teacher gave us a list of possible topics for an opinion essay. The topic I'm most interested in is whether our school should stay open until 6:00 P.M. I've always wanted the school to stay open later.

I listed all the reasons I could think of for keeping the school open later. That was my strategy for getting started.

Writer's Term

Opinion

An **opinion** is a belief that is based on reasons. Unlike a fact, an opinion cannot be proven to be true.

My Opinion: The school building should stay open until 6:00 P.M.

Reasons to Support My Opinion

1. There could be more after-school activities and clubs.
2. Students can wait inside for a ride home.
3. Activities can last longer, and students can get back into the building after outdoor activities.
4. The band and other groups could meet later.

Apply

Choose a topic that you find interesting for an opinion essay. Decide what your opinion is, and then brainstorm a list of reasons that support your opinion.

Prewrite

The Rubric Says   The reasons are organized in a clear order that supports the writer's purpose.

Writing Strategy   Use an Order-of-Importance Organizer.

The rubric reminds me to use strong reasons to support my opinion. An Order-of-Importance Organizer will help me list my reasons in order. I have decided to organize them from most important to least important.

Writer's Term

Order-of-Importance Organizer
An Order-of-Importance Organizer shows reasons in order of their importance. Usually, the most important reason goes first, and the least important reason goes last.

Order-of-Importance Organizer

Most Important:
Students can wait inside for a ride home.

Next in Importance:
Activities can last longer, and students can get back into the building after outdoor activities.

Next in Importance:
The band and other groups could meet later.

Least Important:
There could be more after-school activities and clubs.

Reflect

How will the notes and graphic organizer help Shamari write a good opinion essay?

Apply

Look at your notes. Use an Order-of-Importance Organizer to put your reasons in order.

Draft

Focus on **Ideas**

The Rubric Says   The writer's opinion is clear. The ideas are supported by plenty of strong details.

Writing Strategy   Make sure the opinion and reasons are clear.

Now I can start writing. In order to convince others to believe in my opinion, I need to make sure they understand what my opinion is. I also need to be sure that all my reasons strongly support my opinion. That means I should state my opinion clearly and openly in the first paragraph. Then I should support it with my two most important reasons in the next two paragraphs. In my final paragraph, I'll restate my opinion in a sincere way that convinces my readers.

As I write my draft, I'll do the best I can with spelling and grammar, but I won't worry about mistakes right now. I'll have a chance to fix them later. My draft begins on page 252.

Writer's Term

Reasons

Good **reasons** support a writer's opinion. Strong details and facts that support the writer's reasons can convince others to agree with the writer.

My Opinion (first paragraph)
The school building should stay open until 6:00 P.M.

My Reasons

Reason 1 (next paragraph)
Students can wait inside for a ride home.

Reason 2 (next paragraph)
Activities can last longer, and students can get back into the building after outdoor activities.

My Restatement (final paragraph)
Adams School should keep its doors open until 6:00 P.M.

[DRAFT]

Keep the Doors Open

Adams School is a busy place. The first teachers arrive very early in the morning. There is activity all day long. The doors are locked at 4:30 P.M. Because many people need to use the building after that, the school should stay open until 6:00 P.M.

opinion stated in first paragraph

The most important reason is that sometimes students have to wait for a ride home. Often students have school clubs and

strongest reason in first argument paragraph

activities. They might have sports or band practice. It's stupid to think that all parents get out of work before 5:00 P.M. Miserable, overtired kids who need to wait for a ride should not have to stand outside the building, especially when it is cold, rainy, or dark. If students could wait inside, they could use their time good. They could do homework or read quietly in the school liberry. They could sit comfortable and talk softly with their friends in a warm place.

Proofreading Marks

⌐ Indent	ℓ Take out something
≡ Make a capital	⊙ Add a period
/ Make a small letter	⊄ New paragraph
∧ Add something	⑤℗ Spelling error

[DRAFT]

The second reason the doors should be open is for students who have activities there. After school ends, many activities take place in and around the school building. Some go on after 4:30 P.M. Many sports teams practice on the school fields. Some practices end after 5:00 P.M. Sometimes, students need to go back into the school after practice. Right now, they can't do that. Also, some activities that take place inside the school are cut short because the building closes so early.

next strongest reason in second argument paragraph

Adams School should keep its doors open until 6:00 P.M. Many students are still using the school building or grounds at 4:30 P.M. keeping the school open an hour and a half later would make life easier for them and sometimes for the adults in their lifes, too.

opinion restated in last paragraph

Reflect

Read the draft. What reasons did the writer give for her opinion?

Apply

Use your Order-of-Importance Organizer to write a draft of your opinion essay. Remember to clearly state your opinion and use plenty of strong details to support it.

Revise

Focus on **Organization**

The Rubric Says   Transition words make the essay easy to follow.

Writing Strategy   Use transition words to guide the reader.

It's time to revise my draft. The rubric reminds me to make sure my essay is easy to follow. One way to do that is to use transition words and phrases that act as "direction signs" to guide the reader through my argument. The phrase *for instance* tells the reader that I am about to give an example. The word *also* tells the reader that additional information is coming. Do you think my changes improve my writing?

[DRAFT]

If students could wait inside, they could use their time good.
For instance,
They could do homework or read quietly in the school liberry.
    also
They could sit comfortable and talk softly with their friends in

a warm place.

added transition words

Apply

Read your draft. Look for places to add transition words to help the reader follow your essay.

The Rubric Says	The writer's voice sounds sincere and has a serious tone that matches the writer's purpose. It connects with the reader.
Writing Strategy	Keep the audience in mind as you revise.

I read my draft again. The rubric tells me to sound sincere and serious. I should also connect to the reader. To do that, I need to think about my purpose and audience. My audience is students and others at my school. My purpose is to convince them that the building needs to stay open longer for students to use. I added two sentences that speak directly to the audience about things they care about. Keeping my audience in mind helped me strengthen my introduction.

[DRAFT]

Adams School is a busy place. The first teachers arrive very ~~The problem is that the day ends too early.~~ early in the morning. There is activity all day long. The doors are ~~Everybody must leave before the doors are locked.~~ locked at 4:30 P.M.

connected with audience more

Reflect

Look at Shamari's changes. Does she sound sincere and establish a serious tone in her opening paragraph?

Apply

Read your draft. Be sure to connect with your audience, beginning to end.

Revise

Focus on Word Choice

The Rubric Says	The writer's language is fair and balanced. No loaded words or phrases are used.
Writing Strategy	Replace loaded words with neutral words.

When I reread the rubric, I realized I had to check my opinion essay for loaded words. I want to use strong reasons and details that explain my opinion to my readers. I don't want to trick them by using words with added meanings. I'll replace loaded words with words that are more neutral.

Writer's Term

Loaded Words

Loaded words carry extra meaning. For example, a shack and a house are both places in which to live, but the word **shack** makes the place seem shabby. It creates a feeling that is different from **house**.

replaced loaded words

[DRAFT]

activities. They might have sports or band practice. ~~It's stupid~~
Many parents and other adults don't   until after
~~to think that all parents~~ get out of work ~~before~~ 5:00 P.M.

neutral words

Reflect

Look at the revisions. How do neutral words strengthen the writer's opinion?

Apply

Check your draft for loaded words. Replace any loaded words with neutral words.

The Rubric Says   Adverbs are used correctly. The meaning is clear.

Writing Strategy   Check that adverbs are used correctly.

I know from the rubric that I need to check my essay for errors. First I'll check spelling, punctuation, and capitalization. Next I'll check to see that I used each adverb correctly.

> ✏️ **Writer's Term**
>
> ### Adverbs
> **Adverbs** are words that describe verbs. Many adverbs end in **-ly**. However, some common adverbs, including **fast, later, well,** and **once,** do not.

[DRAFT]

cold, rainy, or dark. If students could wait inside, they could

use their time ~~good~~ well . For instance, They could do homework or read quietly in

the school ~~liberry~~ library . They also could sit ~~comfortable~~ comfortably and talk softly

with their friends in a warm place.

corrected use of adverb

corrected use of adverb

Reflect

Look at the edits. Did the writer proofread her writing and use adverbs correctly?

Apply   Conventions

Check that you have used all adverbs correctly.

For more practice using adverbs correctly, use the exercises on the next two pages.

Adverbs

Know the Rule

Adverbs are describing words. An adverb describes a verb. Adverbs tell how or when. Many adverbs end in *-ly*. The words *well* and *fast* are also adverbs.

Practice the Rule

Number a piece of paper 1–12. Read each sentence below. On your paper, write the word that correctly completes each sentence.

1. Last year, the closing time for the school was (usual/usually) three o'clock.
2. This year, those hours were (quiet/quietly) changed.
3. The officials looked (careful/carefully) at many things.
4. They wanted to use the school building (intelligent/intelligently).
5. (Late/Lately) one afternoon, a meeting was held.
6. Most people behaved (good/well) at the meeting.
7. They listened (polite/politely) to each speaker.
8. The officials (surprising/surprisingly) discovered some interesting facts.
9. Workers (regular/regularly) clean the building each night.
10. Many teachers would (happy/happily) stay after school to oversee activities.
11. The town officials (final/finally) decided to let local groups use the building after school hours.
12. Our teacher (excited/excitedly) told us the news the next day.

Good and Well

Know the Rule

Good is an adjective that describes a noun. **Well** is an adverb that describes a verb.

Example:
The lunchroom offers **good** food. However, some students do not eat **well** at school.

Practice the Rule

Number a piece of paper 1–10. Write the correct adjective (**good/well**) to complete the sentence.

1. My soccer team played _____ last week.
2. The fans had a _____ time watching us win.
3. Afterward, my sister said she had never seen us play so _____.
4. The whole team went out to see a _____ movie.
5. My favorite actor played the "_____ guy."
6. The tickets cost a lot, but it was money _____ spent.
7. Next, we went to a _____ pizza restaurant.
8. They have a _____ selection of toppings there.
9. We ate _____ that night.
10. Finally, everyone went home for a _____ night's sleep.

Publish

+Presentation

Publishing Strategy   Give my essay as a speech on "Sound Off Day."

Presentation Strategy   Use good margins and number the pages.

My opinion essay is finished. Now it's time to publish. Every student in class wrote his or her own essay, so we thought it would be good if everyone could hear all the opinions. That's why we decided to have a "Sound Off Day" when all the students could give their essays as speeches and record them as podcasts. Before I publish my essay, I'll check to be sure I left enough space around the text so that it is easy to read out loud. I'll also number my pages so they don't get lost or out of order. I'll use this final checklist to prepare my final copy.

My Final Checklist

Did I—

✔ check my spelling and punctuation?

✔ use adverbs correctly?

✔ use good margins?

✔ number the pages?

✔ put my name on the paper?

Apply

Make a checklist to check your opinion essay. Then make a final copy. Practice reading your essay aloud before presenting it.

Keep the Doors Open
by Shamari

Adams School is a busy place. The first teachers arrive very early in the morning, and there is activity all day long. The problem is that the day ends too early. Everybody must leave before the doors are locked at 4:30 P.M. Because many people need to use the building after that, the school should stay open until 6:00 P.M.

1

2

The most important reason is that sometimes students have to wait for a ride home. Often students have school clubs and activities. They might have sports or band practice. Many parents and other adults don't get out of work until after 5:00 P.M. Students who need to wait for a ride should not have to stand outside the building, especially when it is cold, rainy, or dark. If students could wait inside, they could use their time well. For instance, they could do homework or read quietly in the school library. They also could sit comfortably and talk softly with their friends in a warm place.

The second reason the doors should be open is for students who have activities there. After school ends, many activities take place in and around the school building. Some go on after 4:30 P.M. For example, many sports teams practice on the school fields. Some practices end after 5:00 P.M. Sometimes students need to go back into the school after practice to get their books, make a phone call, get a drink of water, or use the bathroom. Right now they can't do that. Also, some activities that take place inside the school are cut short because the building closes so early. This happened just last week. Mr. Azar's class was practicing for the holiday play. The cast needed more practice time, but everyone had to leave by 4:30 P.M.

Adams School should keep its doors open until 6:00 P.M. Many students are still using the school building or grounds at 4:30 P.M. Keeping the school open an hour and a half later would make life easier for them and sometimes for the adults in their lives, too.

Reflect

Use the rubric to check Shamari's essay. Are all the traits of a good opinion essay there? How does your opinion essay compare against the rubric?

What's an Editorial?

It's an article I write for a newspaper or magazine that expresses my opinion about a topic. My topic should interest readers of that publication.

What's in an Editorial?

Introduction
That's my first paragraph. I'll get the reader interested in my topic right away. Then I'll state my opinion. One thing I feel strongly about is that my school needs a student newspaper! My friends and I want to take photographs and write articles about life at school.

Body
The body is where I convince the reader that my opinion is correct. I'll give reasons for my opinion and offer examples that support it. I'll also give facts and information that support my reasons.

Conclusion
That's my last paragraph. I'll restate my opinion and summarize my reasons and facts.

Why write an Editorial?

There are many reasons to write an editorial. Here are some reasons I thought of.

To Express an Opinion
Citizens write editorials about articles in newspapers. They may agree or disagree with the article, or they may state an opinion about a current event.

To Entertain
Some people write editorials to share an idea or view that they think is interesting. Sometimes writers use humor to call attention to the issue.

To Inform
Some editorials are written to give information about a topic. The writer may express an opinion, but the main purpose is to call attention to the issue.

Linking Opinion Writing Traits to an Editorial

In this chapter, you will write to present your point of view to readers of a newspaper or magazine. This type of opinion writing is called an editorial. Shamari will guide you through the stages of the writing process: Prewrite, Draft, Revise, Edit, and Publish. In each stage, Shamari will show you important writing strategies that are linked to the Opinion Writing Traits below.

Opinion Writing Traits

- a clear opinion
- strong reasons that are supported by facts and details

- a clear, logical organization
- an introduction, body, and conclusion
- transitions that connect opinions and reasons

- a voice and tone that are appropriate for the audience and purpose

- fair and balanced language
- specific words and phrases

- a variety of sentence patterns that make the writing flow

- no or few errors in spelling, grammar, punctuation, and capitalization

Before you write, read Joaquin Dasilva's editorial on the next page. Then use the editorial rubric on pages 268–269 to decide how well he did. (You might want to look back at What's in an Editorial? on page 264, too!)

Students Deserve Healthy Foods

by Joaquin Dasilva

strong introduction

the issue

opinion

Just eat right. This sounds simple, but it's not always as easy as it sounds, especially when we're in school. As students, what can we do to help ourselves develop healthy eating habits? First we need to remove vending machines that sell junk food and change soda machine choices to water and low-sugar juices. Then we need to work with teachers, staff, and parents to develop a healthy eating program at school.

Why are good eating habits so important? What we eat affects our health now and will continue to affect us in the future. When we eat snack foods and sugary sodas too often, we eat too much fat, sugar, and salt. This type of diet causes many students to gain weight. Children who have poor eating habits tend to have less energy and to get tired quickly. They don't exercise enough and may have trouble paying attention in class. Maybe in the past people thought eating sweets did not harm children, but now we know better.

body

Vending machines encourage students to eat junk. Most of the foods sold in vending machines are bad for our health. The cafeteria should offer us more fresh foods, such as fruits and vegetables. Vending machines make unhealthy snack foods and high-sugar drinks easily available to us. Many kids are in a hurry to eat because they are hungry or they have a short lunch period. Often students would rather buy junk food than wait in a long cafeteria line for healthier choices. We need to get rid of these snack vending machines and fill soda machines with low-sugar juices and water. It also would help to organize lunch lines in the cafeteria so they are shorter and move more quickly.

Students, teachers, staff, and parents should work together to plan a healthy eating program. The program would eliminate unhealthy foods and give us more healthy choices. We need more fresh fruits, vegetables, and salads. We should have sandwiches on whole-grain breads with lean meats like turkey, chicken, ham, and tuna fish. We should also have low-fat dairy products like yogurt and low-fat cheeses. Fried foods such as French fries, fried chicken, and fish sticks should be replaced with baked potatoes, chicken, or fish.

Eating right in school may not always be simple, but it's a challenge we can meet! Together, we can make our school a "Healthy Food Zone."

strong conclusion

Editorial Rubric

Use this 6-point rubric to plan and score an editorial.

	6	5	4
Ideas	The editorial expresses an opinion on one issue. Reasons offer facts and details that clarify and support the opinion.	The editorial expresses an opinion that could be stated more clearly. The reason is supported by facts and details.	The editorial expresses an opinion. Some of the reasons may not support the opinion.
Organization	The editorial has a strong introduction, body, and conclusion. The introduction grabs the reader's attention.	The editorial has an introduction, body, and conclusion. The introduction is fairly strong.	The introduction, body, and conclusion are noticeable but unoriginal.
Voice	The writer uses a convincing tone. First-person point of view connects with the reader.	The tone is convincing most of the time. The writer uses the first-person point of view.	The writer's tone is appropriate but not always convincing. The writer uses first-person point of view.
Word Choice	Words are focused and support the opinion.	Many words support the opinion.	The writing is basically clear. Some words do not relate to the opinion.
Sentence Fluency	Sentences are clear and flow naturally.	Most sentences are clear and flow naturally.	Some sentence beginnings are repetitive.
Conventions	Past-tense verbs are formed correctly. The meaning is clear.	Most past-tense verbs are formed correctly. The meaning is clear.	The writer shows good control of verb tenses. Minor errors do not confuse the reader.

✛ Presentation The editorial is formatted neatly on the computer.

3	2	1	
The editorial expresses an opinion. Too few reasons support the opinion. Facts and details are vague.	The opinion is not clearly stated, and few reasons support it. The reader is confused.	The essay does not express an opinion. The reasons are unrelated.	**Ideas**
The editorial has an introduction, body, and conclusion. The introduction or the conclusion is weak.	The introduction, body, and conclusion are hard to locate.	The editorial does not have a clear introduction, body, or conclusion. It is mostly a list of unrelated information.	**Organization**
The tone is not consistent. The writer switches point of view. Sometimes *you* is used.	The writer's tone is not convincing. The writer does not connect with the reader or use first person.	The writer's tone is missing and/or inappropriate for the purpose and audience.	**Voice**
Words are general or repetitive, and some do not support the opinion.	Many words are misused or unclear.	Words are too general. The writer does not express a clear opinion.	**Word Choice**
Some sentences are not clear. The sentences do not flow naturally.	Choppy, run-on, awkward sentences make the text difficult to read and understand.	Sentences are incomplete or incorrect. The essay is very difficult to read.	**Sentence Fluency**
Several errors in how past-tense verbs are formed confuse the reader.	Frequent, major errors with past-tense verbs distract the reader. The writing is difficult to follow.	The writing contains many major errors. It is very difficult to read.	**Conventions**

See Appendix B for 4-, 5-, and 6-point opinion rubrics.

Using the Rubric to Study the Model
Editorial

Did you notice that the model on page 267 points out some key elements of an editorial? As he wrote his editorial, Joaquin Dasilva used these elements to help him convince others to agree with his opinion. He also used the 6-point rubric on pages 268–269 to plan, draft, revise, and edit the writing. A rubric is a great tool to evaluate writing during the writing process.

Now let's use the same rubric to score the model. To do this, we'll focus on each trait separately, starting with Ideas. We'll use the top descriptor for each trait (column 6), along with examples from the model, to help us understand how the traits work together. How would you score Joaquin on each trait?

- **The editorial expresses an opinion on one issue.**
- **Reasons offer facts and details that clarify and support the opinion.**

Joaquin clearly states his opinion. He then provides examples that support and clarify it. Look at his paragraph about planning a healthy eating program. Joaquin provides a lot of good examples for his readers to think about.

Students, teachers, staff, and parents should work together to plan a healthy eating program. The program would eliminate unhealthy foods and give us more healthy choices. We need more fresh fruits, vegetables, and salads. We should have sandwiches on whole-grain breads with lean meats like turkey, chicken, ham, and tuna fish.

Organization

- The editorial has a strong introduction, body, and conclusion.
- The introduction grabs the reader's attention.

Joaquin expresses his opinion in the editorial's introduction. The body of his editorial is well organized around the issue. Joaquin's introduction hooks readers by stating the problem in a way they can relate to.

Just eat right. This sounds simple, but it's not always as easy as it sounds, especially when we're in school.

Voice

- The writer uses a convincing tone.
- First-person point of view connects with the reader.

Joaquin uses words like *we* and *our health* to connect with his audience—other students. His choice of words creates a convincing tone. Here's a good example.

Most of the foods sold in vending machines are bad for our health. The cafeteria should offer us more fresh foods, such as fruits and vegetables. Vending machines make unhealthy snack foods and high-sugar drinks easily available to us.

Using the **Editorial** Rubric to Study the Model

Word Choice • Words are focused and support the opinion.

Joaquin phrases everything in a way that supports his opinion. He chooses his words and phrases for effect. In this paragraph, he wants the audience to understand why poor eating habits are bad for children. This information supports his opinion that the school should serve healthful foods.

Why are good eating habits so important? What we eat affects our health now and will continue to affect us in the future. When we eat snack foods and sugary sodas too often, we eat too much fat, sugar, and salt. This type of diet causes many students to gain weight. Children who have poor eating habits tend to have less energy and to get tired quickly. They don't exercise enough and may have trouble paying attention in class.

Sentence Fluency • Sentences are clear and flow naturally.

Each sentence should lead smoothly and naturally into the next one. Joaquin does a good job of creating flow. For example, after he explains why vending machines are a problem in school, he follows with a solution to the problem.

Many kids are in a hurry to eat because they are hungry or they have a short lunch period. Often students would rather buy junk food than wait in a long cafeteria line for healthier choices. We need to get rid of these snack vending machines and fill soda machines with low-sugar juices and water. It also would help to organize lunch lines in the cafeteria so they are shorter and move more quickly.

Conventions

- Past tense verbs are formed correctly.
- The meaning is clear.

Joaquin uses correct spelling, capitalization, and punctuation. His writing is easy to understand. When Joaquin uses a past tense verb, he uses it correctly.

Maybe in the past people thought eating sweets did not harm children, but now we know better.

✛Presentation The editorial is formatted neatly on the computer.

My Turn!

Now it's my turn to write an editorial. Follow along to see how I use the rubric and good writing strategies to help me.

Prewrite

The Rubric Says   The editorial expresses an opinion on one issue.

Writing Strategy   Write an opinion on an issue. List reasons for the opinion.

My teacher asked us to imagine that we have been hired to write an editorial for a travel magazine. Our job will be to convince people to visit a special place for vacation. In my opinion, North Carolina is the best place for a vacation!

I'll write down my opinion and a list of the best reasons I know for visiting North Carolina.

> **Writer's Term**
>
> **Reasons**
>
> Reasons are the explanations behind an opinion.

My Opinion: North Carolina is the perfect place for a vacation.

Reasons That Support My Opinion:
the Great Smoky Mountains
the Piedmont Region; historic Stagville
the people are great, too

Things to do: camping, hiking, horseback riding, white-water rafting, swimming, fishing, sailing, shopping, golf, go to a theme park

Apply

Choose a topic for an editorial. Write down your opinion about the topic. Then jot down a list of reasons that support your opinion.

Prewrite

The Rubric Says   The editorial has a strong introduction, body, and conclusion.

Writing Strategy   Use a Main-Idea Table to organize the opinion and reasons.

Now I need to organize my notes. The Main-Idea Table will help me organize my information into an introduction, body, and conclusion. The main idea will be in the introduction and conclusion. The supporting details will be in the body of the editorial.

Writer's Term

Main-Idea Table
A **Main-Idea Table** shows how a main idea is supported by details. It helps you organize information by showing how supporting details hold up the main idea.

Main-Idea Table

Main Idea:
North Carolina is the perfect place for a vacation.

Supporting Detail	**Supporting Detail**	**Supporting Detail**
Great Smoky Mountains —camping, hiking, riding, rafting	Piedmont Region— Stagville, shopping, golf, theme park	the people— warm, kind, welcome visitors

Reflect
Look at the notes and the graphic organizer. How will they help Shamari write a good editorial?

Apply
Look at your notes. Use a Main-Idea Table to put your opinion and list of reasons in order.

Draft

Focus on **Organization**

The Rubric Says The editorial has a strong introduction, body, and conclusion.

Writing Strategy Organize the information in a logical order.

It's time to start writing! I'm going to use my Main-Idea Table to write a draft. The rubric reminds me to organize my notes into an introduction, body, and conclusion. I will state the main idea in the introduction and again in the conclusion. The details in the table are the reasons. They will form the body of the editorial and connect the introduction to the conclusion.

As I write my draft, I'll do the best I can with spelling and grammar, but I won't worry about mistakes right now. I'll have a chance to fix them later. Read the beginning of my draft on the next page.

Writer's Term

Introduction, Body, and Conclusion

The **introduction** is the first paragraph, and it states the main idea.

The **body** is the part that provides reasons and supporting details.

The **conclusion** is the last paragraph of a paper. It ties up loose ends and summarizes main points.

[DRAFT]

opinion

North Carolina is nice. I should know—I live in North

Carolina. During school vacations my family likes to take trips,

and we don't have to travel far. There are exciting things to

share about what we have done.

My very favorite place in North Carolina is the Great Smoky

Mountains in the western part of the state. my family camped at

Great Smoky Mountains National Park. Everyone in the family

enjoyed the outdoor activities.

introduction

first paragraph of body

reason

Reflect

Read the draft. Did Shamari state her opinion in the introduction? What reason does she give to support her opinion?

Apply

Use your Main-Idea Table to write a draft of your editorial. Organize your writing into an introduction, body, and conclusion.

Revise

The Rubric Says	The writer uses a convincing tone. First-person point of view connects with the reader.
Writing Strategy	Use a convincing tone and first-person point of view.

The rubric reminds me that I should connect with my readers and convince them to accept my opinion. The best way to do that is with the words I choose to express my opinion. If the tone of my editorial is sincere and believable, the reader will probably accept my ideas. I should also speak directly to the reader by using first-person point of view (*I, me, we, us*). I want people to feel as enthusiastic about North Carolina as I do!

Writer's Term

Tone

Tone is the way writing sounds. It shows the writer's attitude toward the subject of his or her writing. A writer's tone can be serious, funny, formal, personal, and so forth.

[DRAFT]

looks for adventure

During school vacations my family likes to take trips, and we I'm going to share with you some of the exciting things we have don't have to travel far. There are exciting things to share done. I hope you will be convinced to discover North Carolina on your next vacation! about what we have done.

used first-person point of view

added convincing tone

Apply

Read your draft. Look for places to add a convincing tone. Remember to express your opinion and use first-person point of view.

The Rubric Says   Words are focused and support the opinion.

Writing Strategy   Choose words and phrases to convey ideas precisely.

The rubric says that all the words in my editorial should support my opinion. I read through my draft again. In my last paragraph, I found some information that has nothing to do with my topic. I'll take that out now.

[DRAFT]

Please accept my invitation to visit my home state, North Carolina. ~~I was born in the city of Raleigh.~~ Come and experience the special places my family has thoroughly enjoyed. There are so many more to discover!

> deleted unnecessary words

Reflect

How did Shamari improve her draft?

Apply

Read your draft again. Take out any information that doesn't support your opinion.

Revise

Focus on **Sentence Fluency**

The Rubric Says   Sentences are clear and flow naturally.

Writing Strategy   Combine sentences.

I asked a friend to read my paragraph out loud. While I listened, I noticed some problems. The paragraph about meeting the people of North Carolina seems difficult to read. The ideas are mixed up. I could combine sentences to make my ideas clear. Now both my ideas and my sentences will flow well.

[DRAFT]

~~You get to meet wonderful people here. That's~~ last but not
, , you get to meet wonderful people like my family and me
least, when you take a vacation in North Carolina. ~~For example,~~

~~there's my family and me.~~ North Carolinians are proud to live in

such a beautiful state.

revised for clarity and flow

Apply

Read your draft out loud so you can hear how your writing sounds. Listen for sentences that do not flow smoothly.

The Rubric Says   Past-tense verbs are formed correctly. The meaning is clear.

Writing Strategy   Make sure that past-tense verbs are formed correctly.

The rubric reminds me that I need to check my editorial for errors. I'll begin by checking my spelling, punctuation, and capitalization. Next I'll look over my draft to make sure that I used past-tense verbs correctly.

Writer's Term

Past-Tense Verbs

Past-tense verbs show that an action happened in the past. For example: While we stayed on the Outer Banks, we swam in the ocean. The verbs **stayed** and **swam** are past tense verbs.

[DRAFT]

than one hundred and fifty years ago. It ~~is~~ **was** very interesting to

see how people ~~have~~ **had** to make so many of the things they used.

It was also very sad to see how enslaved people ~~live~~ **lived**.

corrected verb tense

Reflect

How did the way Shamari changed her sentences improve their flow? Did she use past-tense verbs correctly?

Apply   Conventions

Edit your draft for spelling, punctuation, and capitalization. Check that you have used all past-tense verbs correctly.

For more practice with past-tense verbs, use the exercises on the next two pages.

Past-Tense Verbs

Know the Rule

A **past-tense verb** shows an action that happened in the past. Many past-tense verbs end in -ed (*live/lived*). Irregular verbs change spelling in their past-tense form (*speak/spoken*). Make sure the tense of each verb agrees with the time in which the action takes place.

Practice the Rule

Number a piece of paper 1–12. Read each sentence below. On your paper, write the correct past-tense form of the verb in parentheses.

1. Last year, my family (visit) the Great Smoky Mountains National Park.

2. What an incredible vacation we (has)!

3. We hiked, (swim), had picnics, and visited historic sites.

4. We also enjoyed beautiful scenery and (see) lots of wildlife.

5. I even (learn) a little about the history of the park.

6. We (begin) our day with a visit to Cades Cove.

7. We (start) out early in the morning.

8. Long ago, this beautiful forest valley (is) part of the Cherokee Nation.

9. Europeans (settle) in the area in 1818.

10. Sadly, in time, they (force) most of the Cherokee people to leave.

11. Bison, elk, mountain lions, and wolves once (live) in the valley, too, but now are gone.

12. However, when we visited, we (see) whitetail deer, a young black bear, and some wild turkeys.

Irregular Verbs

Know the Rule

Irregular verbs change their spelling in their past-tense form.
Examples:
I **begin** my guitar lessons today. I **began** playing guitar last year.
I **write** in my journal every day. I **wrote** about my birthday party
yesterday. We may **lose** the game today. We **lost** against the same
team last week.

Practice the Rule

Number a piece of paper 1–10. Write the correct past-tense form of
the irregular verb.

1. For my assignment, I (write) about visiting the Great Smoky
   Mountains National Park.

2. I (begin) by writing about our drive to Clingman's Dome.

3. Our trip took a long time because we (lose) our way a couple of
   times.

4. My father (begin) to get nervous when he couldn't find the
   parking lot.

5. Then I (write) about how we had to walk the last half-mile to the top.

6. My brother (lose) his camera when he tripped, but luckily we
   managed to find it.

7. While we looked out at the view, the clouds (begin) to roll in.

8. So we (begin) to walk back to where we had parked our car.

9. I almost (lose) my shoe in the mud!

10. Finally I (write) about how we made it back to our car just as it
    started to pour.

Publish

+Presentation

Publishing Strategy — Publish my editorial in the class newspaper.

Presentation Strategy — Make good design decisions on the computer.

My editorial is finished! It's time to think about ways of publishing it. There are lots of ways to publish an editorial: in newspapers, magazines, and online, to name a few. Since I'd like to give everyone in my class a chance to read my editorial, I'll publish it in the first issue of our class newspaper.

The computer can help me present my work in a very neat and readable way. I will use the computer to make neat margins and spacing on the page. I will also choose clear fonts. I'll use the computer's spell checker, but I should check my spelling, too. Before publishing it, I will read my editorial one last time. Here's the final checklist I'll use.

My Final Checklist

Did I—

✔ form past-tense verbs correctly?

✔ use clear fonts?

✔ make neat margins and spacing?

✔ put my name on the paper?

Apply

Make a checklist. Check your editorial against it. Then make a final draft. Submit your editorial to the editor of your class newspaper or website for publication.

Welcome to North Carolina!
by Shamari

North Carolina is a perfect place for a vacation! I should know—I live in this magnificent state! During school vacations my family looks for adventure, and we don't have to travel far. I'm going to share with you some of the exciting things we have done. I hope you will be convinced to discover North Carolina on your next vacation!

My favorite place in North Carolina is the Great Smoky Mountains in the western part of the state. My family camped at Great Smoky Mountains National Park. Everyone in the family enjoyed hiking parts of the Appalachian Trail. There's horseback riding in the mountain forests and white-water rafting on the Nantahala River.

The Piedmont Region in central North Carolina is where most of our cities are located. There's a fun theme park, great shopping, and nice golf courses. There are fascinating historic sites like the plantation in Stagville. On our visit, we learned about life on a plantation more than one hundred and fifty years ago. It was very interesting to see how people had to make so many of the things they used. It was also very sad to see how enslaved people lived. I'm sure glad life is very different in North Carolina now!

Last but not least, when you take a vacation in North Carolina, you get to meet wonderful people like my family and me. North Carolinians are proud to live in such a beautiful state. We are warm and kind, and we always welcome visitors.

Please accept my invitation to visit my home state, North Carolina. Come and experience the special places my family has thoroughly enjoyed. There are many more to discover!

Reflect

Use the rubric to check Shamari's editorial. Are all the traits of a good editorial there? How does your editorial compare against the rubric?

What's a Friendly Letter?

I like writing friendly letters to my family members and friends. When I express an opinion in the letter, I try to convince the person who reads the letter to agree with me.

What's in a Friendly Letter?

Personal Tone
In a friendly letter, I want to use a personal tone. My letter should sound like I am talking to the reader in a conversation. I'll use first-person point of view and sound casual yet polite.

Organization
I want to be organized and convincing. I'll state my opinion in an introduction, support it with facts and reasons in the body, and restate it in a conclusion.

Five Parts
A friendly letter has certain words and pieces of information in a particular place on the page. The five parts of a friendly letter are the heading, greeting, body, closing, and signature.

Why write a Friendly Letter?

There are a lot of reasons to write a friendly letter. Here are three reasons for writing a friendly letter.

To Express an Opinion
I may write a friendly letter to convince a friend or family member to come visit me or to watch a movie I saw.

To Resolve a Disagreement
If a friend and I disagree about something, a friendly letter can help resolve the issue.

To Entertain
Sometimes it's fun to debate about something. I can carry on a debate long distance by writing my opinions in a friendly letter.

Linking Opinion Writing Traits to a Friendly Letter

In this chapter, you will write a letter to convince someone you know to agree with your opinion. This type of opinion writing is called a friendly letter. Shamari will guide you through the stages of the writing process: Prewrite, Draft, Revise, Edit, and Publish. In each stage, Shamari will show you important writing strategies that are linked to the Opinion Writing Traits below.

Opinion Writing Traits

- a clear opinion
- strong reasons that are supported by facts and details

- a clear, logical organization
- an introduction, body, and conclusion
- transitions that connect opinions and reasons

- a voice and tone that are appropriate for the audience and purpose

- fair and balanced language
- specific words and phrases

- a variety of sentence patterns that make the writing flow

- no or few errors in spelling, grammar, punctuation, and capitalization

Before you write, read Samuel Taylor's friendly letter on the next page. Then use the friendly letter rubric on pages 290–291 to decide how well he did. (You might want to look back at What's in a Friendly Letter? on page 286, too!)

100 West Street
Rivertown, MN 52045
October 3, 2012

greeting

heading

Dear Chase,

personal tone

I am very happy that you are coming to visit me next summer. It will be fun to spend a whole week together. My parents said that we can either go to our campsite or stay here. I think we'll have more fun if we go to my family's campsite than if we stay at my house the whole time.

introduction

First there's a lot to do at the campsite. There is a lake, so we can go swimming any time we want. We can also go fishing or hike up Overlook Hill. There are bike paths, so we can ride our bikes. At night we can have bonfires and roast marshmallows. At home there's nothing to do except watch TV. We don't have a pool, and there aren't any hills to go hiking. Of course, there's no place to fish, either. So we wouldn't have as much fun at home.

body of the letter

Camping would be good for us, too. We can get a bunch of exercise. At my house, we would just sit around. If we go camping, we would get to spend a lot of time outdoors, so we'd get lots of fresh air. As a result, we would both feel great! At home, we would probably stay indoors most of the time. Because of that, we wouldn't feel as good.

When you come to visit, I hope that you will want to go to my family's campsite. I know we'll have lots of fun there, and it will be good for us, too.

conclusion

closing

Your friend,

Samuel

signature

Friendly Letter Rubric

Use this 6-point rubric to plan and score a friendly letter.

	6	**5**	**4**	
Ideas	The letter clearly states an opinion. Strong, convincing facts support the reasons.	The letter clearly states an opinion. Many facts support the reasons.	The letter clearly states an opinion. Somewhat convincing facts support the reasons.	
Organization	Introduction, body, and conclusion are clear. Focused transition words connect ideas.	Introduction, body, and conclusion are clear. One or two more or better transition words would help connect ideas.	Introduction, body, and conclusion are clear. Ordinary transition words are used.	
Voice	The writer uses a personal, friendly tone. The voice is appropriate for the purpose and audience.	The writer's tone of voice is personal, friendly, and appropriate for the purpose and audience most of the time.	The writer's tone of voice is personal, friendly, and appropriate for the purpose and audience some of the time.	
Word Choice	The writer's language is fair. No loaded words are used.	The writer's language is fair and balanced most of the time. One loaded word may be present.	The writer's language is fair some of the time. One or two words are loaded.	
Sentence Fluency	The sentences vary in length and structure. They flow naturally.	Most of the sentences are varied and flow naturally.	Some of the sentences are varied and flow naturally. A few sentences are too short.	
Conventions	All five parts of the friendly letter are present and punctuated correctly.	All five parts of the friendly letter are present, and most are punctuated correctly.	One part of the letter might be missing. There are a few punctuation errors, but they do not interfere with meaning.	

✛ Presentation The letter has all five parts placed neatly and correctly.

3	2	1	
The letter states an opinion. Supporting facts are weak.	The purpose/opinion of the letter is vague. Reader has to guess or assume what the message is. Facts are repetitive and/or weak.	The letter does not state an opinion. Supporting facts are missing.	**Ideas**
Introduction, body, and/or conclusion are not clear. Transition words are basic, and few are used. Some may be misleading.	Introduction, body, and/or conclusion are not clear. Transition words are missing.	The writing does not have an introduction or conclusion. Transition words are missing.	**Organization**
The writer's tone of voice is inconsistent. It seems to come and go. It may not be appropriate for the purpose and audience.	The writer's tone is too formal, informal, or critical. The writer seems distant from the reader.	The voice is weak or absent. The writer does not connect with the reader.	**Voice**
The writer's language is sometimes biased. Some words are loaded.	Many words are emotional or disrespectful. Some words may offend the reader.	The writer doesn't appear to give much thought to the language used. The message is unclear.	**Word Choice**
Many sentences are short. The letter sounds choppy.	There is little sentence variety. Many sentences begin alike and are of the same length.	Sentences are incomplete or incorrect.	**Sentence Fluency**
Some of the parts of the friendly letter are missing. Some punctuation errors are distracting.	Most of the parts of the letter are unclear or missing. Several punctuation errors confuse the reader. The text is difficult to read and understand.	Letter format is not followed. The writing contains many errors. It is very difficult to read.	**Conventions**

See Appendix B for 4-, 5-, and 6-point opinion rubrics.

Using the Rubric to Study the Model

Friendly Letter

Did you notice that the model on page 289 points out some key elements of a friendly letter? As he wrote his letter, Samuel Taylor used these elements to help him introduce his opinion to others. He also used the 6-point rubric on pages 290–291 to plan, draft, revise, and edit the writing. A rubric is a great tool to evaluate writing during the writing process.

Now let's use the same rubric to score the model. To do this, we'll focus on each trait separately, starting with Ideas. We'll use the top descriptor for each trait (column 6), along with examples from the model, to help us understand how the traits work together. How would you score Samuel on each trait?

Ideas

- **The letter clearly states an opinion.**
- **Strong, convincing facts support the reasons.**

Samuel states his opinion clearly in the introduction—the first paragraph of his letter. Samuel doesn't just tell Chase that staying at the campsite would be more fun than staying at home. He gives Chase a lot of good reasons why he thinks this is true. Here's an example.

First there's a lot to do at the campsite. There is a lake, so we can go swimming any time we want. We can also go fishing or hike up Overlook Hill. There are bike paths, so we can ride our bikes. At night we can have bonfires and roast marshmallows.

Organization

- Introduction, body, and conclusion are clear.
- Focused transition words connect ideas.

Samuel's letter has a clear introduction, body, and conclusion. Each paragraph leads into the next. I've learned that focused transition words help tie ideas together. Samuel uses transition words such as *so*, *as a result*, and *because of* to show the connections between his ideas.

> If we go camping, we would get to spend a lot of time outdoors, so we'd get lots of fresh air. As a result, we would both feel great! At home, we would probably stay indoors most of the time. Because of that, we wouldn't feel as good.

Voice

- The writer uses a personal, friendly tone.
- The voice is appropriate for the purpose and audience.

In writing, I know that tone reveals your attitude toward your topic and your reader. Samuel chose just the right tone for his letter. I could tell that he was writing to a friend. His language was casual and friendly and set a personal tone that showed respect for his friend Chase.

> I am very happy that you are coming to visit me next summer. It will be fun to spend a whole week together. My parents said that we can either go to our campsite or stay here.

Using the Friendly Letter Rubric to Study the Model

Word Choice

- The writer's language is fair.
- No loaded words are used.

Samuel uses fair language to explain why he would rather go camping when his friend comes to visit. He doesn't use loaded words to try to convince Chase. His language is honest and straightforward.

> When you come to visit, I hope that you will want to go to my family's campsite. I know we'll have lots of fun there, and it will be good for us, too.

Sentence Fluency

- The sentences vary in length and structure.
- They flow naturally.

In his letter, Samuel uses a variety of long and short, simple and complex sentences. Each sentence begins differently, too. This made his writing flow and his letter interesting to read.

> At home there's nothing to do except watch TV. We don't have a pool, and there aren't any hills to go hiking. Of course, there's no place to fish, either. So, we wouldn't have as much fun at home.

Conventions

- All five parts of the friendly letter are present and punctuated correctly.

If you look again at the letter on page 289, you'll see that the parts of Samuel's letter have been labeled. He included all five parts of a friendly letter: the heading, the greeting, the body of the letter, the closing, and the signature. Also, he was careful to use capital letters and commas correctly in all the parts and to end each sentence with correct punctuation.

✛Presentation The letter has all five parts placed neatly and correctly.

My Turn!

Now it's my turn to write a friendly letter. I'll use what I've learned from studying the model. Follow along as I use the rubric and good writing strategies to help me.

Prewrite

The Rubric Says   The letter clearly states an opinion.

Writing Strategy   Decide what to write about and research facts about the issue.

My teacher asked us to write a letter to convince someone about something. I have the perfect topic. My parents said we could have a pet. My grandparents are going to get it for us, but they haven't decided on a puppy or a kitten. My dad helped me find a couple of books and websites on the Internet with information about cats and dogs. I took notes from these sources.

> ✏️ **Writer's Term**
>
> **Fact**
> A **fact** is a statement that can be proven to be true. Facts support a writer's reasons.

Dogs	Cats
loving	loving, but also independent
playful	playful, but mostly as kittens
can learn tricks	don't learn tricks easily
can help people	don't help people
can protect their owners	don't protect their owners

Apply

Choose a topic for a friendly letter. Use print or Internet resources to research facts about the issue. Make a list of important things to remember about the topic.

Prewrite

The Rubric Says   Introduction, body, and conclusion are clear.

Writing Strategy   Use a Network Tree to organize facts and reasons.

I know from the rubric that my letter must have an introduction, body paragraphs, and a conclusion. I think adding a puppy to our family would be better for us than a kitten. I'll use a Network Tree to organize my notes and plan my letter.

Writer's Term

Network Tree
A **Network Tree** organizes information. The writer's opinion goes at the top of the tree. Reasons for the opinion go on the next level. Facts and other details go on the lowest level.

Network Tree

Opinion
My grandparents should get us a puppy.

Reason 1
Dogs are more fun than cats.

Reason 2
Dogs can be useful to people.

Fact
Dogs love being with people.

Fact
Dogs like to play games and go for walks.

Fact
Dogs can be trained to do tricks.

Fact
Dogs can be trained to help or guide humans.

Fact
Dogs have rescued their owners.

Fact
Dogs can protect their owners.

Reflect

Look at the notes and the Network Tree. How will they help Shamari write a good letter?

Apply

Look at the notes you took. Use a Network Tree to organize your opinion, reasons, and facts and details.

Draft

Focus on **Voice**

The Rubric Says   The writer uses a personal, friendly tone. The voice is appropriate for the purpose and audience.

Writing Strategy   Use first-person point of view and casual language.

My audience is my grandparents, and my purpose is to convince them to get a dog for our family. I want my own voice to come through. Yet, I also have to remember that I am writing to adults. Since this will be a letter to my grandparents, I'll keep my language casual but polite. Because my letter will express my personal opinion, I'll use first-person point of view (*I, me, we, us*).

As I write my draft, I'll set it up in the form of a friendly letter. I'll also do the best I can with spelling and grammar, but I won't worry about mistakes right now. I'll have a chance to fix them later. Here's the start of my letter to my grandparents.

[DRAFT]

Proofreading Marks

⅂ Indent   ℓ Take out something

≡ Make a capital   ⊙ Add a period

∕ Make a small letter   ⌗ New paragraph

∧ Add something   SP Spelling error

1000 martin st
Raleigh, Nc 27601
march 16, 2012

Dear Grandma and Grandpa

> personal tone

I am very grateful that you are going to get a pet for our family. Mom and dad said we could have either a puppy or a kitten. I think you should get us a puppy. Dogs are much more fun than cats. They are also more useful than cats.

> first-person point of view

Dogs have always make better pets than cats because dogs are more fun. Dogs go on walks with people and play games like fetch. They can learn tricks like lying down and rolling over. A dog will wag its tail, bark, and jump around. Dogs are very loving animals. A dog will put its head on your lap or nuzzle you to be petted. Cats are useless. Cats do not go for walks. They don't play games. They don't learn tricks very easily. They don't jump around. They don't join in the fun. Cats can be loving, but a cat has to be in the mood to be stroked or petted.

Reflect

Read the beginning of Shamari's draft. Did she use a personal tone that shows respect for the reader?

Apply

Use your Network Tree to write a draft of your friendly letter. Set the right tone by choosing your words thoughtfully.

Revise

Focus on **Ideas**

The Rubric Says   The letter clearly states an opinion. Strong, convincing facts support the reasons.

Writing Strategy   Add facts to support the reasons.

When I write, I always look back at the rubric. It reminds me that I should have facts to support my opinion. When I read the third paragraph of my letter, I noticed that I didn't have enough facts to support my opinion. I'll add some facts to that paragraph.

added supporting facts

[DRAFT]

Dogs also make better pets than cats because dogs are

Some dogs are trained to assist or guide people. Others have saved or rescued their owners. Many dogs will bark if a stranger comes into their homes.   these

useful to people. Cats don't do helpful kinds of things for their owners.

Apply

Read your draft. Look for places to add facts to support your reasons. Add these facts to your draft.

The Rubric Says   The writer's language is fair. No loaded words are used.

Writing Strategy   Replace loaded words with neutral ones.

The rubric reminds me to use fair language. I've learned that loaded words can cause strong emotions in the reader. Sometimes the use of loaded words can distract or upset the reader. If I use loaded words, the reader may even stop reading. When I reread my draft, I noticed a loaded word I should replace with a neutral one.

[DRAFT]

very different

Cats are ~~useless~~. Cats do not go for walks. They don't play

games. They don't learn tricks very easily. They don't jump around.

They don't join in the fun.

replaced loaded word

Reflect

Look at the revision. How does using neutral language help Shamari be more convincing?

Apply

Read your draft. Look for loaded words and replace them with neutral ones.

Revise

Focus on Sentence Fluency

The Rubric Says The sentences vary in length and structure. They flow naturally.

Writing Strategy Combine short, choppy sentences to make the writing flow.

I reread my draft out loud. This time I listened for a smooth flow. I found a lot of short, choppy sentences in my second paragraph. If I combine some of them, that will add variation and make my writing flow.

[DRAFT]

petted. Cats are very different. Cats do not go for walks. They

don't play games. ~~They don't~~ learn tricks very easily. They don't
                or

jump around. ~~They don't~~ join in the fun.
              and

combined short, choppy sentences

Apply

Read through your draft. Combine short, choppy sentences to make your writing flow.

Edit

The Rubric Says   All five parts of the friendly letter are present and punctuated correctly.

Writing Strategy   Use punctuation correctly.

I'll check my spelling, capitalization, and punctuation. Then I'll check that my letter has all five parts. My letter won't make a very good impression if it has a lot of errors in it.

Writer's Term

Punctuating a Friendly Letter

Capitalize	Use Commas
• street	• between day and year
• city	• between city and state
• state	
• month	• after greeting
• words in greeting	• after closing
• closing	
• signature	

[DRAFT]

capital letters

1000 martin st
Raleigh, Nc 27601
march 16, 2012

period needed

Reflect

Look at how Shamari combined sentences. Do her sentences flow well? Has she fixed all the errors in punctuation?

Apply   Conventions

Edit your draft for spelling, capitalization, and punctuation. Check that you have included all five parts of a friendly letter.

For more practice with friendly letters and abbreviations, use the exercises on the next two pages.

Parts of a Friendly Letter

Know the Rule

A friendly letter has five parts.
- The **heading** gives your address and the date. Use a comma to separate the name of a city or town from the name of a state. Use another comma to separate the month and the day from the year.
- The **greeting** includes the name of the person you are writing to. It begins with a capital letter and ends with a comma.
- The **body** of the letter is your message.
- The **closing** is a friendly way to say goodbye. It begins with a capital letter and ends with a comma.
- The **signature** is your name.

A letter's envelope has two parts.
- The **address** of the person receiving the letter.
- The **return address** of the person sending the letter.

Note: When addressing an envelope, use all capital letters and no punctuation.

Practice the Rule

Number a piece of paper 1–7. Read the letter and envelope below and on the next page. Write the name of each numbered part of this friendly letter.

1. 32 Lake St.
Duluth, MN 50800
November 12, 2012

2. Dear Samuel,

3.   Thanks for inviting me to visit. I really had a great time. I liked meeting your parents, and staying at the campsite was a lot of fun. Maybe you can come to Duluth for a visit sometime soon.

4. Your friend,

5. Chase

6. CHASE SIMONS
32 LAKE ST
DULUTH MN 50800

U.S. POSTAGE

7. SAMUEL TAYLOR
100 WEST ST
RIVERTOWN MN 52045

Abbreviations and Initials

Know the Rule

Abbreviations are short forms of words. In a letter, you might use abbreviations for a title (*Mr.*) and a street name (*Elm St.*). An **initial** is a capital letter with a period after it. An initial takes the place of a name. For example, *D.J. Connors* stands for *David Jacob Connors*.

Practice the Rule

Number a piece of paper 1–10. Match the abbreviations and initials to their written-out forms. Write the letter of the abbreviation or initial.

1. Doctor Lewis

2. Saint Mary's Hospital

3. Broad Road

4. Market Street

5. Warren Avenue

6. Mister Jackson

7. Cleveland Boulevard

8. Clive Staples Lewis

9. John Fitzgerald Kennedy

10. Frank Mahoney, Senior

a. J.F.K.

b. St.

c. Mr.

d. Sr.

e. Rd.

f. Blvd.

g. St.

h. Dr.

i. C.S.

j. Ave.

Publish

+Presentation

Publishing Strategy   Address an envelope and ask my parents to mail my letter.

Presentation Strategy   Check all the parts of the letter.

My friendly letter is finished. I used this assignment to write about something that really mattered to me. When it came time to publish it, I decided to mail the letter to my grandparents! There are other ways to publish a friendly letter, too. Some of my classmates used their computers to send their letters through e-mail.

Before I put my letter in the envelope, I looked it over one last time. In addition to making sure my letter has all five parts, I made sure it was written neatly and carefully. Here is my final checklist.

My Final Checklist

Did I—

✔ make sure my letter has all five parts?

✔ correctly punctuate all five parts of my letter?

✔ use abbreviations and initials correctly?

✔ use my best handwriting or careful word processing?

Make a checklist to check your friendly letter. Then make a final copy. Address an envelope to the person you are writing to, and then mail the letter.

1000 Martin St.
Raleigh, NC 27601
March 16, 2012

Dear Grandma and Grandpa,

I am very grateful that you are going to get a pet for our family. Mom and Dad said we could have either a puppy or a kitten. I think you should get us a puppy. Dogs are much more fun than cats. Dogs are also more useful than cats.

Dogs have always made better pets than cats because dogs are more fun. First, dogs go on walks with people and play games like fetch. Also, they can learn tricks like lying down and rolling over. A dog will wag its tail, bark, and jump around. In addition, dogs are very loving animals. A dog will put its head on your lap or nuzzle you to be petted. However, cats are very different. Cats do not go for walks. They don't play games or learn tricks very easily. They don't jump around and join in the fun. Cats can be loving, but a cat has to be in the mood to be stroked or petted.

Dogs also make better pets than cats because dogs are useful to people. Some dogs are trained to assist or guide people. Others have saved or rescued their owners. Many dogs will bark if a stranger comes into their homes. Cats don't do these helpful kinds of things for their owners.

When you make your decision, I hope you will consider my reasons for getting a puppy. It's important to have a pet we can have fun with. It's also good to have a pet that can help us.

Love,

Shamari

Reflect

Use the rubric to check Shamari's friendly letter. Are all the traits of a good friendly letter there? How does your friendly letter compare against the rubric?

What's a Response to Literature?

It's an opportunity to share my opinion of a book I've read. My response will be a book review that includes a short description of the plot and characters, the author's main message, and my opinion of the book.

What's in a Response to Literature?

Summary
A response to literature should include a summary of the book. A summary is a brief description of the plot and the important characters. It usually does not reveal the ending of the book, especially if it's a surprise.

Theme
The theme of a book is the author's main point or message to the reader. Sometimes the reader has to figure it out. Sometimes the author tells exactly what it is.

Supporting Evidence
The writer's opinion needs to be supported with information from the book, such as details and direct quotations. Some information can be paraphrased, or put into the writer's own words. Writers can also use their own knowledge to support their opinion.

Why write a Response to Literature?

There are many reasons to respond to literature.
Here are three I can think of. Can you add another?

To Express an Opinion
Sometimes I am very excited about a book I've read. I like to write about it to convince readers to agree with my opinion and get them to read the book. Then we can discuss the book among ourselves.

To Inform
I often learn so much new information from a great book! Writing a book review is a good way to give my friends the opportunity to learn new things, too.

To Understand
When I write a book review, I learn a lot about what I am thinking and feeling. Sometimes I even surprise myself!

Linking Opinion Writing Traits to a Response to Literature

In this chapter, you will write to convince your readers to agree with your opinion about a book. This type of opinion writing is called a response to literature. Shamari will guide you through the stages of the writing process: Prewrite, Draft, Revise, Edit, and Publish. In each stage, Shamari will show you important writing strategies that are linked to the Opinion Writing Traits below.

Opinion Writing Traits

	• a clear opinion • strong reasons that are supported by facts and details
	• a clear, logical organization • an introduction, body, and conclusion • transitions that connect opinions and reasons
	• a voice and tone that are appropriate for the audience and purpose
	• fair and balanced language • specific words and phrases
	• a variety of sentence patterns that make the writing flow
	• no or few errors in spelling, grammar, punctuation, and capitalization

Before you write, read Toshio Mori's response to literature on the next page. Then use the response to literature rubric on pages 312–313 to decide how well he did. (You might want to look back at What's in a Response to Literature? on page 308, too!)

A Magic Tree House Book with a Message

by Toshio Mori

I just finished reading two Magic Tree House books by Mary Pope Osborne. Each book takes Jack and his sister Annie on an adventure. In *Pirates Past Noon*, they go back in time to the days of the Caribbean pirates. In *Tigers at Twilight*, they explore a jungle in India. I enjoyed reading both books. In my opinion, *Tigers at Twilight* sends an important message. The title means that time is running out for the tigers. The book helped me to care about what happens to them.

theme

In *Tigers at Twilight*, Annie and Jack are amazed at the beautiful jungle, with playful monkeys, colorful peacocks, and small deer. Then they find out that the jungle is also home to many large wild animals. One tiger came too close, and Jack and Annie had to escape on an elephant! Later, they found out that the tiger they saw was being hunted. Read the book to find out how they help the tiger.

summary

Tigers at Twilight is filled with interesting facts about jungle animals, like how much a wild tiger eats and how a python can "swallow an animal the size of a full-grown deer." Unfortunately, poachers—people who hunt illegally—kill too many animals.

Did you know that once animals become extinct they're gone forever? Their future depends on what we do today! Read *Tigers at Twilight* to learn how we can work together to save them.

supporting evidence

Response to Literature Rubric

Use this 6-point rubric to plan and score a response to literature.

	6	5	4
Ideas	The writer's opinion is clearly stated. Reasons are supported by strong evidence (quotations, paraphrases, facts, or details).	The writer's opinion is clearly stated. Most evidence is strong and supports the reasons.	The writer's opinion is stated. Some evidence does not support the reasons.	
Organization	The book review is organized logically. Transition words are used effectively.	The parts of the book review are in order. Most transition words are used effectively.	Most parts of the book review are in order. Transition words are used but not effectively.	
Voice	The writer uses a formal tone that sounds knowledgeable and convincing.	The writer uses a formal tone that sounds knowledgeable most of the time.	The writer sounds convincing in the beginning and then fades somewhat.	
Word Choice	Specific nouns and strong verbs are used to convince the reader.	Specific nouns and strong verbs convince the reader most of the time.	A few of the words are vague and should be replaced.	
Sentence Fluency	A variety of sentence patterns makes the writing flow smoothly.	Most sentences are varied. Most of the writing flows smoothly.	Several sentences in a row share the same pattern.	
Conventions	The writing has been edited carefully. Pronouns are used correctly.	A few errors are present but do not confuse the reader. Pronouns are used correctly.	Several errors confuse the reader. One or two pronouns may be used incorrectly.	

✛Presentation The use of multimedia strengthens the message.

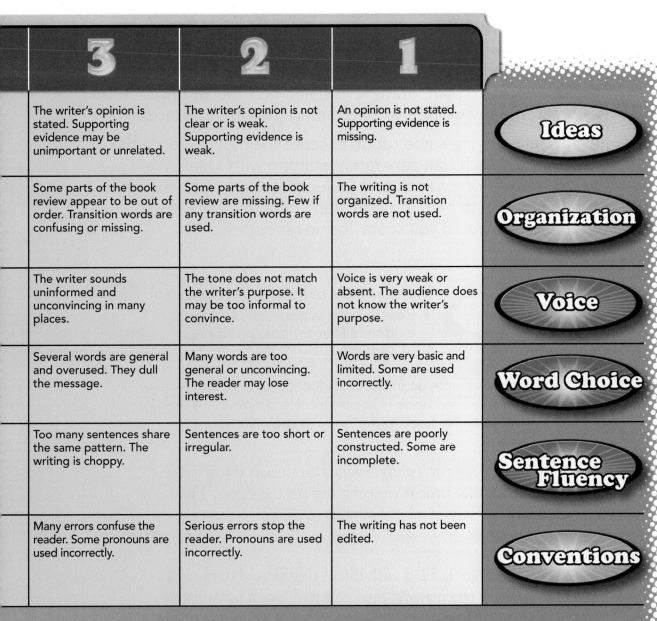

3	2	1	
The writer's opinion is stated. Supporting evidence may be unimportant or unrelated.	The writer's opinion is not clear or is weak. Supporting evidence is weak.	An opinion is not stated. Supporting evidence is missing.	**Ideas**
Some parts of the book review appear to be out of order. Transition words are confusing or missing.	Some parts of the book review are missing. Few if any transition words are used.	The writing is not organized. Transition words are not used.	**Organization**
The writer sounds uninformed and unconvincing in many places.	The tone does not match the writer's purpose. It may be too informal to convince.	Voice is very weak or absent. The audience does not know the writer's purpose.	**Voice**
Several words are general and overused. They dull the message.	Many words are too general or unconvincing. The reader may lose interest.	Words are very basic and limited. Some are used incorrectly.	**Word Choice**
Too many sentences share the same pattern. The writing is choppy.	Sentences are too short or irregular.	Sentences are poorly constructed. Some are incomplete.	**Sentence Fluency**
Many errors confuse the reader. Some pronouns are used incorrectly.	Serious errors stop the reader. Pronouns are used incorrectly.	The writing has not been edited.	**Conventions**

See Appendix B for 4-, 5-, and 6-point opinion rubrics.

Using the Rubric to Study the Model

Did you notice that the model on page 311 points out some key elements of a response to literature? As he wrote "A Magic Tree House Book with a Message," Toshio used these elements to help him write his book review. He also used the 6-point rubric on pages 312–313 to plan, draft, revise, and edit the writing. A rubric is a great tool to evaluate writing during the writing process.

Now let's use the same rubric to score the model. To do this, we'll focus on each trait separately, starting with Ideas. We'll use the top descriptor for each trait (column 6), along with examples from the model, to help us understand how the traits work together. How would you score Toshio on each trait?

Ideas

- **The writer's opinion is clearly stated.**
- **Reasons are supported by strong evidence (quotations, paraphrases, facts, or details).**

Toshio states his opinion in the introduction of his book review. He tells why the second book is important. He supports his opinion with evidence from the book in the body of the review.

In my opinion, *Tigers at Twilight* sends an important message. The title means that time is running out for the tigers. The book helped me to care about what happens to them.

Tigers at Twilight is filled with interesting facts about jungle animals, like how much a wild tiger eats and how a python can "swallow an animal the size of a full-grown deer." Unfortunately, poachers—people who hunt illegally—kill too many animals.

Organization

- The book review is organized logically.
- Transition words are used effectively.

Toshio gives his opinion in the introduction. He summarizes the book and gives supporting evidence in the body. Toshio uses transition words, such as *then* and *later*, to make the book review easy to follow. His conclusion invites the audience to read the book.

Then they find out that the jungle is also home to many large wild animals. One tiger came too close, and Jack and Annie had to escape on an elephant! Later, they found out that the tiger they saw was being hunted.

Voice

- The writer uses a formal tone that sounds knowledgeable and convincing.

You can tell that Toshio liked reading and learning from *Tigers at Twilight*. He shares some of the things he learned and invites his audience to read the book, too. However, he keeps his language formal throughout the book review.

Did you know that once animals become extinct they're gone forever? Their future depends on what we do today! Read *Tigers at Twilight* to learn how we can work together to save them.

Using the Rubric to Study the Model

Word Choice

- Specific nouns and strong verbs are used to convince the reader.

Toshio names specific animals that Annie and Jack saw in the jungle. He also uses specific words from the book as supporting evidence. I'm glad he defined the word *poachers* to help me understand what it means.

Unfortunately, poachers—people who hunt illegally—kill too many animals.

Sentence Fluency

- A variety of sentence patterns makes the writing flow smoothly.

Toshio's book review had sentences of different types and lengths. They kept the book review flowing smoothly. I like the conclusion. It contains three very different types of sentences. Each sentence is punctuated for effect.

Did you know that once animals become extinct they're gone forever? Their future depends on what we do today! Read *Tigers at Twilight* to learn how we can work together to save them.

Conventions
- The writing has been edited carefully.
- Pronouns are used correctly.

Toshio is careful to spell, punctuate, and capitalize correctly in his book review. This example also shows that he used pronouns correctly.

Each book takes Jack and his sister Annie on an adventure. In *Pirates Past Noon*, they go back in time to the days of the Caribbean pirates. In *Tigers at Twilight*, they explore a jungle in India. I enjoyed reading both books.

+Presentation The use of multimedia strengthens the message.

My Turn!

Now it's my turn to write a response to literature. I'll use the rubric and good writing strategies to help me.

Prewrite

Focus on **Ideas**

The Rubric Says The writer's opinion is clearly stated.

Writing Strategy Decide on a topic. Make a list of details.

My class has read several books by the same author, Jerry Spinelli. Now my teacher wants us to write a book review about our favorite book. That's easy to decide! I know which one I liked the best.

I'll state my opinion and make some notes to help me get ideas for my essay.

> **Writer's Term** ___
>
> **Opinion**
> Your **opinion** is what you believe about something. When you state an opinion, be prepared to give reasons for why you think as you do.

Fourth Grade Rats

by Jerry Spinelli

My opinion: <u>Fourth Grade Rats</u> is a great book because it

1. is fun to read
2. makes you laugh
3. teaches an important lesson about growing up

Apply

Choose a book you can recommend to others. Make notes about the book and tell why it is your favorite.

Prewrite

The Rubric Says The book review is organized logically.

Writing Strategy Use a Four-Paragraph Organizer to plan the response.

The rubric reminds me to organize my book review logically. A Four-Paragraph Organizer will help me put the proper information in each paragraph.

✏️ **Writer's Term** _____

Four-Paragraph Organizer
A Four-Paragraph Organizer shows the flow of ideas in an essay. Use it to organize the Introduction, Summary, Supporting Evidence, and Conclusion.

Four-Paragraph Organizer

Introduction	State my opinion Fun to read Teaches a lesson
Summary	Joey wants Suds to toughen up Later, Suds learns lesson about growing up
Evidence from Story	My favorite chapter "Training Camp"
Conclusion	Recommend book

Reflect

Look at the graphic organizer. How will it help Shamari write her book review?

Apply

Use your notes to make a Four-Paragraph Organizer. Arrange ideas into the four parts of a book review.

Revise

Focus on **Ideas**

The Rubric Says	Reasons are supported by strong evidence (quotations, paraphrases, facts, or details).
Writing Strategy	Include information from the book, such as quotations.

I asked Darian to read my draft. He thought that I could add some more information from the story so that readers would understand better why I liked the book so much.

The rubric reminds me to use quotations from the book. I'm going to add one that made me laugh out loud. I'll make sure to put the author's words in quotation marks so my readers will know that they aren't mine. This will support my opinion that the book is fun to read.

[DRAFT]

For example, Joey tells Suds that the worse food tastes, "the faster you grow up." Suds replies, "All I gotta do is go find a dead skunk and eat it and poof, I'll be thirty years old."

Suds and Joey say some very funny things about food.

∧ *added quotations*

Apply

Read your draft. Look for places to add quotations to support your response to the story. Be sure to use quotation marks to separate the author's words from yours.

Revise

The Rubric Says   Transition words are used effectively.

Writing Strategy   Use transitions to show how ideas are related.

Transition words connect one idea to another. When I read the rubric for Organization, I checked my draft for transition words. I found places in the summary where I could use transition words. Do my revisions help show how the ideas are related?

Writer's Term

Transition Words

Transition words connect ideas. Words such as **at first, as a result, finally, for example, next,** and **then** guide the reader through the essay to the writer's conclusion.

[DRAFT]

At first,
Suds doesn't really want to change. He prefers being an angel!

Then,
Suds sees how the other kids look up to Joey. All the girls like

Finally,
him. Suds gives in and lets Joey teach them to be a tough,

fearless, and rude rat, just like Joey.

added transition words

Reflect

Look at the transition words the writer added in the revision. Are they effective?

Apply

Check your draft for places where you can add transition words to connect ideas.

Revise

Focus on Sentence Fluency

The Rubric Says A variety of sentence patterns makes the writing flow smoothly.

Writing Strategy Combine sentences.

The rubric reminded me that my sentences should flow smoothly. I read my draft aloud. I noticed right away that my introduction sounded too choppy. So I revised it. Do you think I improved the flow?

[DRAFT]

"First grade babies! Second grade cats! Third grade angels! Fourth grade rats!" *Fourth Grade Rats* by Jerry Spinelli is a great book. ~~It is~~ about growing up. Joey and Suds are best friends. until Joey tries to change Suds into a rat. It is fun to read ~~It~~ , makes you laugh, and it —making someone change to fit in the group teaches an important lesson about peer pressure.

combined sentences

Apply

Read through your draft aloud. Are there places where you can combine sentences to improve the flow?

Edit

The Rubric Says   The writing has been edited carefully. Pronouns are used correctly.

Writing Strategy   Check the use of all pronouns.

The rubric reminds me to check my writing carefully. I see a place where I could use pronouns in place of names. I also found an error. I think my changes make my writing clearer.

Writer's Term _____

Pronouns

A **pronoun** is a word that takes the place of one or more nouns. A singular pronoun must replace a singular noun. A plural pronoun must replace a plural noun.

[DRAFT]

used pronouns correctly

I
~~We~~ recommend this book to everyone! You're going to love the

surprise turn at the end of the story. I don't want to spoil it for

you
~~them~~, but both Joey and Suds learn an important lesson about

doing the right thing and what it really means to grow up.

Reflect

Look at Shamira's revisions and edits. What do you think of her sentences? Does she use pronouns correctly?

Apply   Conventions

Edit your draft for spelling, punctuation, and capitalization. Check that you have used all pronouns correctly.

For more practice using pronouns correctly, use the exercises on the next two pages.

Personal and Possessive Pronouns

Know the Rule

Personal pronouns can be used in place of names of people and things. **Possessive pronouns** show ownership.

Personal Pronouns
I   me   you   we   he   him   she   her   they   them   it

Possessive Pronouns
my   your   his   her   its   their   our   ours

Practice the Rule

Number a piece of paper 1–10. Write the pronoun from one of the lists that correctly completes the sentence. Remember to capitalize the first letter if the word begins a sentence.

1. Jeff biked to the library. _____ wanted to check out a book.
2. Jeff found the book and took _____ to the check-out desk.
3. "Can I see _____ library card?" the librarian asked Jeff.
4. Jeff gave the librarian _____ card.
5. Then Jeff saw Lisa. _____ was checking out a book, too.
6. Jeff asked, "What book are _____ going to read?"
7. "*Cliques, Phonies, and Other Baloney,*" _____ replied.
8. Jeff had a big smile on _____ face.
9. "I read that book already! Let _____ know what you think!"
10. Jeff and Lisa headed home, eager to read _____ books.

Relative Pronouns

Know the Rule

Relative pronouns are used to connect one part of a sentence to another part. They make the meaning in the sentence clear. *Who, whose, whom, which,* and *that* are relative pronouns.

Examples:
The students **who** have read *Diary of a Wimpy Kid* love it.
It's the book **that** everyone loves to read.
Can you tell me in **which** year it was published?
I think Jeff Kinney is the author to **whom** you are referring.
He is the author **whose** books are all 224 pages long!

Note: A **relative adverb** (*when, where, why*) sometimes can be used in place of a relative pronoun with a preposition to shorten a sentence and improve the flow, as in this example: *Can you tell me* **when** *it was published?*

Practice the Rule

Number a piece of paper 1–10. Write the correct relative pronoun to complete each sentence.

1. I know (who/which) book I would like to read first.

2. *Backpack Stories* is a great book (which/whose) author likes to write humorous stories.

3. A book (whom/that) I'm interested in is *Adventures in Cartooning*.

4. The girl (who/which) recommended it to me loves to draw.

5. Tell me about the books (that/who) you recommend.

6. The book (that/whose) title interests me is *Bug-a-licious*.

7. It tells about different cultures (whom/that) eat bugs.

8. There are people (who/whom) think that bugs taste delicious!

9. I like the book *Blueberry Girl,* (who/which) has beautiful pictures.

10. Yes, the illustrator of that book is Charles Vess, (that/who) is very talented.

Publish

+Presentation

Publishing Strategy	Present the book review as part of a class-published book.
Presentation Strategy	Make a video to go with the book review.

My book review is finished. I can't wait to publish it! It will be part of a class book called "Our Best Books Ever." It will be on display in the library for everyone to see.

Before I make a final copy, I have two things to do. One is to find information about the author on the Internet and add it to my review. I think this is great information to share with others who read my review. Then I am going to ask a couple of friends to help me make a video that will be just like a movie trailer. That will really support my claim that *Fourth Grade Rats* is a great book. The video can run on a library computer near the book display.

My teacher says we have to make sure that our reviews are neat and attractive. I'm using a computer to prepare my final copy. I'll set good margins, center the title and my name, and use clear, easy-to-read fonts. To prepare my final copy, I'll use this checklist.

My Final Checklist

Did I—

✔ edit carefully?

✔ use pronouns correctly?

✔ make a neat final copy?

✔ put a title and my name at the top of the page?

Apply

Use the checklist to prepare your final copy. You could also make a short video of a favorite scene from the book.

A Rat Grows Up
by Shamari

"First grade babies! Second grade cats! Third grade angels! Fourth grade rats!" *Fourth Grade Rats* by Jerry Spinelli is a great book about growing up. Joey and Suds are best friends until Joey tries to change Suds into a rat. It is fun to read, makes you laugh, and teaches an important lesson about peer pressure—making someone change to fit in the group.

Joey is proud of his new ratlike ways, and he wants Suds to follow his example. At first, Suds resists changing. He prefers being an angel! Then, Suds notices how the other kids idolize Joey. All the girls swarm around him, even Judy Billings, the girl Suds has liked since first grade. Finally, Suds gives in and lets Joey teach him to be a tough, fearless, and rude rat, just like Joey.

Suds and Joey say some very funny things about food. For example, Joey tells Suds that the worse food tastes, "the faster you grow up." Suds replies, "All I gotta do is go find a dead skunk and eat it and poof, I'll be thirty years old." In my favorite chapter, "Training Camp," Joey makes Suds toughen up. For example, Suds has to stop crying during sad movies and learn to conquer his fears of spiders and heights.

I recommend this book to everyone! You're going to love the surprise turn at the end of the story. I don't want to spoil it for you, but both Joey and Suds learn an important lesson about doing the right thing and what it really means to grow up.

Reflect

Which evidence from the book did Shamari use to back up her opinion?

Opinion test writing

Read the Writing Prompt

When you begin a writing test, the first thing you will read is the writing prompt. Most writing prompts have three parts.

Setup This part of the writing prompt gives you the background information you need to get ready for writing.

Task This part of the writing prompt tells you exactly what you're supposed to write: an opinion essay to convince your community to support, or not to support, a law that requires bicyclists to wear a safety helmet.

Scoring Guide This section tells how your writing will be scored. To do well on the test, you should include everything on the list.

Think about the rubrics you've been using in this book. When you take a writing test, you don't always have all the information that a rubric gives you. No problem! The scoring guide lists everything you need to think about to write a good paper. Many scoring guides will include the six important traits of writing that are in the rubrics we've looked at:

Many states in the United States have laws that require bike riders to wear safety helmets. Even so, there is a lot of debate over whether these laws are helpful. Some people believe that wearing a helmet prevents injury and death. Others believe that the dangers of bicycling have been exaggerated and that helmets should not be required.

Write an opinion essay to persuade your community to support, or not to support, a law that requires bicyclists to wear a safety helmet.

Be sure

- your essay states an opinion clearly and includes details that strengthen explanations and reasons.

- the reasons are organized from the strongest reason to the weakest.

- your voice is appropriate for the audience and purpose of your essay.

- your essay explains the meaning of any unfamiliar words.

- your essay has a variety of sentence patterns.

- your essay has correct grammar, spelling, capitalization, and punctuation.

Writing Traits
in the Scoring Guide

The scoring guide in the prompt on page 331 has been made into this chart. Does it remind you of the rubrics you've used? Not all prompts include all of the writing traits, but this one does. Use them to do your best writing. Remember to work neatly and put your name on each page.

Ideas
- Be sure your essay states an opinion clearly and includes details that strengthen explanations and reasons.

Organization
- Be sure the reasons are organized from the strongest reason to the weakest.

Voice
- Be sure your voice is appropriate for the audience and purpose of your essay.

Word Choice
- Be sure your essay explains the meaning of any unfamiliar words.

Sentence Fluency
- Be sure your essay has a variety of sentence patterns.

Conventions
- Be sure your essay has correct grammar, spelling, capitalization, and punctuation.

Let's look at the opinion essay by Jasmyn Hill on the next page. Did she follow the scoring guide?

Heads Up — We Need a Helmet Law

by Jasmyn Hill

We need a helmet law in this state, and we need it now. The law would require every bike rider under the age of 16 to wear a helmet. There are many reasons this law is needed. The main reason is that a law would mean that more kids would wear helmets. This would save lives.

Let's take a look at a few facts. Every year bike accidents send about 500,000 children to the hospital or doctor's office. What's worse is that more than 600 of these children die. Up to four out of five of these deaths or serious injuries are caused by head injuries. The fact is that helmets protect the head. A bike helmet can cut the risk of head injury by up to 85 percent.

The sad truth is that very few children wear helmets while riding bikes. Studies show that only about 15 percent wear them all the time. Why do so few wear helmets? For some kids, one reason is fashion. They don't want to ruin their look with a helmet. Helmets, though, are far from unfashionable. Every official bike race requires riders to wear helmets. This means that all the very best bicycle riders wear helmets. Would anyone call Lance Armstrong unfashionable? I don't think so. He has won the Tour de France multiple times, and he always wears a helmet.

Another reason kids ride bareheaded—or without helmets—is that they say helmets are hot and uncomfortable. However, today's helmets are better than ever. They are lightweight, and they fit better. Many helmets are ventilated, which means they have holes in them to let in a cool breeze.

If kids would wear helmets voluntarily, or on their own, we wouldn't need a law. Studies have shown that helmet use increases greatly after a law is passed. In other words, helmet laws work. Today at least 21 states have helmet laws. We need to follow the lead of these states and pass a helmet law here.

With all the dangers of daily life, it makes sense to do whatever we can to lessen the risk of injury. Wearing a helmet when riding a bike is one of the easiest ways to prevent serious injury and even death.

Using the Scoring Guide to Study the Model

Okay, let's use the scoring guide to check Jasmyn's writing test, "Heads Up—We Need a Helmet Law." See if you can find examples from her writing to show how well she did on each part of the scoring guide.

- **The essay states an opinion clearly and includes details that strengthen explanations and reasons.**

Jasmyn's first sentence states her opinion. The reader knows right away that she is in favor of a helmet law. The scoring guide says to use reasons that are supported by strong details. Jasmyn does a good job with these, too. Look at this example.

> The sad truth is that very few children wear helmets while riding bikes. Studies show that only about 15 percent wear them all the time. Why do so few wear helmets?

- **The reasons are organized from the strongest reason to the weakest.**

Jasmyn states her opinion very clearly in the first paragraph, the introduction of her essay. Each paragraph in the body of her essay supports her opinion with reasons. She starts with her strongest reason.

> Let's take a look at a few facts. Every year bike accidents send about 500,000 children to the hospital or doctor's office.

 **Voice**

- **The writer's voice is appropriate for the audience and purpose of the essay.**

Jasmyn's voice is respectful and direct. Her essay is directed toward voters in her state. The purpose of her essay is to convince readers that a helmet law is needed right away, so she needs to use strong facts and clear sentences.

Every year bike accidents send about 500,000 children to the hospital or doctor's office. What's worse is that more than 600 of these children die. Up to four out of five of these deaths or serious injuries are caused by head injuries. The fact is that helmets protect the head. A bike helmet can cut the risk of head injury by up to 85 percent.

 **Word Choice**

- **The essay explains the meaning of any unfamiliar words.**

Words that are unfamiliar to the reader can cause confusion. The scoring guide reminds you that it's important to explain the meaning of unfamiliar words. In her essay, Jasmyn makes sure that she clarifies any words she thinks might be misunderstood by her reader.

Another reason kids ride bareheaded—or without helmets—is that they say helmets are hot and uncomfortable. However, today's helmets are better than ever. They are lightweight, and they fit better. Many helmets are ventilated, which means they have holes in them to let in a cool breeze.

Using the Scoring Guide to Study the Model

- The essay has a variety of sentence patterns.

Your writing is more interesting to read when you use a variety of sentences. A variety of sentences also helps move the writing along for the reader. In this example, Jasmyn asks a question to keep the reader engaged.

Every official bike race requires riders to wear helmets. This means that all the very best bicycle riders wear helmets. Would anyone call Lance Armstrong unfashionable? I don't think so. He has won the Tour de France multiple times, and he always wears a helmet.

- The essay has correct grammar, spelling, capitalization, and punctuation.

Looking back at the scoring guide, you can see the reminder to check your grammar, spelling, capitalization, and punctuation. Don't overlook this step! Take the time to check your essay for mistakes you made and correct them. Watch for errors that you make often. Jasmyn has done a good job in her essay. Her final draft is free from errors.

Planning My Time

Before giving us the writing prompt, my teacher always tells us how much time we have to complete the test. Since I know how much time I have, I can plan how to use it. First I think about how much time I have. Then I divide the time into the different parts of the writing process. In my plan, I always give myself some time to study the writing prompt. Here's how I divide my time into four steps.

Step 4:
Edit
5 minutes

Step 1:
Prewrite
25 minutes

Step 3:
Revise
15 minutes

Step 2:
Draft
15 minutes

Prewrite

Focus on **Ideas**

Writing Strategy | Study the writing prompt to find out what to do.

Once my teacher has given me the writing prompt, I study it to make sure I know exactly what I'm supposed to do. Remember that most writing prompts have three parts. You should find each part and label it: the setup, the task, and the scoring guide. Then you can circle key parts in the writing prompt that tell you what kind of writing to do and what to write about. Look below to see how I did this.

My Writing Test Prompt

Setup — Many people believe that music lessons provide benefits for children beyond musical knowledge or skill. Moreover, they believe all children should have some kind of musical training.

Task — Write an opinion essay to convince parents in your school that all children (or not all children) should take music lessons.

Be sure your essay

Scoring Guide
- states an opinion clearly and includes details that strengthen explanations and reasons.
- organizes the reasons from strongest to weakest.
- uses a voice that is appropriate for the audience and purpose of your essay.
- explains the meaning of any unfamiliar words.
- has a variety of sentence patterns.
- has correct grammar, spelling, capitalization, and punctuation.

Now that I've studied the prompt, I'll think about how the scoring guide relates to the six writing traits I've studied in the rubrics. Not all the writing traits will be included in every scoring guide, but I need to remember them all in order to write a good essay.

Ideas

- Be sure your essay states an opinion clearly and includes details that strengthen explanations and reasons.

I'll let my reader know what my opinion is. I'll keep all my information focused on that opinion.

Organization

- Be sure your essay organizes the reasons from the strongest reason to the weakest.

I'll use a graphic organizer to help me organize my reasons from the strongest to the weakest.

Voice

- Be sure your essay uses a voice that is appropriate for the audience and purpose of your essay.

I'll use strong facts, exact words, and clear sentences to sound sincere and convincing.

Word Choice

- Be sure your essay explains the meaning of any unfamiliar words.

I'll clarify any words my reader might not know.

Sentence Fluency

- Be sure your essay has a variety of sentence patterns.

When I write, I'll be sure to vary my sentence patterns. I should use statements, questions, and exclamations.

Conventions

- Be sure your essay has correct grammar, spelling, capitalization, and punctuation.

Whenever I write anything, I always check grammar, spelling, capitalization, and punctuation.

Prewrite

Focus on **Ideas**

Writing Strategy   Respond to the task.

Writers gather information to help them write. This is a key step when you write for a test. You can gather a lot of information from the writing prompt. Take another look at the task in the writing prompt. The task explains what you are supposed to write.

From my writing prompt, I know I'm supposed to write an opinion essay. I also know the topic. First I'll decide on my opinion, and then I'll quickly jot down some of my reasons for it.

Task — Write an opinion essay to convince parents in your school that all children (or not all children) should take music lessons.

My Opinion: Yes, all children should take music lessons!
Reasons to Support My Opinion:

It's great to learn how to make music—music is forever.
Kids have less time for video games & television.
Music lessons make children smarter in math and language.
Kids learn to concentrate and keep trying.
When you get better, you have interesting opportunities.

Apply

Before you write, think about how you'll respond to the task. To gather information, decide on your opinion, and then quickly jot down some reasons and details that support your position.

Writing Strategy   Choose a graphic organizer.

I need to start organizing my ideas. A good graphic organizer for an opinion essay is an Order-of-Importance Organizer. It will help me put my list of reasons in order from most important to least important.

Most Important: Music lessons make children smarter in math and language.

Next in Importance: Kids learn to concentrate and keep trying.

Next in Importance: Kids have less time for video games & television.

Next in Importance: It's great to learn how to make music—music can carry into adulthood.

Least Important: When you get better, you have interesting opportunities.

Reflect

Look at the graphic organizer. Does it include the reasons the writer will need to write a good opinion essay?

Apply

Choose the best graphic organizer for the assignment. Use it to organize the reasons in a clear order that supports your purpose.

Prewrite

Writing Strategy Check the graphic organizer against the scoring guide.

In a writing test, you don't always have much time to revise. That's why prewriting is so important! So before I start drafting, I'll check my Order-of-Importance Organizer against the scoring guide in the writing prompt.

Most Important: Music lessons make children smarter in math and language.

Next in Importance: Kids learn to concentrate and keep trying.

Next in Importance: Kids have less time for video games & television.

Next in Importance: It's great to learn how to make music—music can carry into adulthood.

Least Important: When you get better, you have interesting opportunities.

Ideas
- Be sure your essay states an opinion clearly and includes details that strengthen explanations and reasons.

I'll be sure to start off by clearly stating my opinion. I'll keep all the information focused on that opinion.

Organization
- Be sure your essay organizes the reasons from the strongest to the weakest.

Since my graphic organizer arranges my reasons from strongest to weakest, I'll use it as a guide while I write.

Voice
- Be sure your essay uses a voice that is appropriate for the audience and purpose of your essay.

I'll use strong facts, exact words, and clear sentences to convince my readers of my opinion.

Word Choice
- Be sure your essay explains the meaning of any unfamiliar words.

As I write and edit my draft, I'll look for words that might need explaining.

Sentence Fluency
- Be sure your essay has a variety of sentence patterns.

I'll keep this in mind as I write. I will vary my sentences by using statements, questions, and exclamations.

Conventions
- Be sure your essay has correct grammar, spelling, capitalization, and punctuation.

I need to check my grammar, spelling, capitalization, and punctuation when I edit my draft.

Reflect

Does the graphic organizer cover all the points of the scoring guide?

Apply

Before you begin drafting, be sure you understand what to do.

Draft

Focus on **Ideas**

Writing Strategy State your opinion in the opening sentence. Make sure everything in your essay supports your opinion.

A good opinion essay lets the reader know right away what point of view the writer has on the issue. So I'll state my opinion. Next I'll use my Order-of-Importance Organizer as a guide for writing the body of my essay. It reminds me of the reasons that support my opinion.

Music Lessons: Good for Your Child, Now and Forever

my opinion

[DRAFT]

All parents should consider haveing their kids take music lessons. Many kids will be glad they took the lessons when they get older.

Studys by scientists have shown that taking music lessons can make children smarter. Music students are learning more than how to play notes. They are learning how to consentrate and to keep trying until they reach their goals. Learning music also

Proofreading Marks

⌐ Indent	ℓ Take out something
≡ Make a capital	⊙ Add a period
/ Make a small letter	¶ New paragraph
∧ Add something	⒮⒫ Spelling error

helps children get better at math and at langauge That means that kids who take music lessons are more likely to be able to learn other subjects faster and easier, too.

Another good thing about taking music lessons is that kids will use less of their leisure time playing video games or watching television. Not only do music students have to spend some time taking the lessons, they also have to practice.

As kids get better at playing the instruments of their choice, they will have other opportunities.

Finally, playing a musical instrument is a talent that kids can carry with them into adulthood. That's why it's important for them to at least try taking music lessons with their parents' encouragement and support.

Reflect

Read the draft. Does the essay begin with a clear statement of the writer's opinion? Does all the information that follows support her opinion?

Apply

Every opinion essay needs a clear opinion and strong reasons. Your essay should begin with a sentence that clearly states your point of view. Then all the information that follows should support the opinion.

Revise

Focus on **Organization**

Writing Strategy Make sure the reasons are in a clear order.

Now it's time to check my draft against the scoring guide. I want to be sure I've included all the points I'll be graded on.

The scoring guide reminds me to organize my reasons from strongest to weakest. I noticed that my last two reasons are listed out of order, according to my graphic organizer. I'll switch them so that the stronger reason comes first.

[DRAFT]

Playing an instrument is also a talent that kids can carry with them into adulthood.
~~As kids get better at playing the instruments of their choice,~~

~~they will have other opportunities.~~
Finally, as kids get better at playing the instruments of their choice, they will have other opportunities.
~~Finally, playing a musical instrument is a talent that kids can~~
These are all reasons
~~carry with them into adulthood.~~ ~~That's~~ why it's important for

them to at least try taking music lessons with their parents'

encouragement and support.

changed order of reasons

Apply

Read your draft. Are your reasons in order?

Revise

Writing Strategy   Use a sincere, convincing voice that matches the purpose of your essay.

Since the purpose of my essay is to get my readers to agree with me, I need to sound confident and knowledgeable from beginning to end. When I read my draft again, I noticed that I didn't sound convincing enough in my introduction. Do you think my revision improves my voice?

[DRAFT]

Many kids will be glad they took the lessons when they
~~They'll find that taking music lessons has had many positive effects on them, helping them in many ways.~~

get older. ∧

improved voice

Reflect

Look at the revision. How does it improve the writer's voice? Do you think it will convince the reader?

Apply

Look at your draft. Make sure your voice is sincere and matches the purpose of your essay.

Revise

Focus on **Word Choice**

Writing Strategy   Explain the meaning of any unfamiliar words.

The scoring guide reminds me to explain the meaning of any words that may be unfamiliar to my reader. This will make my essay easier to read and understand. I'll read my draft again. If I find any words that might be unclear or confusing, I'll add an explanation.

[DRAFT]

Another good thing about taking music lessons is that kids

will use less of their leisure **, or free,** time playing video games or

watching television.

added explanation

Reflect

Did her explanation of the unfamiliar word make her idea easier to understand?

Apply

Read your draft. Explain any words that may be unfamiliar to your reader.

Writing Strategy Check the grammar, spelling, capitalization, and punctuation.

The scoring guide reminds me to check and correct my grammar and spelling. I also need to make sure that I've used capitalization and punctuation correctly. It's a good thing that I planned how to use my time. Now I have time to check for errors.

Music Lessons: Good for Your Child, Now and Forever
by Shamari

[FINAL DRAFT]

All parents should consider ~~haveing~~ having their kids take music

lessons. Many kids will be glad they took the lessons when they

get older. They'll find that taking music lessons has had many

positive effects on them, helping them in many ways.

~~Studys~~ Studies by scientists have shown that taking music lessons can

make children smarter. Music students are learning more than

how to play notes. They are learning how to con~~s~~entrate concentrate and to

keep trying until they reach their goals. Learning music also

helps children get better at

math and at ~~langauge~~ language ⊙ That

Apply

Every time you write for a test, you need to check your grammar, spelling, capitalization, and punctuation.

[FINAL DRAFT]

means that kids who take music lessons are more likely to be able to learn other subjects faster and easier, too.

Another good thing about taking music lessons is that kids will use less of their leisure ∧ time playing video games or
, or free,
watching television. Not only do music students have to spend some time taking the lessons, they also have to practice.
∧

After all, how many of those games or TV shows will they be able to use or enjoy when they grow up? Probably none, and music is forever.

Playing an instrument is also a talent that kids can carry with them into adulthood.

∧ ~~As kids get better at playing the instruments of their choice, they will have other opportunities.~~
Finally, as kids get better at playing the instruments of their choice, they will have other opportunities.
∧ ~~Finally, playing a musical instrument is a talent that kids can~~
These are all reasons
~~carry with them into adulthood.~~ That's why it's important for
∧
them to at least try taking music lessons with their parents' encouragement and support.

Reflect

Use the scoring guide to check Shamari's opinion essay. Did the writer include everything she will be graded on?

Wow! We're done! We used information in the writing prompt and the six writing traits to complete an opinion essay. Remember these important tips when you write for a test.

TEST TIPS

1. **Study the writing prompt before you begin to write.** Most writing prompts have three parts: the setup, the task, and the scoring guide. Remember, they won't be labeled. You'll have to figure them out for yourself.

2. **Make sure you understand the task before you begin to write.**
   - Find and label the three parts of the writing prompt. Then read them carefully.
   - Circle key words in the task. These tell you what kind of writing you need to do.
   - Read the scoring guide. Make sure you know how you'll be graded.

3. **Plan your time. Then keep an eye on the clock.** Be sure you know exactly how much time you will have to write. Then decide how much time you'll spend on each part of the writing process. Stick to your plan as closely as possible. Give yourself time to revise and edit your draft.

4. **Use the scoring guide to check your draft.** A scoring guide on a writing test is like a rubric, and it's a valuable writing tool. Like the rubrics you've used on other papers, it reminds you of what is important. Read your draft at least twice, and compare it to the scoring guide. Make sure that it does what the scoring guide says it should do.

5. **Plan and use your time carefully.** Leave yourself time to carefully read your draft a final time and make any necessary corrections.

6. **Write neatly.** Remember: The people who score your test must be able to read it!

Descriptive writing

uses words to give a clear picture of objects, people, places, or events.

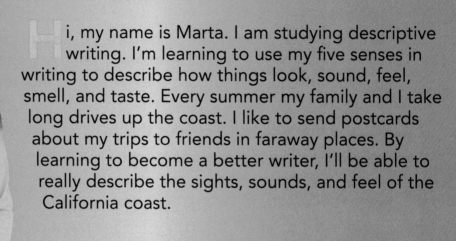

Hi, my name is Marta. I am studying descriptive writing. I'm learning to use my five senses in writing to describe how things look, sound, feel, smell, and taste. Every summer my family and I take long drives up the coast. I like to send postcards about my trips to friends in faraway places. By learning to become a better writer, I'll be able to really describe the sights, sounds, and feel of the California coast.

IN THIS UNIT

- **Descriptive Paragraph**
- **Character Sketch**
- **Poetry Review: Response to Literature**
- MATH CONNECTION ▷ **Poem**
- **Writing for a Test**

Name: Marta

Home: California

Favorite
Activities: sailing, reading,
and writing
poetry

Pets: angelfish

Favorite Book: *Emily's Runaway
Imagination* by
Beverly Cleary

What's a Descriptive Paragraph?

It's a clear, detailed picture in words of a specific person, place, or thing.

What's in a Descriptive Paragraph?

Topic

This is what my paragraph is all about. It could be the day I spent at the beach with my family or a biking trip with my friends. The details I write will support the topic.

Sensory Details

I can bring my paragraph to life with details related to the five senses. By creating word pictures, I can tell my readers how something looks, sounds, smells, feels, or tastes.

Why write a Descriptive Paragraph?

Describing is important for all writers. I can think of a lot of reasons to write a descriptive paragraph. Here are a few.

To Entertain

Writers of stories use descriptive paragraphs to make the characters, setting, and action seem real. Good descriptions help the readers picture the story in their minds. The reader can enjoy an amazing imaginary world.

To Inform

Describing is one way to give people information. Describing what you observe is an important activity of scientists. The observations that they write are detailed descriptions of what they see or hear. I can write about something I've seen or heard to share with others.

To Express an Opinion

How a writer describes something can influence a reader's opinion about it. That's why historians try hard to describe events in history without giving an opinion.

Fiction writers have a different goal. They often use opinion words like *beautiful, scary, awful*, and *delicious* to bring emotion to a story. They want to make the readers think and feel a certain way.

Linking Descriptive Writing Traits to a Descriptive Paragraph

In this chapter, you will describe a special place. This type of descriptive writing is called a descriptive paragraph. Marta will guide you through the stages of the writing process: Prewrite, Draft, Revise, Edit, and Publish. In each stage, Marta will show you important writing strategies that are linked to the Descriptive Writing Traits below.

Descriptive Writing Traits

Ideas	• a clear and complete topic • sensory details and examples that help the reader "see" what is being described
Organization	• well-organized paragraphs that each tell about one main idea • transitions that guide the reader through the text
Voice	• a voice and tone that are appropriate for the purpose and connect with the audience
Word Choice	• precise, descriptive language that creates a picture for the reader
Sentence Fluency	• different kinds of sentences that make the writing flow
Conventions	• no or few errors in grammar, usage, mechanics, and spelling

Before you write, read Andrea Baum's descriptive paragraph on the next page. Then use the descriptive paragraph rubric on pages 358–359 to decide how well she did. (You might want to look back at What's in a Descriptive Paragraph? on page 354, too!)

OUR SECRET HIDING PLACE

Descriptive **MODEL** Paragraph

by Andrea Baum

topic

For a quiet, happy afternoon, away from my little brothers, there is nothing like the special place that Sarah and I found. It is in the woods, not far from my house. To get there, we walk a half-mile down a dirt path, turn off just before a wooden walkway, and go down another short trail. Suddenly, there it is! With a few more steps, we reach a quiet, open place about eight feet by ten feet. In that one place, there are no trees, but the sunlight cuts through the leaves of the surrounding trees with bright knives of light. It is an ideal hideaway! Sarah and I spend hours there playing. We talk, plan, listen, and sit quietly together. We hear the *rat-a-tat-tat* of woodpeckers and the soft whistles of nuthatches. We listen as the breeze whispers in the leaves of the maple trees. We watch orange and black butterflies flutter nearby. The soft pine needles make a scented cushion. Sometimes, we sit and imagine the country when the pioneers came here, and we pretend we are explorers. All friends should have a secret place as special as ours.

sensory details

Descriptive Paragraph Rubric

Use this 6-point rubric to plan and score a descriptive paragraph.

	6	5	4
Ideas	The writer's topic is clear. Sensory details create a clear, focused picture of one place.	The writer's topic is clear. A few more sensory details would help create a clearer picture.	The writer's topic is fairly clear. Sensory details would help create a clearer picture.
Organization	A clear topic sentence introduces the topic. Well-chosen transitions guide the reader through the description.	A clear topic sentence introduces the topic. Most transitions guide the reader through the description.	A topic sentence introduces the topic. Some transitions guide the reader through the description.
Voice	The writer's personality comes across clearly. The voice speaks directly to the reader.	The writer's voice is sincere and natural in most places.	The writer's personality comes through. The voice is ordinary in a few places.
Word Choice	Descriptive language creates a vivid picture for the reader.	Most of the language is descriptive and helps the reader "see" the place.	Some descriptive language is vague or overused.
Sentence Fluency	A mix of sentence types and lengths makes the writing enjoyable to read.	Most of the writing has a mix of sentence types and lengths.	Some sentences are different types and lengths, but a few more would improve the writing.
Conventions	Articles and plural nouns are used correctly. The writing is easy to read.	The use of articles and plural nouns is mostly correct.	Few errors in articles and plural nouns are noticeable.

✛ Presentation The paragraph is neat and legible.

3	2	1	
The topic is somewhat clear. Sensory details are needed to complete the picture.	The topic is not clear. Sensory details are needed to form a picture.	The writing is not focused. Sensory details not used.	**Ideas**
A topic sentence is present. Few transitions guide the reader through the description.	A topic sentence is present. Transitions are confusing or missing.	A topic sentence is not present. Transitions are not used.	**Organization**
The writer's personality comes through sometimes. The voice is inconsistent.	The voice may be inappropriate or very inconsistent. The reader is confused or distracted.	The writer's voice is absent. The reader does not feel a connection with the writer.	**Voice**
Most of the language is very general. The words are not descriptive enough.	The language is vague or dull. Too few words describe the topic.	No descriptive language is used. The reader cannot "see" the topic.	**Word Choice**
Most of the sentences are the same length and type.	Sentences are repetitive, choppy, and/or run on.	Incomplete or incorrect sentences make the writing impossible to follow.	**Sentence Fluency**
Noticeable errors with articles and plural nouns confuse the reader.	Several major errors in articles and plural nouns cause confusion and rereading.	The writing contains many errors in articles and plural nouns. It is very difficult to read.	**Conventions**

See Appendix B for 4-, 5-, and 6-point descriptive rubrics.

Descriptive Paragraph

Using the Rubric to Study the Model

Did you notice that the model on page 357 points out some key elements of a descriptive paragraph? As she wrote "Our Secret Hiding Place," Andrea Baum used these elements to help her describe a special place. She also used the 6-point rubric on pages 358–359 to plan, draft, revise, and edit the writing. A rubric is a great tool to evaluate writing during the writing process.

Now let's use the same rubric to score the model. To do this, we'll focus on each trait separately, starting with Ideas. We'll use the top descriptor for each trait (column 6), along with examples from the model, to help us understand how the traits work together. How would you score Andrea on each trait?

Ideas

- **The writer's topic is clear.**
- **Sensory details create a clear, focused picture of one place.**

Andrea writes a description about a secret hiding place she found with her friend. She uses her senses to describe their special place. Read how the writer describes what their hideaway looks like.

With a few more steps, we reach a quiet, open place about eight feet by ten feet. In that one place, there are no trees, but the sunlight cuts through the leaves of the surrounding trees with bright knives of light.

Organization

- A clear topic sentence introduces the topic.
- Well-chosen transitions guide the reader through the description.

Andrea introduces the topic right away. Her topic sentence gives the main idea of the paragraph. It also creates a lot of interest in the place. In the paragraph, I notice that Andrea uses transitions like *in the woods, half-mile down,* and *just before.* The words help me follow the description.

> It is in the woods, not far from my house. To get there, we walk a half-mile down a dirt path, turn off just before a wooden walkway, and go down another short trail.

Voice

- The writer's personality comes across clearly.
- The voice speaks directly to the reader.

Andrea's personality comes through in her writing. You can tell she likes her secret place and her friend Sarah. You see her secret place from her point of view.

> It is an ideal hideaway! Sarah and I spend hours there playing. We talk, plan, listen, and sit quietly together.

Using the Rubric to Study the Model

Descriptive Paragraph

Word Choice
- Descriptive language creates a vivid picture for the reader.

Andrea uses interesting descriptive words. She creates word pictures by describing the sights, sounds, and smells of her secret hiding place. I can picture her secret place in my mind!

> We listen as the breeze whispers in the leaves of the maple trees. We watch orange and black butterflies flutter nearby. The soft pine needles make a scented cushion.

Sentence Fluency
- A mix of sentence types and lengths makes the writing enjoyable to read.

The writer uses a variety of sentence types and lengths in her writing. She includes exclamations to add excitement to the paragraph. When she describes the way to her secret place, she starts with a very short sentence. It is an exclamation that shows the excitement of the moment.

> Suddenly, there it is! With a few more steps, we reach a quiet, open place about eight feet by ten feet.

Conventions
- Articles and plural nouns are used correctly. The writing is easy to read.

I read the description very carefully. Every word is spelled correctly. There are no errors in capitalization or punctuation either. The writer uses articles and plural nouns correctly. Look at this example. It has six plural nouns. Can you find them?

We hear the *rat-a-tat-tat* of woodpeckers and the soft whistles of nuthatches. We listen as the breeze whispers in the leaves of the maple trees. We watch orange and black butterflies flutter nearby.

⁺Presentation The paragraph is neat and legible.

My Turn!

Now it's my turn to write a descriptive paragraph! I'll use the 6-point rubric on pages 358–359 and good writing strategies to help me. Follow along to see how I do it.

Prewrite

Focus on **Ideas**

The Rubric Says The writer's topic is clear. Sensory details create a clear, focused picture of one place.

Writing Strategy Make some notes about an interesting place you know.

I love visiting Splash Zone at the Monterey Bay Aquarium. I can see and even touch a lot of sea creatures there. My teacher asked us to think of a place we had visited and liked. Right away, I thought of Splash Zone. My strategy will be to jot down notes about what I saw, heard, and smelled.

Notes for My Paragraph

- Splash Zone—best part of the aquarium
- a place for families
- different species of fish
- salty smell of the sea
- can hold starfish
- a beautiful coral reef
- walls of bubbling water
- hear excited children
- a window that puts you next to penguins
- giant clam chair
- sounds of fish eating
- hear "talking" penguins
- walls that feel like coral
- smell of animals
- water play area

Apply

Think about an interesting place you know well. Jot down notes about it. What would a visitor want to know about it?

The Rubric Says A clear topic sentence introduces the topic. Well-chosen transitions guide the reader through the description.

Writing Strategy Make a Web to organize your notes.

I know from the rubric that organization is important. To organize my notes, I'm going to make a Web. I'll put the main idea of my paragraph in the middle of my Web. Then I'll use my five senses to put the details in circles around my topic. The Web will make writing my paragraph easier because all of the information will be right there as I write.

Writer's Term

Web

A **Web** organizes information about one main topic. The main topic goes in a center circle. Related details go in outside circles.

Web

smell:
salty smell of seawater, smell of animals

taste:
nothing—but I felt AS IF I could taste bubbling coral reef water!

Splash Zone

see:
colorful fish, beautiful coral, huge clam chair, water tunnel. LOTS more!

touch:
hold starfish, water play area, walls that feel like coral

hear:
fish eating, bubbling water, excited children, penguins "talking"

Reflect

Look at the notes and the Web. How will they help Marta write a descriptive paragraph?

Apply

Look at the notes you made. Choose notes with the most vivid details about the place. Make a Web to organize your ideas.

Draft

Focus on Ideas

The Rubric Says The writer's topic is clear. Sensory details create a clear, focused picture of one place.

Writing Strategy Select details that will help the reader "see" the place.

Now it's time to write my descriptive paragraph. I'll use the center of my Web to write my topic sentence. Then I'll choose information from the other circles to write detail sentences. I know from the rubric that my topic sentence needs to be so clear that my reader can almost "see" my subject.

I won't worry about checking grammar or spelling right now. I know I'll get a chance to fix any mistakes later when I edit my writing.

Writer's Term

Topic Sentence and Detail Sentences

A **topic sentence** states the main idea of a whole paragraph.

Detail sentences go with, tell about, or give examples of the topic sentence.

[DRAFT]

detail
sentence

Wet, Wild, and Wonderful

topic
sentence

No one should miss Splash Zone at the Monterey Bay Aquarium. It is

the best place to learn about a life of sea animals. Where else can

kids sit in a giant clam chair or hear fish eating? Where else is there

a coral reef with bubbling walls of water. I can crawl through

detail
sentence

a tunnel. As I crawl, I see sea horses, eeles, reef sharks, and

all kinds of fish. The bubbling water looked cold. Then there are

model starfish and other creatures. In the water play area, kids

can make waves and tide pooles. Then there are the blackfooted

detail
sentence

penguins. They hop and swim around there home with rocks by the

water. They talk like donkys. A neat special window makes it seem as

if I suddenly popped up next to them. I can even stand behind a big

wall where I can put my head inside cutout faces on top of

detail
sentence

painted penguin bodies.

Reflect

Read the draft. Does the topic sentence describe a real place that the reader might like to visit?

Apply

Use your notes and Web to write your own draft. Remember to write a clear topic sentence and choose details that will help the reader "see" what you describe.

Revise

The Rubric Says   Well-chosen transitions guide the reader through the description.

Writing Strategy   Use words and phrases that help the reader follow the description.

After I wrote my paragraph, I decided to add transitions. The rubric says that well-chosen transitions guide the reader. Phrases that begin with *at* will help the reader feel as if they are following me through Splash Zone. I can explain where we found the model starfish and the blackfooted penguins.

> **Writer's Term**
>
> **Transitions**
> **Transitions** guide the reader from one idea to the next. In a paragraph, transitional words and phrases help link the details in a logical order.

[DRAFT]

added transition

At the touch pool,
~~Then~~ there are model starfish and other creatures. In the water play area, kids can make waves and tide pooles. ~~Then there~~ are the   At the end of Splash Zone,

blackfooted penguins. They hop and swim around there home with

rocks by the water.

added transition

Apply

Read your draft. Find places where you can add transitions to guide the reader.

Revise

The Rubric Says The writer's personality comes across clearly. The voice speaks directly to the reader.

Writing Strategy Use first-person point of view to share your feelings.

The rubric says that I should let my personality come through in my writing. I should also speak directly to the reader.

By sharing my feelings about my visit to Splash Zone, the reader will get to know a little bit about my personality. By using first person (*I, me, my, we*), I help the reader share my personal experience.

[DRAFT]

used first-person words

if I suddenly popped up next to them. I can even stand behind

a big wall where I can put my head inside cutout faces on top of

My parents and I looked silly in the picture

we took there. I remember Splash Zone

and laugh whenever I look at the photograph

of my family as penguins!

painted penguin bodies. ~~We took pictures. Splash Zone was fun.~~

Reflect

Look at the revisions. What do they tell you about the writer's personality?

Apply

Read your draft again. Look for places where you can add personal feelings about your experience. Remember to use *I, me, we,* and *our* to talk about your feelings.

Revise

The Rubric Says   Descriptive language creates a vivid picture for the reader.

Writing Strategy   Include word pictures to improve my description.

After I wrote my draft, I decided to write a word picture to support my topic. At Splash Zone, we had a picture taken of us behind the painted penguins with cutout faces. I'll revise my new sentence to make a funny word picture describing that photograph. That way, my audience will be able to "see" how much fun Splash Zone is.

✏️ Writer's Term

Word Picture

A **word picture** is a vivid description of something in words. By painting pictures with words, you help the reader imagine the place you are describing.

[DRAFT]

created a word picture

                    like a family of chubby birds wearing tuxedos
My parents and I looked silly in the picture we took there.

I remember Splash Zone and laugh whenever I look at the

photograph of my family as penguins!

Apply

Read your draft. Find places where you can create word pictures to help the reader imagine what you are describing.

Edit

The Rubric Says   Articles and plural nouns are used correctly.

Writing Strategy   Make sure plural nouns and articles are correct.

Next I'll check my spelling, capitalization, and punctuation. Also the rubric reminds me to make sure that all my plural nouns and articles are formed correctly.

Writer's Term

Plural Nouns

A **plural noun** names more than one thing. Add **-s** to most singular nouns to form the plural. Add **-es** to singular nouns that end in **s, x, ch,** or **sh.** Some nouns form the plural in other ways, like *children* or *geese.*

[DRAFT]

No one should miss Splash Zone at the Monterey Bay Aquarium. It is
                                              the lives
the best place to learn about a life of sea animals.

corrected article and plural noun

Reflect

What do you think of Marta's revisions to make a word picture? Look at the edits. Are the plural nouns and articles correct?

Apply   Conventions

Edit your draft for spelling, capitalization, and punctuation. Make sure all your plural nouns and articles are correct.

For more practice with plural nouns and articles, use the exercises on the next two pages.

Plural Nouns

Know the Rule

A **noun** is a word that names a person, place, or thing. A singular noun names one thing. A plural noun names more than one thing. Most singular nouns become plural when you add -s.

> **Example: dog/dogs**

If a singular noun ends in *s, x, ch,* or *sh,* add -es to make it a plural noun.

> **Example: tax/taxes**

If a singular noun ends in *y,* change the *y* to *i* before adding -es.

> **Example: daisy/daisies**

Many singular nouns that end in *f* change the *f* to *v* to form the plural.

> **Example: shelf/shelves, hoof/hooves**

However, not all singular nouns that end in *f* do this.

> **Example: roof/roofs, chief/chiefs, cliff/cliffs**

Practice the Rule

Number a separate sheet of paper from 1–10. Read each sentence below. Write the plural form of the noun in parentheses.

1. We spent two (week) at a national park.
2. The (beach) had soft white sand.
3. We ate many picnic (lunch) there.
4. One beach was divided into two (half).
5. People could swim and have (party) on one side.
6. Birds raised their (baby) on the other side.
7. Sometimes (fox) would raid a nest.
8. Some people pitched (tent) at a nearby campground.
9. Campers were careful not to leave any (mess) behind.
10. People always carried their trash and (dish) away.

Articles

Know the Rule

A, an, and the are special adjectives called **articles**. Use a before a noun that begins with a consonant sound. Use an before a noun that begins with a vowel sound. Use a and an when talking about any one person, place, or thing. Use the when talking about specific persons, places, or things.

Examples:
The moon shone brightly until **a** cloud blocked it out.
An ant crawled into **the** tent.

Practice the Rule

Number a separate sheet of paper from 1–10. Read each sentence below. Write the correct article (a, an, the) to complete each sentence.

1. Our campsite was by _____ edge of the lake.
2. I had _____ air mattress to put in my tent.
3. We brought wood to build _____ fire.
4. I looked for _____ stick to roast marshmallows.
5. _____ roasted marshmallows were delicious.
6. We kept warm by _____ fire my dad built.
7. During the night, I heard _____ owl in the trees.
8. _____ nighttime animal sounds kept me awake.
9. I saw _____ sun come up in the morning.
10. I helped pack up and take _____ tents down.

Publish

✚Presentation

Publishing Strategy Publish the description as part of a brochure.

Presentation Strategy Use a limited number of clear fonts.

My descriptive paragraph is done! My next step is to publish it. I think I should publish my description as part of a brochure. In a brochure, I can describe what it's like to be at Splash Zone and invite others to visit, too. Then my classmates will see why they should go! I will prepare my brochure on the computer. The rubric tells me to use clear fonts. Too many fonts will distract from my writing. So I will choose a few fonts that are attractive and easy to read. I will use this checklist to check my descriptive paragraph one more time.

My Final Checklist

Did I—

✔ check to make sure all plural nouns are correct?

✔ make sure I used articles correctly?

✔ use a few clear fonts?

✔ put my name on the brochure?

Apply

Use the checklist to check your own descriptive paragraph. Then make a final copy and publish it as part of a brochure. Make copies of your brochure to share with your classmates.

Wet, Wild, and Wonderful
by Marta

No one should miss Splash Zone at the Monterey Bay Aquarium. It is the best place to learn about the lives of sea animals. Where else could I sit in a giant clam chair or hear fish eating? Where else could I visit a coral reef with bubbling walls of water? I can crawl through a tunnel and touch walls that feel like rough and soft coral. As I crawl, I see sea horses, eels, reef sharks, and all kinds of brightly colored fish. I smell the salty sea air, and I can almost taste the bubbling, cold water. At the touch pool, I can pick up live and model starfish and other creatures. In the water play area, I can make waves and tide pools. At the end of Splash Zone are the blackfooted penguins. They hop and swim around their rocky home. They bray like donkeys! A special window makes it seem as if I suddenly pop up next to them. I can even stand behind a big wall where I can put my head inside cutout faces on top of painted penguin bodies. My parents and I looked like a family of chubby birds wearing tuxedos in the picture we took there. I remember Splash Zone and laugh whenever I look at the photograph of my family as penguins!

Reflect

Use the rubric to score Marta's paragraph. How did she do? Now, use it to score your own paragraph.

What's a Character Sketch?

It's a description of a real person or a character in a book.

What's in a Character Sketch?

Thoughts
That's what my character thinks. Describing what my character thinks will make the person more interesting.

Appearance
That's what my character looks like. Describing my character will help the reader "see" the person.

Words
That's what my character says. Describing what a character says makes the person seem real.

Actions
That's what my character does. My character's actions will tell a lot about his or her personality. The actions could be adventuresome like an astronaut in space or thoughtful like an author.

Why write a Character Sketch?

Describing a person can be fun, but it's also helpful.
Here are some good reasons for writing a character sketch.

To Entertain

People are so interesting! Characters can be quiet
or adventuresome, heroes or villains. They make
good decisions or bad ones. Exploring the world
of people—real and imaginary—is fascinating!

To Inform

Biographers write character sketches
to help us get to know the people they are writing
about. Reporters may write character sketches of
people in the community. I can write a character
sketch about an interesting person to share with others.

To Understand

No two people are exactly the same. Writing
about real people and characters in books can help
us understand others. We can recognize what we
have in common. We can learn to appreciate our
differences.

Linking Descriptive Writing Traits to a Character Sketch

In this chapter, you will describe a person. This type of descriptive writing is called a character sketch. Marta will guide you through the stages of the writing process: Prewrite, Draft, Revise, Edit, and Publish. In each stage, Marta will show you important writing strategies that are linked to the Descriptive Writing Traits below.

Descriptive Writing Traits

 **Ideas**	• a clear and complete topic • sensory details and examples that help the reader "see" what is being described
 **Organization**	• well-organized paragraphs that each tell about one main idea • transitions that guide the reader through the text
 **Voice**	• a voice and tone that are appropriate for the purpose and connect with the audience
 **Word Choice**	• precise, descriptive language that creates a picture for the reader
 **Sentence Fluency**	• different kinds of sentences that make the writing flow
 **Conventions**	• no or few errors in grammar, usage, mechanics, and spelling

Before you write, read Ed Lee's character sketch on the next page. Then use the character sketch rubric on pages 380–381 to decide how well he did. (You might want to look back at What's in a Character Sketch? on page 376, too!)

JOHNNY APPLESEED

Character MODEL Sketch

by Ed Lee

Johnny Appleseed is the title of a book by Reeve Lindbergh. It is also the name of the folk hero who is the main character in the book. Johnny Appleseed was a real person, but Appleseed wasn't his real last name. The name given to him at birth was John Chapman. He was later called Johnny Appleseed because he traveled around the country planting apple trees.

appearance → Johnny Appleseed was a thin man with a lean face. He traveled barefoot, sometimes in rain and snow. His clothes were old and worn, but he did not care about how he looked. He cared about what he did with his life.

actions → The life he chose was to plant apple trees across the country. He knew that apples were a very important crop in early America, and they could be grown easily. However, pioneers did not have room to carry small trees with them. Johnny Appleseed carried young, healthy apple trees to families who were settling the western frontier. Sometimes he shared a meal and talked with the families, but he never stayed long in any one place. Wherever he went next, he scattered his precious apple seeds. **actions**

Johnny Appleseed was a very gentle man. He walked alone through unsettled territory filled with wild animals, but he never carried anything to protect himself. He told people that he would never harm a living creature. He was also a very grateful person, and he appreciated the beauty around him. He spoke about his love for the grand, green forests, the vast prairies, and the wide rivers. He spoke about his respect for the rich and fertile land he traveled. **words**

Johnny Appleseed gave a lot to people. The wilderness blossomed with his apple trees. Even so, he did not believe that **thoughts** anyone owed him any special thanks. In our day, people express their thanks by writing books about him. The next time you take a bite of fresh-baked apple pie, think of Johnny Appleseed!

Character Sketch Rubric

Use this 6-point rubric to plan and score a character sketch.

	6	5	4
Ideas	The writer's topic is clear. Descriptive details bring the subject to life for the reader.	The writer's topic is clear. Many important details bring the character to life.	The writer's topic is clear. More descriptive details would help the reader.
Organization	The strong introduction, body, and conclusion fit together well. A variety of helpful transitions guides the reader through the description.	The strong introduction, body, and conclusion fit together. Most transitions help the reader follow the description.	The introduction, body, and conclusion fit together. In one or two places, transitions help the reader follow the description.
Voice	The writer's personality comes through. The reader can tell the writer knows about and likes the subject.	The writer's personality and feelings come through most of the time.	Some of the writer's personality and feelings come through. The voice is appropriate.
Word Choice	The words paint a clear picture. Concrete words and phrases help the reader "see" the subject.	Most of the words and phrases are concrete and help the reader "see" the subject.	Some words and phrases are too general. The reader cannot always picture the subject.
Sentence Fluency	Sentence lengths and structures are varied effectively.	Most of the sentence structures and lengths are varied.	Many of the sentences are the same length and/or structure.
Conventions	The writing is free from errors. Compound sentences are written correctly. There are no run-on sentences.	There are minor errors in compound sentences and no run-on sentences. Errors do not impair meaning.	There are a few errors in compound sentences and one or two run-on sentences. However, the errors do not confuse the reader.

✛Presentation   A title and the writer's name are on the sketch. Paragraphs are indented.

3	2	1	
The writer's topic is unclear in places. Descriptions are not specific, confusing the reader.	The writer's topic is not clear. Few descriptive details help the reader.	The writer's topic is not clear. Details are unrelated or not provided.	**Ideas**
The introduction, body, and conclusion do not fit together well. Transitions, if used, may mislead or confuse the reader.	The introduction, body, and conclusion are not clear. Transitions are not used.	The writing does not have an introduction and/or a conclusion. Transitions are not used.	**Organization**
The writer's personality and feelings are inconsistent and not creatively expressed.	The writer's voice is very weak. It is difficult to sense personality or feelings. The voice may be inappropriate.	The reader cannot sense the writer's personality. The writer seems not to know or care about the subject.	**Voice**
Some of the words and phrases are dull. Some phrases are hard for the reader to understand.	The words and phrases are ordinary. They do not describe the subject well.	Many words or phrases are misused, confusing, and vague. The reader feels lost.	**Word Choice**
Repetitive sentence beginnings and length make text choppy and awkward.	Lack of sentence variety makes text very difficult to read and understand.	Many sentences are incomplete or incorrect. They are difficult to read.	**Sentence Fluency**
Several run-on sentences and incorrect compound sentences make the reader stop to reread.	Too many run-on sentences and incorrect compound sentences confuse the reader.	Many run-on sentences and poor compound sentences make the writing very hard to understand.	**Conventions**

See Appendix B for 4-, 5-, and 6-point descriptive rubrics.

Using the Rubric to Study the Model
Character Sketch

Did you notice that the model on page 379 points out some key elements of a character sketch? As he wrote "Johnny Appleseed," Ed Lee used these elements to help him describe a person. He also used the 6-point rubric on pages 380–381 to plan, draft, revise, and edit the writing. A rubric is a great tool to evaluate writing during the writing process.

Now let's use the same rubric to score the model. To do this, we'll focus on each trait separately, starting with Ideas. We'll use the top descriptor for each trait (column 6), along with examples from the model, to help us understand how the traits work together. How would you score Ed on each trait?

Ideas

- **The writer's topic is clear.**
- **Descriptive details bring the subject to life for the reader.**

Ed makes it clear right away that he wants to tell his readers about Johnny Appleseed. He gives lots of specific details about his subject. This part tells me about Johnny Appleseed's personality. Details about what he said and did helped me really understand what kind of person he was.

Johnny Appleseed was a very gentle man. He walked alone through unsettled territory filled with wild animals, but he never carried anything to protect himself. He told people that he would never harm a living creature.

Organization

- The strong introduction, body, and conclusion fit together well.
- A variety of helpful transitions guides the reader through the description.

The first paragraph introduces us to Johnny Appleseed. The body of the sketch tells us details about Johnny Appleseed's life and why he is remembered. Ed's paragraphs flow together well. Helpful transitions like *In our day* and *The next time* guide the reader all the way through the sketch.

In our day, people express their thanks by writing books about him. The next time you take a bite of fresh-baked apple pie, think of Johnny Appleseed!

Voice

- The writer's personality comes through.
- The reader can tell the writer knows about and likes the subject.

The writer's voice comes through in his description of Johnny Appleseed. He shares with readers what he thinks makes Johnny Appleseed so special. In the last paragraph, the writer shows his respect for his subject.

Johnny Appleseed gave a lot to people. The wilderness blossomed with his apple trees. Even so, he did not believe that anyone owed him any special thanks.

Using the Rubric to Study the Model
Character Sketch

Word Choice

- The words paint a clear picture.
- Concrete words and phrases help the reader "see" the subject.

Ed uses a lot of specific phrases like *a thin man with a lean face* that help the reader picture Johnny Appleseed. Look at these sentences.

> Johnny Appleseed was a thin man with a lean face. He traveled barefoot, sometimes in rain and snow. His clothes were old and worn, but he did not care about how he looked.

Sentence Fluency

- Sentence lengths and structures are varied effectively.

The writer varies the sentence lengths to keep the reader interested. Look at the first paragraph. He uses both long and short sentences to introduce Johnny Appleseed. A variety of sentence lengths helps the writing to flow.

> *Johnny Appleseed* is the title of a book by Reeve Lindbergh. It is also the name of the folk hero who is the main character in the book. Johnny Appleseed was a real person, but Appleseed wasn't his real last name. The name given to him at birth was John Chapman.

Conventions

- The writing is free from errors.
- Compound sentences are written correctly.

I carefully read through the sketch again. All the compound sentences are correct. I looked for run-on sentences, but I couldn't find any.

He was also a very grateful person, and he appreciated the beauty around him. He spoke about his love for the grand, green forests, the vast prairies, and the wide rivers. He spoke about his respect for the rich and fertile land he traveled.

✚ Presentation The title and author's name are on the paper. Each paragraph is indented.

My Turn!

Now it's my turn to write my own character sketch. Follow along to see how I'll use the rubric and good writing strategies.

Prewrite

The Rubric Says The writer's topic is clear. Descriptive details bring the subject to life for the reader.

Writing Strategy Choose a character from a book and jot down some details about him or her.

When my teacher said we could write about a character from a book, I decided to write about Pecos Bill. He is a funny, wild character from a tall tale. Heroes in tall tales do things that regular people can't do. Everyone would probably enjoy reading about Pecos Bill's fantastic adventures.

First I'll jot down a list of details about Pecos Bill.

My Notes

The Book: Pecos Bill
by Steven Kellogg
The Character: Pecos Bill
Details from the Book:

- falls in a river
- grows up with coyotes
- feels like a member of the coyote pack
- always looks happy and smiling
- looks strong
- decides to become a Texan
- tells outlaws he'll turn them into cowboys
- chases and catches a horse named Lightning
- says Lightning can go free
- ropes a tornado
- sure of himself

Apply

Think about an interesting character from a book that you would like to write about. Jot down details about your character.

Prewrite

The Rubric Says   The strong introduction, body, and conclusion fit together well.

Writing Strategy   Use a Spider Map to organize details about the character.

I know that the purpose of a character sketch is to tell all about a character. So I need details about how my character acts, talks, thinks, and looks. I'm going to use a Spider Map to be sure I have those kinds of details. I'll also use the Spider Map to organize them.

Writer's Term

Spider Map

A **Spider Map** organizes information about a topic. The topic goes in the center, the categories go on the spider's "legs," and specific details about the categories are attached to the "legs."

Spider Map

Pecos Bill

Appearance
- always looks happy and smiling
- strong

Actions
- falls in a river
- grows up with coyotes
- chases and catches Lightning
- ropes a tornado

Words
- says Lightning can go free
- tells outlaws he'll turn them into cowboys

Thoughts
- sure of himself
- feels like a member of the coyote pack
- decides to become a Texan

Reflect

Look at the notes and the Spider Map. How will they help Marta write a good character sketch?

Apply

Look at your list. Choose the details that best describe your character. Organize these details using a Spider Map.

Draft

The Rubric Says   The strong introduction, body, and conclusion fit together well. A variety of helpful transitions guides the reader through the description.

Writing Strategy   Organize the information in an introduction, body, and conclusion. Use helpful transitions.

Now I'm ready to describe my character. I'll use my Spider Map to help me write a draft.

First I need to tell my readers what I am writing about. My introduction should tell the book I read, the character's name, and the reason I chose to write about the character. The body of the sketch is where I will put all the details I have collected.

Finally I will wrap up my description in the conclusion. Maybe I will leave the reader with a question to think about.

The rubric also reminds me to use transitions, like *one day* and *then*, to help readers follow my description. I will include as many as I can as I write my draft. But I can always go back and add them later. In fact, I can check my transitions as well as my grammar, punctuation, and spelling at the end.

[DRAFT]

Pecos Bill

In the book <u>Pecos Bill</u> by Steven Kellogg, the main character is an interesting person. He is called Pecos Bill because as a child he falls into the Pecos River. That action makes changes that make new actions happen in his whole life.

introduction

A coyote rescues baby Bill from the river in the nick of time. Bill grows up in a family of coyotes. He believes he is a coyote

One day Pecos Bill is taking a coyote nap a Texan on a horse discovers him. Bill becomes a Texan instead of a coyote. Always happy and smiling. he grows strong and sure of himself. He wrestles with creetures like a giant rattlesnake. The fiercest outlaws in Texas are amazed. He informs outlaws that he will turn them into honest cowboys they agree! They promise to round up all the steers in Texas for him.

body

transitions

Then Pecos Bill trys to catch a wild horse named Lightning. Bill chases Lightning from the Arctic Circle to the Grand Canyon. He leaps onto the silver stallion's back and sings to it in its own language. He offers the horse freedom. Lightning decides to stay with Pecos Bill forever.

conclusion

Reflect

Read the draft. Is the sketch organized with an introduction, body, and conclusion?

Apply

Use your Spider Map to write your own draft. Remember to organize your information in an introduction, body, and conclusion. Use transitions to guide the reader.

Revise

The Rubric Says   The writer's personality comes through. The reader can tell the writer knows about and likes the subject.

Writing Strategy   Let the reader know what you think about the character.

I know from the rubric that I should let my personality come through in my writing. To do that, I will explain what I think about Pecos Bill. There are other ways to show my voice, too. The details I choose, the kinds of words I use, and the kinds of sentences I write will all combine to show my voice.

[DRAFT]

a funny, fantastic hero named Bill.

In the book <u>Pecos Bill</u> by Steven Kellogg, the main character is ^

He has wild, exciting adventures.

~~an interesting person.~~ He is called Pecos Bill because as a child he ^

falls into the Pecos River. That action makes changes that make

new actions happen in his whole life.

improved voice

Apply

Read your draft. Choose details, words, and sentence types that help your personality come through in your writing.

Revise

Focus on **Word Choice**

The Rubric Says The words paint a clear picture. Concrete words and phrases help the reader "see" the subject.

Writing Strategy Replace clichés with concrete words and phrases.

I read my draft to myself. I remembered from the rubric that I should use concrete words and phrases in my writing.

Writer's Term _

Cliché

A **cliché** is an expression that has been overused. These expressions lose their meaning or freshness. For example, "flat as a pancake" and "good as gold" are clichés.

I looked back and found a place in my draft where I had used a cliché. See what I did to make my writing more specific.

just as he is sinking

replaced overused expression

A coyote rescues baby Bill from the river ~~in the nick of time.~~ Bill grows up in a family of coyotes.

Reflect

Look at the changes. What words replace the cliché? How do they improve Marta's draft?

Apply

Read your draft again. Look for clichés. Replace any worn-out words and phrases with specific ones.

Revise

Focus on  Sentence Fluency

The Rubric Says   Sentence lengths and structures are varied effectively.

Writing Strategy   Use short, simple sentences to make a point.

The rubric says to vary sentence lengths and structures effectively. A variety of sentences helps the writing flow. Sometimes you want to get the reader's attention to make a point. A short, simple sentence can do that. I will look for places where I can change a longer sentence to a shorter sentence to make a point.

used short sentence to make a point

He is called Pecos Bill because as a child he falls into the Pecos

That accident changes more than Bill's name.
It changes his whole life.

River. ~~That action makes changes that make new actions happen~~
   ∧
~~in his whole life.~~

[DRAFT]

Apply

Look for places in your draft where you can vary sentence lengths to make a point.

The Rubric Says	Compound sentences are written correctly. There are no run-on sentences.
Writing Strategy	Make sure there are no run-on sentences.

Next I'll check my spelling, capitalization, and punctuation. As I checked my writing, I found a run-on sentence. I'll correct it now by joining the two thoughts in the sentence with a comma and the word *and*.

Writer's Term ___

Run-on Sentences

A **run-on sentence** is made of two sentences that have been run together without a comma and a conjunction. To correct a run-on sentence, turn it into a **compound sentence** by adding a comma and a conjunction, such as **and, or,** or **but,** between the two complete thoughts.

[DRAFT]

corrected run-on sentence

, and

One day Pecos Bill is taking a coyote nap⌃a Texan on a horse

discovers him. Bill becomes a Texan instead of a coyote. Always

Reflect

What do you think of the way Marta revised her sentences? Look at the edits. How else can a run-on sentence be fixed?

Apply   Conventions

Edit your draft for spelling, punctuation, and capitalization. Fix any run-on sentences.

For more practice fixing run-on sentences, use the exercises on the next two pages.

Run-on Sentences

Know the Rule

Begin every sentence with a capital letter and end with the correct punctuation mark. There should be no run-on sentences. A **run-on sentence** is two complete thoughts that run together without punctuation and a conjunction.

Example: Her story was long it was very interesting.
Use a comma followed by **and, but,** or **or** to join two sentences to make a compound sentence.

Example: Her story was long, **but** it was very interesting.

Practice the Rule

Number a sheet of paper from 1–10. Rewrite each sentence, correcting any errors in capitalization or punctuation. Correct any run-on sentences by adding a comma and a conjunction.

1. on a hot June day in 1778, an important battle was fought.
2. One hero of the battle was Molly Hays most now call her Molly Pitcher.
3. Washington planned to attack the British and Molly knew there would be a terrible battle.
4. the sound of musket and cannon fire soon filled the air.
5. It was a hot summer day men began falling from the heat.
6. Molly saw the problem she heard the men cry for water.
7. Molly spotted a cool stream nearby she filled a pitcher with water.
8. again and again, she brought pitchers of cool water to the thirsty soldiers.
9. Who was the woman who brought the water
10. Her family called her Molly Hays the grateful soldiers called her Molly Pitcher.

Compound Sentences

Know the Rule

A **compound sentence** is made up of two simple sentences. A simple sentence has one subject and one predicate. To write a compound sentence, include a comma (,) followed by **and, but,** or **or. And, but,** and **or** are joining words. They are called conjunctions.

Examples:

I wrote about Annie Oakley, **and** I included information about her childhood.

She was born a long time ago, **but** her story lives on in books, plays, and songs.

I might watch a movie about Annie Oakley, **or** I could read a book about her life.

Practice the Rule

Number a sheet of paper from 1–8. Each compound sentence below contains two simple sentences. Write the two sentences and circle the comma and conjunction that join them.

1. Annie Oakley was a famous sharpshooter, and she is remembered in books, movies, and plays.

2. Annie Oakley was born in 1860, and she lived in a log cabin.

3. Her mother named her Phoebe Ann, but her sisters called her Annie.

4. Annie Oakley learned to shoot at nine years of age, and she won her first shooting contest at 16.

5. Annie Oakley beat Frank Butler in a shooting contest, and then she married him.

6. The Butlers traveled to Europe, and they performed for Queen Victoria.

7. Annie Oakley had a difficult childhood, but she was a successful adult.

8. You can learn more about Annie Oakley by reading a biography about her, or you could see the famous play *Annie Get Your Gun*.

Publish

Publishing Strategy   Illustrate the character sketch and post the final copy on the class bulletin board or website.

Presentation Strategy   Put the title and your name on the paper. Indent every paragraph.

I've finished my character sketch! Now I have to decide how to publish it. I think my classmates will want to "see" Pecos Bill in two ways. I will draw a picture of him to go along with my character sketch, and I will post them both on our class bulletin board. Since my sketch will be on the bulletin board, I need to clearly put the title and my name on the paper. The rubric also reminds me to indent each paragraph. That way, my story will be neat and easier to read.

My Final Checklist

Did I—

✔ fix any run-on sentences?

✔ form compound sentences correctly?

✔ put the title and my name on the paper?

✔ indent every paragraph?

Apply

Use the checklist to check your own character sketch. Then make a final copy for the class bulletin board. You may want to post it to your class website, too.

Pecos Bill
by Marta

In the book <u>Pecos Bill</u> by Steven Kellogg, the main character is a funny, fantastic hero named Bill. He has wild, exciting adventures. He is called Pecos Bill because as a child he falls into the Pecos River. That accident changes more than Bill's name. It changes his whole life.

A coyote rescues baby Bill from the river just as he is sinking, and Bill grows up in a family of coyotes. He runs with the coyotes during starry nights. He howls with them at the full, yellow moon. He believes he is a coyote.

One day Pecos Bill is taking a coyote nap, and a Texan on a horse discovers him. Bill becomes a Texan instead of a coyote. He is always happy and smiling, and he grows strong and sure of himself. He wrestles with creatures like a giant rattlesnake. The fiercest outlaws in Texas are amazed. He informs them that he will turn them into honest cowboys, and they agree! They promise to round up all the steers in Texas for him.

Then Pecos Bill tries to catch a wild horse named Lightning. Bill chases Lightning from the Arctic Circle to the Grand Canyon. Finally, he leaps onto the silver stallion's back and sings to it in its own language. Then he offers the horse freedom, but Lightning decides to stay with Pecos Bill forever.

Pecos Bill saves his bride, Slewfoot Sue, by roping a tornado in outer space! He and Sue are blown down to Earth, and they land on his family's wagon in California. What other character in a book has ever had adventures like that?

Reflect

Use the rubric to check the story. Are the traits of a good character sketch there? Then, use the rubric to check your character sketch.

What's a Poetry Review?

It's an essay that describes the writer's experience of reading a poem.

What's in a Poetry Review?

Evidence of Careful Reading
The writer's ideas come from reading a poem carefully. A poetry review focuses on the feelings and images that the poem evokes. Reading a poem about the beauty of nature would make me want to spend time in a garden or at a lake.

Examples and Details
The writer supports his or her central idea with examples and details from the poem.

A Central Idea
The writer expresses a central idea about the poem. The central idea may be whether or not the writer liked the poem, or how the writer felt after reading the poem.

Why write a Poetry Review?

There are different reasons for writing a poetry review. Here are a few.

To Reflect
Poems can touch me in different ways. Writing about my response to a poem helps me put my feelings into words.

To Entertain
If I really love a poem, I enjoy sharing my response to it with others. My readers may find it interesting to compare my response with theirs.

To Teach a Lesson
Sometimes a poem can teach a lesson. By giving the poem a closer look and writing about it, I can learn something of value.

Poetry Review Rubric

Use this 6-point rubric to plan and score a poetry review.

	6	5	4	
Ideas	The topic is introduced clearly. The review has a central idea, and several examples offer support.	The topic is introduced clearly. The review has a central idea. One more example is needed.	The topic is introduced. The central idea is somewhat clear. More examples are needed.	
Organization	All examples and details are organized logically. A variety of transitions links ideas from one sentence to the next.	Most of the examples and details are organized logically. A variety of transitions links ideas from one sentence to the next.	Some of the examples seem to be out of order. More or better transitions are needed.	
Voice	The personal tone connects with the reader. The writer shares feelings and ideas.	The writer connects with the reader most of the time. A more personal tone would help.	The writer connects with the reader some of the time. The tone is personal some of the time.	
Word Choice	Comparisons and well-chosen adjectives convey the meaning precisely.	Most comparisons and adjectives convey the meaning precisely.	Some comparisons are vague or confusing. More adjectives would help convey meaning.	
Sentence Fluency	Varied sentence beginnings help the writing flow. The review is enjoyable to read.	In one or two places, sentence beginnings are not varied. The review is enjoyable to read.	Writing is easy to read, but a few sentences start the same way.	
Conventions	Different types of adjectives are used correctly. The writing is easy to read.	Minor errors in the use of adjectives do not distract the reader.	There are a few errors in the use of adjectives, but they do not interfere with meaning.	

✛ Presentation   The review is legible and neat. The title and the writer's name are at the top of the page.

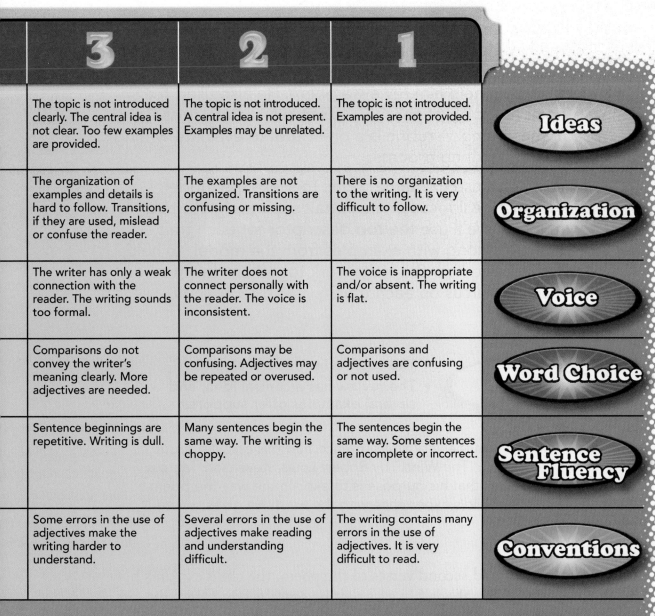

3	2	1	
The topic is not introduced clearly. The central idea is not clear. Too few examples are provided.	The topic is not introduced. A central idea is not present. Examples may be unrelated.	The topic is not introduced. Examples are not provided.	**Ideas**
The organization of examples and details is hard to follow. Transitions, if they are used, mislead or confuse the reader.	The examples are not organized. Transitions are confusing or missing.	There is no organization to the writing. It is very difficult to follow.	**Organization**
The writer has only a weak connection with the reader. The writing sounds too formal.	The writer does not connect personally with the reader. The voice is inconsistent.	The voice is inappropriate and/or absent. The writing is flat.	**Voice**
Comparisons do not convey the writer's meaning clearly. More adjectives are needed.	Comparisons may be confusing. Adjectives may be repeated or overused.	Comparisons and adjectives are confusing or not used.	**Word Choice**
Sentence beginnings are repetitive. Writing is dull.	Many sentences begin the same way. The writing is choppy.	The sentences begin the same way. Some sentences are incomplete or incorrect.	**Sentence Fluency**
Some errors in the use of adjectives make the writing harder to understand.	Several errors in the use of adjectives make reading and understanding difficult.	The writing contains many errors in the use of adjectives. It is very difficult to read.	**Conventions**

See Appendix B for 4-, 5-, and 6-point descriptive rubrics.

Poetry Review
Using the Rubric to Study the Model

Did you notice that the model on page 401 points out some key elements of a poetry review? As he wrote "My Playful Friend, 'The Wind,'" Marcus West used these elements to help him review a poem. He also used the 6-point rubric on pages 402–403 to plan, draft, revise, and edit the writing. A rubric is a great tool to evaluate writing during the writing process.

Now let's use the same rubric to score the model. To do this, we'll focus on each trait separately, starting with Ideas. We'll use the top descriptor for each trait (column 6), along with examples from the model, to help us understand how the traits work together. How would you score Marcus on each trait?

 **Ideas**

- **The topic is introduced clearly.**
- **The review has a central idea, and several examples offer support.**

I knew from the very first sentence that this essay is about a poem called "The Wind" by Robert Louis Stevenson. Marcus makes it clear that his purpose is to explain the way the poem describes a child's experience with the wind. He gives several examples.

In the first and second verses of the poem, the child explains how he knows the wind is there. He says that he saw the wind "toss the kites on high."

Organization

- All examples and details are organized logically.
- A variety of transitions links ideas from one sentence to the next.

Marcus organizes his thoughts around a central idea. Each paragraph talks about a particular feeling or image that the poem brings to mind. In this example, he explains how Stevenson made the wind seem real.

Stevenson makes both the child speaker of the poem and the wind real characters. He makes the wind seem lively and real. He treats it like a person. The child always speaks to the wind directly. He says, "O wind," "O you," and "O blower." Maybe he is teasing the wind a little. In fact, the reader almost expects the wind to answer the child back.

Voice

- The personal tone connects with the reader.
- The writer shares feelings and ideas.

I really like the way Marcus uses a personal tone to describe the poem. Here's a good example. He says that the poet helps the reader feel what it is like to play in the wind. He supports that idea by imagining how readers might respond to "The Wind."

A child who reads the poem might think, "Yes, I know that feeling." An older person reading the poem might feel like a child again.

Using the Rubric to Study the Model
Poetry Review

Word Choice

- Comparisons and well-chosen adjectives convey the meaning precisely.

Sometimes the writer uses comparisons to make his descriptions clear. He compares something he is describing to something else that is familiar to the reader. In this example, he is describing the rhythm and rhyme of the poem. The adjective *playful* is a good choice. Then, when he compares rhythm and rhyme to skipping and singing, he makes his meaning clearer to me.

The rhythm in this poem makes it seem playful. It is easy to imagine a little boy or girl outside, pretending the wind is a friend. The rhythm goes *tah-DUM*, *tah-DUM*, like a child skipping. Each two lines end with words that rhyme, like a child's song.

Sentence Fluency

- Varied sentence beginnings help the writing flow.
- The review is enjoyable to read.

The writer does a good job of varying the beginnings of his sentences. Almost every sentence begins differently from the one before it. This makes his writing easy to read and understand. It also makes it more interesting.

In the first and second verses of the poem, the child explains how he knows the wind is there. He says that he saw the wind "toss the kites on high." He also heard it make sounds like the swish of "ladies' skirts across the grass." The child also shows how strong the wind is when he says, "I felt you push."

Conventions • Different types of adjectives are used correctly. The writing is easy to read.

I read through the whole review, and the writer uses adjectives correctly to describe and compare. In this example, the writer uses the adjectives *lively* and *easier* to describe and compare the wind.

The child knows the wind is there and has seen the things it does. Yet everything the lively wind does is easier to see than the wind itself.

⁺Presentation The review is legible and neat. The title and the writer's name are at the top of the page.

My Turn! Now it's my turn to write a poetry review! I'll use the rubric and good writing strategies to help me. Follow along to see how I do it.

Prewrite

The Rubric Says   The topic is introduced clearly. The review has a central idea, and several examples offer support.

Writing Strategy   Jot down some ideas about a poem you find interesting.

Today my teacher asked us to look through some poetry books and choose a poem that we find interesting. Whatever poem we choose will be the subject of an essay—a poetry review. I found a poem by Edna St. Vincent Millay that I really liked. It's called "Afternoon on a Hill."

I read the poem carefully and jotted down some notes. I included what I think the poem is about, how the poem makes me feel, and what it helps me to see.

My Notes

- painted pictures in my mind
- describes a happy day on a hill
- Verse 1: happy in the sun
- happy like a child
- a hundred flowers
- "gladdest"—a funny, happy word

- Verse 2: time passing
- cliffs and clouds
- the grass bowing and rising
- looking "with quiet eyes"
- Verse 3: going home
- getting dark
- lights from town

Apply

Choose a poem that you find interesting. Read it. Then jot down your thoughts and feelings about it.

Prewrite

The Rubric Says All examples and details are organized logically. A variety of transitions links ideas from one sentence to the next.

Writing Strategy Make a Network Tree to organize examples and details.

I know that I need to organize my ideas before I write. I'll use a Network Tree. The central idea goes at the top. The verses go in the second level. The details are grouped by verse and go in the third level. Each set of details will become a paragraph.

Writer's Term

Network Tree

A **Network Tree** organizes information according to the level of ideas. At the top is the central idea. Key details that support the central idea go on the next level. Details that support these go on the bottom level.

Network Tree

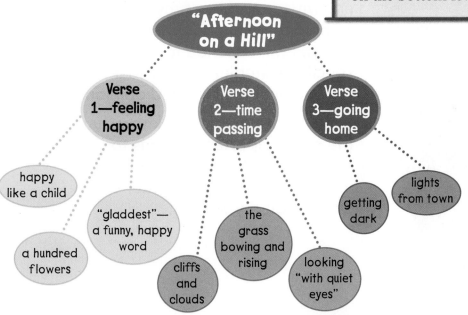

Reflect

Look at the notes and the Network Tree. How will they help Marta write a good review?

Apply

Look at the notes that you made about your poem. Use a Network Tree to organize your ideas.

Draft

The Rubric Says   The personal tone connects with the reader. The writer shares feelings and ideas.

Writing Strategy   Use first person (*I, me, my*) to share your thoughts about the poem.

Now it's time to write my draft. The rubric tells me that I need to use a personal tone to connect with the reader. To do that, I should use first-person point of view when I tell readers about the poem. That means I should use the words *I, me,* and *my* to talk about my reactions. To help readers understand the poem, I will describe it and offer specific examples. I will also include my personal feelings and opinions.

As I write my draft, I know that the most important thing is to express my ideas. If I make any mistakes, I will fix them later on when I edit my writing.

[DRAFT]

"Afternoon on a Hill"
a poem by Edna St. Vincent Millay

personal tone

The words of Edna St. Vincent Millay's poem "Afternoon on a Hill" seem to paint pictures in my mind. The words she chose help me see and feel the things that she imagined. This poem is about being happy wherever you are.

Millay tells a story in this poem. She goes out in the country during the day. She sits in the sunshine on top of a hill. She looks at flowers and clouds. At the end of the day, when it gets dark, she goes back home.

Reflect

Read the beginning of Marta's draft. What personal feelings about the poem does the writer share in her review?

Apply

Use your notes and Network Tree to write your own draft. Remember to show your personal tone by sharing your feelings about the poem. Use *I*, *me*, and *my*.

Revise

Focus on **Ideas**

The Rubric Says   The review has a central idea, and several examples offer support.

Writing Strategy   Use examples from the poem.

I've finished my draft. Now I'll check to make sure I've used the best examples from the poem to support my central idea, an afternoon on a hill.

example from the poem →

She says, "I will be the gladdest thing."
"Gladdest" is a funny word but a good choice.
Millay's choice of words is important. ⌄ Some words sounds

like a little child who is really happy and excited. The poet
    She says that even though she will see "a
    hundred flowers," she will "not pick one."
shows that she wants to protect nature, too. ⌄

[DRAFT]

example from the poem

Read your draft. Look for places to add good details and examples.

Revise

The Rubric Says   Comparisons and well-chosen adjectives convey the meaning precisely.

Writing Strategy   Use *like* to compare one thing to another.

The rubric tells me that using comparisons will help make my writing clearer. I read my draft again. My thoughts about the second verse are not very clear. I put in some comparisons that will help the reader understand just what I mean. I'll use good adjectives like *bending* and *floating* in the comparison, too.

[DRAFT]

In the second verse, Millay compares the clouds and bending

grass with time. She describes how she watches "with quiet

It feels slow, like time passing. ← **added comparison**

eyes" as clouds move across the sky. When the wind makes the

added comparison → The bending grass and floating clouds are like clocks in nature.

grass bow down and rise, she has time to watch it rise.

used helpful adjectives

Reflect

Look at the revisions. How do the comparisons make the descriptions clearer?

Apply

Read your draft again. Look for descriptions that aren't clear. Add comparisons that will make them clearer.

Revise

The Rubric Says   Varied sentence beginnings help the writing flow.

Writing Strategy   Start sentences in different ways.

It's time for me to revise my writing. According to the rubric, it's important to use different types of sentence beginnings. If I start every sentence the same way, my writing won't flow and will be hard to understand.

I looked over my essay and found a place where too many sentences began the same way. Three sentences in a row began with *She*! Do you think my changes improve this part of my review?

varied sentence beginnings

[DRAFT]

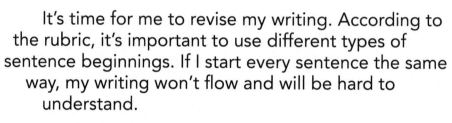

Millay tells a story in this poem. She goes out in the country during the day. ~~She sits~~ Sitting in the sunshine on top of a hill, She looks at flowers and clouds. At the end of the day, when it gets dark, she goes back home.

Apply

Read through your draft. Make sure your sentences begin in different ways.

Edit

The Rubric Says   Different types of adjectives are used correctly.

Writing Strategy   Make sure adjectives are used correctly.

Now I'll proofread my review for spelling, punctuation, and capitalization. The rubric says to make sure I've used adjectives correctly. I'll look for places where I've described and compared people, places, or things.

> ✎ **Writer's Term** _____
>
> ### Comparative Adjectives
> **Comparative adjectives** describe the differences between two things. If an adjective has one syllable, the comparative is formed by adding **-er**. Adjectives with two syllables or more form the comparative by adding the word **more**. When a two-syllable adjective ends in **-ly**, the **-y** is changed to **-ier**.

corrected comparative adjectives

The poet can see her house from the hilltop. Maybe its light

       brighter

seems ~~more bright~~ than the others. When I come home after

       better

dark, I feel ~~good~~ if there are lights on.

[DRAFT]

Reflect

First look at how Marta revised her sentences. Do her revisions help the writing flow better? Then look at the edits. Do you think the adjectives are used correctly and effectively?

Apply

Check your draft. Make sure you have used adjectives correctly to describe and compare.

For more practice using adjectives, use the exercises on the next two pages.

Adjectives

Know the Rule

An **adjective** describes a noun. It tells what the noun is like. When two or more adjectives describe a noun, they are listed in a particular order. Look at the chart to see the order of certain kinds of adjectives.

Size	Age	Color	Material
big	young	red	wooden
little	old	blue	silk
teeny	teenaged	yellow	golden
tall	elderly	purple	woolen
short	antique	green	cotton

Practice the Rule

Number a sheet of paper 1–10. Complete each sentence below with one or two adjectives. If you use two adjectives, make sure they are in the order shown in the chart.

1. The poem is about a mother and her _____ son.
2. The mother and the son live in a(n) _____ house.
3. One day, the mother plays her _____ harp.
4. Soon a _____ pile of clothes forms on the ground.
5. The son tries on a(n) _____ sweater.
6. The mother chooses a(n) _____ blouse.
7. They call to their _____ neighbors to share the clothes.
8. One neighbor picks out a(n) _____ coat.
9. The neighbors carry home some clothing in a(n) _____ basket.
10. At the end, the mother says that tomorrow she will play her _____ flute!

Comparative Adjectives

Know the Rule

Comparative adjectives are used to describe the differences between two nouns or pronouns.

When an adjective has only one syllable, the comparative is often formed by adding *-er*.

> **Example: bright/brighter**

When an adjective has two syllables or more, the comparative is often formed by using the word **more** before the adjective.

> **Example: important/more important**

When a two-syllable adjective ends in *-ly*, drop the *-y* and add *-ier*.

> **Example: early/earlier**

Practice the Rule

Number a sheet of paper 1–8. Read each sentence. Write the correct form of the adjective in parentheses.

1. I used to think that poetry would be (difficult/more difficult) to understand than prose.

2. I discovered that reading poems is (fun/more fun) than I expected.

3. Understanding poetry is a lot (easy/easier) than I thought it would be.

4. There is one form of poetry that I think is (good/better) than other forms.

5. It is called haiku, and, in my opinion, it is (beautiful/more beautiful) than other kinds of poetry.

6. With only three lines, haiku is (short/shorter) than most other poems.

7. The way haiku uses language is much (exciting/more exciting) than other forms of poetry.

8. The poet must paint a mental picture in (few/fewer) words than most poetry forms allow.

Publish

✛Presentation

Publishing Strategy   Read your response aloud to the class.

Presentation Strategy   Use neat handwriting or word processing. Put your name and the page number on each page.

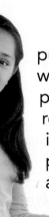

My poetry review is finished! Now I have to think about publishing it. I'd like to share the poem and my review with the rest of the class. I could hand out copies of the poem or read it aloud to the class, and then follow up by reading my response to the poem. To make sure my work is easy to read, I will use neat handwriting or word processing. I also need to remember to put my name and the page number on the bottom of each page. Here's the checklist I'll use.

My Final Checklist

Did I—

✔ use adjectives correctly to describe and compare?

✔ indent every paragraph?

✔ use neat handwriting or word processing?

✔ put my name and the page number on each page?

Apply

Use the checklist to check your own poetry review. Then make a final draft. Practice reading the poem and your essay before reading them aloud to your class.

"Afternoon on a Hill"
a poem by Edna St. Vincent Millay
a review by Marta

The words of Edna St. Vincent Millay's poem "Afternoon on a Hill" paint pictures in my mind. The words she chose help me see and feel the things that she imagined. I think this poem is about being happy wherever you are.

Millay tells a story in this poem. She goes out in the country during the day. Sitting in the sunshine on top of a hill, she looks at flowers and clouds. At the end of the day, when it gets dark, she goes back home.

In the first verse, Millay shows what it is like to feel happy. She says, "I will be the gladdest thing." At first I thought this might be a mistake in writing. I thought it was more correct to say, "I will be the most glad thing." Then I decided that "gladdest" makes the poet sound like a happy child. I think Millay is trying to show how a child feels. These words make me feel very happy, too. Poets often use words in surprising ways to express their feelings.

In the second verse, Millay compares the clouds and bending grass with time. She describes how she watches "with quiet eyes" as clouds move across the sky. It feels slow, like time is passing. When the wind makes the grass bow down and rise, she has time to watch it rise. The bending grass and floating clouds are like clocks in nature. They also make me think about how things change as time goes by. I think the second verse is a tiny bit sadder than the first verse.

In the third verse, Millay shows that a lot of time has gone by. The sky must be darker than it was earlier in the day. People in the town are starting to turn lights on in their houses. The poet can see

Marta, page 2

her house from the hilltop. Maybe its light seems brighter than the others. When I come home after dark, I feel better if there are lights on. Lighted windows make a house feel welcoming. I think Millay feels good about going home.

Millay's choice of words is important. She says, "I will be the gladdest thing." "Gladdest" is a funny word but a good choice. It sounds like a little child who is really happy and excited. The poet shows that she wants to protect nature, too. She says that even though she will see "a hundred flowers," she will "not pick one."

The poet likes being alone on the hill, looking at the flowers and clouds as she sits in the sun. She also likes going back to her family. One place is not better than the other. They are both important, and you can be happy wherever you are.

Marta, page 3

Reflect

Use the rubric to check Marta's poetry review. Are all the traits of a good poetry review there? Don't forget to use the rubric to check your own.

What's a Poem?

It's a special form of writing that expresses feelings and impressions. Precise words and descriptive language create vivid imagery.

What's in a Poem?

Lines

A poem is written in lines. Lines may be written as whole or partial sentences. In a shape poem, the lines are arranged to look like the subject of the poem.

Figurative Language

Figurative language is used to create interesting comparisons. *Metaphor* and *simile* are two types of comparisons. A *simile* compares two unlike things using the word *like* or *as*. A *metaphor* compares without using the word *like* or *as*. Can you tell which comparison is used in this example? *The tiny, red car looked like a giant ladybug.*

Alliteration

Alliteration is the repetition of beginning consonant sounds. Can you tell which consonant sound repeats in this example? *Two twigs on a tree tapped a merry tune for me.*

Why write a Poem?

Writing poems is a great way to express yourself! Here are a few reasons to write poems on a variety of subjects.

To Express Yourself

Writing a poem is a good way to express your feelings. You might write a poem to express your feelings about the beauty you see in nature. You might also write to express your feelings on a topic that you feel strongly about, such as saving the rainforests. Poetry is a great way to express personal thoughts and emotions.

To Describe

Many poems describe a person, a place, or a thing. A poem could also describe something humorous or sad, or anything in between. Descriptive poems include vivid words and comparisons that create a clear picture of the subject.

To Understand

Many poets write about a subject in order to learn more about it. You might write a poem about a math term, such as decimals or fractions, and learn more about it in the process. Writing to explore a subject is a great way to expand your understanding of it.

Linking Descriptive Writing Traits to a Poem

In this chapter, you will write a poem to describe something you have learned in math class. Marta will guide you through the stages of the writing process: Prewrite, Draft, Revise, Edit, and Publish. In each stage, Marta will show you important writing strategies that are linked to the Descriptive Writing Traits below.

Descriptive Writing Traits

Ideas
- a clear and complete topic
- sensory details and examples that help the reader "see" what is being described

Organization
- well-organized paragraphs that each tell about one main idea
- transitions that guide the reader through the text

Voice
- a voice and tone that are appropriate for the purpose and connect with the audience

Word Choice
- precise, descriptive language that creates a picture for the reader

Sentence Fluency
- different kinds of sentences that make the writing flow

Conventions
- no or few errors in grammar, usage, mechanics, and spelling

Before you write, read Owen O'Reilly's poem on the next page. Then use the poem rubric on pages 426–427 to decide how well he did. (You might want to look back at What's in a Poem? on page 422, too!)

Do-Si-Do

Poem MODEL

by Owen O'Reilly

Round
and round, like a
dot or a dime, spinning
through space, O, shape of mine,
curving, closing, completing circumference,
widening, like a ripple on a pond, rocking, rolling,
rounding, no beginning or ending, like a playground
hoop or a Ferris wheel, a carousel or a steering wheel,
intersecting line through the center, forming diameter,
dividing into two, equal halves, twin faces on a coin or
on the moon, then dance the line from center, do-si-do
along the rim, and form a radius, like the big hand
on a clock turns 360, pointing to perimeter, the
first spoke on a wheel, O, shape of mine,
spinning through space, like a
dot or a dime, round
and round.

alliteration

simile

metaphor

simile

Poem Rubric

Use this 6-point rubric to plan and score a poem.

	6	5	4	
Ideas	Descriptive details create a clear picture of the subject.	Most of the details are descriptive and create a clear picture.	Several details are not descriptive enough to create a clear picture.	
Organization	The poem's form or shape fits the subject.	The poem's form or shape fits the subject fairly well.	The form or shape somewhat fits the subject.	
Voice	The writer's personality comes through and connects with the audience.	The writer's personality comes through and connects most of the time.	The writer's personality comes through in a few places.	
Word Choice	Descriptive words and figurative language bring meaning to the writer's message.	Most words are descriptive. Figurative language adds meaning.	Some words are descriptive. Figurative language adds some meaning.	
Sentence Fluency	The words and lines flow naturally and smoothly.	Most of the words and lines flow smoothly.	Some of the words and lines flow smoothly.	
Conventions	The writing contains no errors. Prepositional phrases are formed correctly.	A few errors are present but do not confuse the reader. Prepositions are formed correctly.	Several errors confuse the reader. Some prepositions may be confused, such as *to* and *by*.	

✛ Presentation   The poem is legible and placed neatly on the page.

3	2	1	
Some details stray from the subject. Some do not create a picture.	Vague details do not create a clear picture.	Details are not descriptive or related to the subject.	**Ideas**
The form or shape does not fit the subject.	The form or shape is not appropriate.	The writing is not in poem form.	**Organization**
The writer's personality fades away by the final line(s).	The writer's personality does not match the topic or audience.	The writer's personality is hidden or absent.	**Voice**
Few descriptive words are used. Comparisons are weak.	Words are ordinary or vague. Comparisons are not used.	Words are not descriptive. Many are used incorrectly.	**Word Choice**
Many lines do not flow smoothly.	Lines do not flow well.	The writing is not arranged in lines.	**Sentence Fluency**
Many errors confuse the reader. Prepositional phrases are not formed correctly.	Serious errors stop the reader. Prepositional phrases are not formed correctly.	The writing has not been edited.	**Conventions**

See Appendix B for 4-, 5-, and 6-point descriptive rubrics.

Using the Poem Rubric to Study the Model

Did you notice that the model on page 425 points out some key elements of a poem? As he wrote "Do-si-do," Owen O'Reilly used these elements to help him describe a math concept, the circle. He also used the 6-point rubric on pages 426–427 to plan, draft, revise, and edit the writing. A rubric is a great tool to evaluate writing during the writing process.

Now let's use the same rubric to score the model. To do this, we'll focus on each trait separately, starting with Ideas. We'll use the top descriptor for each trait (column 6), along with examples from the model, to help us understand how the traits work together. How would you score Owen on each trait?

**Ideas** • **Descriptive details create a clear picture of the subject.**

The writer uses interesting details to describe the properties of a circle, such as circumference, diameter, and radius. His descriptions and the page design help the audience "see" his subject.

O, shape of mine, curving, closing, completing
circumference, widening, like a ripple on a pond,

Organization
- The poem's form or shape fits the subject.

Owen's poem looks like a circle on the page. I noticed that each line grows longer to the middle of the poem. Then, the lines become shorter to fit the shape. I like the way he divides the shape poem in half by placing details about diameter in the middle of the poem. The middle line is the longest line in the poem.

intersecting line through the center, forming diameter,
dividing into two

Voice
- The writer's personality comes through and connects with the audience.

Owen's enthusiasm for his subject comes through loud and clear. It's also clear that he knows the properties of circles. I wonder if he wants to be a math teacher when he grows up. I'm sure his students would have fun writing shape poems of their own!

from center, do-si-do
along the rim, and form a radius, like the big hand
on a clock turns 360, pointing to perimeter, the
first spoke on a wheel, O, shape of mine,

Using the Poem Rubric to Study the Model

• Descriptive words and figurative language bring meaning to the writer's message.

Owen uses a lot of descriptive words and figurative language to describe a circle, especially alliteration and similes. Alliteration—the repetition of beginning consonant sounds—is an effective way to use words that make an impression on the audience. Can you find where Owen used alliteration and simile in these lines?

> widening, like a ripple on a pond, rocking, rolling,
> rounding, no beginning or ending, like a playground
> hoop or a Ferris wheel, a carousel or a steering wheel,

• The words and lines flow naturally and smoothly.

Owen's poem is actually one very long sentence. Did you notice that the first and last set of lines repeat? Even though they don't rhyme, they do help create the poem's rhythm and flow. I think the poem would be fun to read aloud in rounds, like one big circle!

> first spoke on a wheel, O, shape of mine,
> spinning through space, like a
> dot or a dime, round
> and round.

Conventions
- The writing contains no errors.
- Prepositional phrases are formed correctly.

I read the poem again carefully. Every word is spelled correctly and the commas help the reader pause at the right places. Owen also uses prepositional phrases that add details. Many of them can be found in the comparisons. Here's my favorite: *like a ripple on a pond*. How many can you find in these lines?

equal halves, twin faces on a coin or
on the moon, then dance the line from center, do-si-do
along the rim, and form a radius,

⁺Presentation The poem is legible and placed neatly on the page.

My Turn!

Now it's my turn to write a shape poem! I'll use the rubric and good writing strategies to help me. Follow along to see how I do it.

Prewrite

The Rubric Says   Descriptive details create a clear picture of the subject.

Writing Strategy   Choose a topic. Make a list of details.

My teacher has asked us to show what we have learned in math class by writing a poem. The assignment is to describe a concept from math class. To do this, I must choose a topic. The model poem is a shape poem about a circle. I think I'll write a shape poem about a triangle.

I want my reader to be able to "see" what I'm describing. First I'll look through my math book and make a list of the properties of triangles. Then I'll list some everyday examples of objects that look like triangles.

My Notes

Triangles
- 3 sides
- 3 vertices (corners)
- 3 angles

Kinds of Triangles
- right triangle
- isosceles triangle
- equilateral triangle

Right Triangle
- one long side
- two shorter sides
- right angle

Everyday Examples
- road sign
- slice of pizza
- musical triangle
- scout badge
- half a diamond
- 3-cornered scarf
- jack-o'-lantern teeth
- guitar pick

Apply

Choose a geometric shape. Jot down some math terms that tell more about the shape. Then list examples of the shape.

Prewrite

The Rubric Says The poem's form or shape fits the subject.

Writing Strategy Use a Three-Column Chart to plan the poem.

I'm going to write a shape poem about a triangle. When I'm finished, I want my poem to look like a triangle on the page.

First, I need to decide which details about triangles I will write about at the beginning of my poem. Then I will decide which details to put in the middle, and, last, how to end it.

> **Writer's Term**
>
> **Three-Column Chart**
> A **Three-Column Chart** organizes information into three categories.

Three-Column Chart

Beginning	Middle	End
• introduce my subject, a triangle	• describe a right triangle	• restate properties of a right triangle
• name the properties of a triangle	• name the properties of a right triangle	
• compare to everyday examples	• compare to everyday examples	

Reflect

Look at the organizer. How will it help Marta write her shape poem?

Apply

Use a Three-Column Chart to plan your poem. Choose details to put in the beginning, middle, and end.

Draft

The Rubric Says   Descriptive words and figurative language bring meaning to the writer's message.

Writing Strategy   Use figurative language.

Now it's time for me to write my shape poem. Words are always important, but I know they are especially important in poetry because there are fewer words in poems. Each word I use has a big job to do.

I know that figurative language can help the reader understand or "see" the topic. I want to include similes or metaphors in my poem.

As I write my draft, I will also look out for mistakes in grammar and spelling, but I know I can fix my mistakes later. Here's my draft.

> ✏️ **Writer's Term** ___
>
> **Simile and Metaphor**
> A **simile** compares two unlike things using the word *like* or *as.*
> A **metaphor** compares without using the word *like* or *as.*

[DRAFT]

The Right Triangle

A

triangle

has three

vertices and

three sides,   *simile*

just <u>like a</u> ←

<u>tasty slice of pizza</u>

<u>or a plastic pick.</u> To tell

if a triangle is truly a right

triangle, look at the right angle,

one that has a square corner. The sides   *alliteration*

join together to make a <u>perpindiculer place.</u>

Yes, it sure is the right triangle in this triangle poem,

one right angle, two other vertices, and three sides.

Reflect

What is the subject of Marta's poem? Did she write a shape poem? How can you tell?

Apply

Use your notes and chart to write your poem. Remember to describe the subject with figurative language. Try to write the poem in the shape of its subject.

Revise

The Rubric Says   Descriptive details create a clear picture of the subject.

Writing Strategy   Use details that help the reader "see" the subject.

After I wrote my draft, I decided that my poem could use more figurative language. I found lines near the end of my poem that were not very descriptive. I added comparisons that will create a clear picture of my subject. Do they help you "see" what I'm describing?

[DRAFT]

added figurative language

one that has a square corner. The sides
, like the corner on a piece of paper, even a classroom door
join together to make a perpindiculer place.

Apply

Remember to use figurative language that helps your reader "see" your subject. Replace any dull lines with creative ones.

Revise

The Rubric Says The poem's form or shape fits the subject.

Writing Strategy Make sure to follow the shape of the poem.

The rubric says the poem's shape should fit the subject. Here's what I did to shape the beginning lines of my poem:

- The word *triangle* can be divided to make shorter lines. I used a hyphen to connect the syllables.

- Even though *tasty* is descriptive, I am describing a triangle, not a pizza.

- The word *truly* makes the line too long. I'll remove it.

[DRAFT]

Before revising:	After revising:
A	A
triangle	tri-
has three	angle
vertices and	has three
three sides,	vertices and
just like a	three sides, like
tasty slice of pizza	a slice of pizza or a
or a plastic pick. To tell	plastic pick. To tell if a
if a triangle is truly a right	triangle is a right triangle,

Reflect

How did Marta improve the shape of her poem?

Apply

Check where your lines end. Make sure they match the shape of your subject.

Revise

The Rubric Says   The words and lines flow naturally and smoothly.

Writing Strategy   Adjust the length of lines for a smooth flow.

To help me hear how my lines flow, I read my poem aloud. I found that several lines were uneven and interrupted the flow. Here are the changes I made. Do you think I've improved the lines?

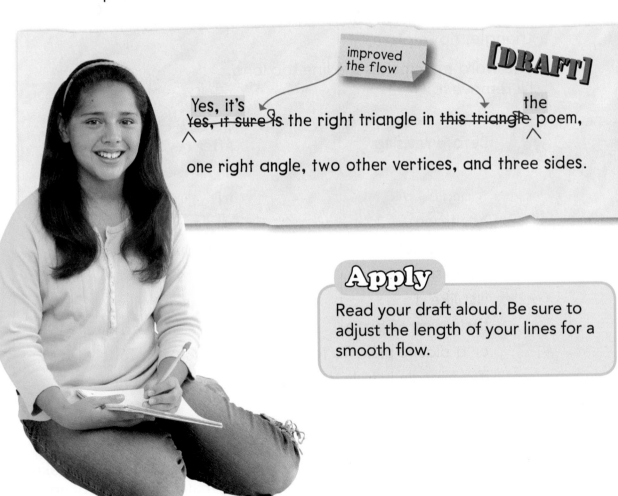

[DRAFT]

improved the flow

Yes, it's

~~Yes, it sure is~~ the right triangle in ~~this triangle~~ the poem,

one right angle, two other vertices, and three sides.

Apply

Read your draft aloud. Be sure to adjust the length of your lines for a smooth flow.

The Rubric Says	The writing contains no errors. Prepositional phrases are formed correctly.
Writing Strategy	Check prepositions and prepositional phrases.

Next I'll check my spelling, capitalization, and punctuation. Also, the rubric reminds me to make sure that I've used prepositions correctly.

Writer's Term

Prepositional Phrases

A **preposition** is a word that shows the relationship between its object (a noun or a pronoun) and another word in the sentence. The preposition and the words that follow it form a **prepositional phrase**.

Example: The tiny, red car flew **down the road**.

[DRAFT]

used correct preposition

for

look ~~at~~ the right angle, one that has a square corner. The sides

perpendicular

join together to make a ~~perpindicular~~ place.

corrected spelling

Reflect

Look at Marta's sentence revisions and corrections. How do they make the poem easier to understand?

Apply   Conventions

Edit your draft for spelling, capitalization, and punctuation. Make sure all your prepositions are correct.

For more practice with prepositions, use the exercises on the next two pages.

Prepositional Phrases

Know the Rule

A **prepositional phrase** can tell *how, when, what, how much,* or *where.* A prepositional phrase begins with a preposition and ends with a noun. Some common prepositions are *for, in, of, on, to, under,* and *with.*

Example: The cat sleeps **under** the bed **in** my guitar case.

Practice the Rule

Number a sheet of paper 1–10. Write the prepositional phrase in each sentence.

1. The poem has the shape of a right triangle.
2. It describes the properties of a right triangle.
3. Look for a right angle in the lower left corner.
4. Three sides are joined together in a triangle.
5. Do you know about musical triangles?
6. Last year I played the triangle in a concert.
7. On a road trip, we saw a triangle-shaped sign.
8. Did you ever play a guitar with a triangle pick?
9. I borrowed one from my brother.
10. Look for triangles everywhere you go!

More Prepositional Phrases

Know the Rule

A **preposition** tells about the relationship between a noun or pronoun and another word in a sentence. Prepositions include words that help tell where, such as *above, at, below, in, of, on,* and *through*. The preposition and the words that follow it make a **prepositional phrase**. Some prepositional phrases help tell *where* something is.

Practice the Rule

Number a sheet of paper 1–10. Write each sentence with the correct preposition. Underline the prepositional phrase.

1. I see right triangles (on/with) that welcome mat.
2. We decorated a large flowerpot (by/with) colorful triangle shapes.
3. The pot sits (above/between) a rose bush and a maple tree.
4. Some leaves fell (into/through) the pot.
5. A creek flows (through/over) the rose garden.
6. A narrow footpath follows the creek (in/on) one side.
7. The path continues (over/with) a small bridge and then ends.
8. Metal rods (beneath/by) the bridge form triangles.
9. A yellow sign (on/through) the bridge says "Yield."
10. We hung copper triangles (at/in) trees as wind chimes.

Publish ✛Presentation

Publishing Strategy   Submit poem to a magazine or online publisher of children's poetry.

Presentation Strategy   Make the poem look great on the page.

My poem is finished! My next step is to publish it. I have decided to submit my poem to a student magazine that we read in my English class. My teacher will help me write a cover letter to the editor.

I'll type my poem on the computer, using a font that is the right size for the shape of my poem. I'll remember to save my work often! When my poem is ready to go, it will be easy to submit it electronically. To make sure my poem looks great on the page, I'll use this checklist.

My Final Checklist

Did I—
- ✔ check the prepositions and prepositional phrases?
- ✔ look over the words and sentences for correct spelling, grammar, and punctuation?
- ✔ give my poem a title and put my name on the page?
- ✔ make sure the poem is neat and easy to read?

Apply

Use the checklist to prepare your final copy. Write a cover letter, and send your poem to a magazine that publishes poetry written by students. You may even want to enter a poetry-writing contest!

The Right Triangle
by Marta

A

tri-

angle

has three

vertices and

three sides, like

a slice of pizza or a

guitar pick. To tell if a

triangle is a right triangle,

look for its right angle, one that

has a square corner. See how its sides

join together to make a perpendicular

place, like the corner on a piece of paper,

even a classroom door. Yes, it's the right triangle

with one right angle, two other vertices, and three sides.

Reflect

Think about the process of writing a shape poem. How did the traits help you improve your poem? Be sure to use the rubric to score your poem.

Descriptive test writing

Read the Writing Prompt

Every writing test starts with a writing prompt. As you begin the test, look for three helpful parts in the writing prompt.

Setup This part of the writing prompt gives you the background information you need to get ready for writing.

Task This part of the writing prompt tells you exactly what you're supposed to write: a descriptive essay about what you saw.

Scoring Guide This section tells how your writing will be scored. To get the best score on your test, you should include everything on the list.

Think about the rubrics that you've been using in this book. When you take a writing test, you won't always have all the information that's on a rubric. Don't worry—the scoring guide is a lot like a rubric. It lists everything you need to think about to write a good paper. Many scoring guides will include the six important traits of writing that are in all of the rubrics in this book:

 Ideas

 Organization

 Voice

 Word Choice

 Sentence Fluency

 Conventions

Writing MODEL Prompt

Imagine that you witnessed an amazing event or saw an incredible sight.

Write a descriptive essay about what you saw.

Be sure

- your topic is clear and you use sensory details.
- your essay is organized in a natural sequence and uses transitions.
- you use first-person point of view.
- your essay has descriptive words and phrases.
- your sentences vary in length.
- your essay has correct grammar, spelling, and punctuation.

Writing Traits
in the Scoring Guide

The scoring guide in the prompt on page 445 has been made into this chart. Does it remind you of the rubrics you've used? Not all prompts include all of the writing traits, but this one does. Use them to do your best writing. Don't forget to work neatly and put your name on each page.

- Be sure your topic is clear and you use sensory details.

- Be sure your essay is organized in a natural sequence and uses transitions.

- Be sure you use first-person point of view.

- Be sure your essay has descriptive words and phrases.

- Be sure your sentences vary in length.

- Be sure your essay has correct grammar, spelling, and punctuation.

Let's look at Katy O'Connor's essay on the next page. Did she follow the scoring guide?

Dolphins at Play

by Katy O'Connor

The sky was blue, and the summer sun was hot and bright out on the ocean when we went looking for dolphins. The captain of our boat said the water was smooth, but waves rocked us from side to side. I was standing by the railing, the wind pulling at my jacket. Suddenly a splash from a big wave cooled my face and I tasted salt.

Then—swoosh!

A dolphin leapt from the water just a few feet away. He flew through the air and then dove back into the water. His back was dark gray, but his sides were tan-colored. His belly was smooth and white. He was so near that I could see the black stripe that circled his eye. Just then I saw another dolphin, and then another! I began to count. There were at least ten of them.

The captain stood next to me. "Those are called Common Dolphins," he said. "It looks like a group of young males."

The dolphins looked like they were surfing the waves that came off the front of the boat. Then they seemed to play a game of tag. Sometimes one dolphin would chase another. If he got close enough, he'd nip at the other's tail! Then the group of dolphins swam as fast as they could toward each other. I was sure they were going to crash, but at the very last second they'd bend sharply away and disappear in the waves.

Every now and then we'd see a piece of seaweed floating by. One of the dolphins caught a piece of seaweed on his nose. He tossed it into the air, and another dolphin jumped out of the water and batted it back! More dolphins joined them in this funny game of catch.

We could just see the shore in the distance. Before the dolphins left, however, they put on one last performance. The biggest dolphin rose straight up out of the deep blue water and then crashed back down, making a huge splash. The sea spray dampened my face. A smaller one followed him. A third dolphin rose up on his tail and traveled backwards across the waves while another did a spin in the air. They looked like clowns at a circus, each one trying to do the most amazing trick. Their chatter sounded like squeaky laughter as they disappeared.

Using the Scoring Guide to Study the Model

Now, let's use the scoring guide to check Katy's writing test, "Dolphins at Play." See if you can find examples from her writing to show how well she did on each part of the scoring guide.

Ideas

- **The topic is clear, and the writing includes sensory details.**

Katy writes about an exciting event. Her essay describes the day she went out on the ocean in a boat, looking for—and finding—dolphins. Katy brings her paragraph to life with details related to the five senses. She tells how something looks, sounds, smells, feels, or tastes. Here is an example.

The biggest dolphin rose straight up out of the deep blue water and then crashed back down, making a huge splash. The sea spray dampened my face. A smaller one followed him. A third dolphin rose up on his tail and traveled backwards across the waves while another did a spin in the air. They looked like clowns at a circus, each one trying to do the most amazing trick. Their chatter sounded like squeaky laughter as they disappeared.

Organization

- **The essay is organized in a natural sequence and uses transitions.**

Katy organizes her essay around her topic—her experience watching dolphins play. Here's how she describes her first dolphin sighting. Notice that she uses transitions such as *when* and *suddenly* to guide the reader.

The sky was blue, and the summer sun was hot and bright out on the ocean when we went looking for dolphins. The captain of our boat said the water was smooth, but waves rocked us from side to side. I was standing by the railing, the wind pulling at my jacket. Suddenly a splash from a big wave cooled my face and I tasted salt.

 **Voice**

- **The essay uses first-person point of view.**

Katy describes her experience as if she were talking directly to the reader. Notice how she puts herself in the story by using first-person point of view (*I*, *me*, and *my*).

Just then I saw another dolphin, and then another! I began to count. There were at least ten of them.

 **Word Choice**

- **The essay has descriptive words and phrases.**

In her essay, Katy uses descriptive words and phrases so the reader can "see" what she saw. This is a good example. Look at how she describes her first dolphin sighting.

Then—swoosh!
A dolphin leapt from the water just a few feet away. He flew through the air and then dove back into the water. His back was dark gray, but his sides were tan-colored. His belly was smooth and white. He was so near that I could see the black stripe that circled his eye.

Using the Scoring Guide to Study the Model

• The essay has sentences that vary in length.

The scoring guide reminds you that sentences in your essay should vary in length. Katy uses long and short sentences in her description. The mix of sentence lengths helps the essay flow and makes it enjoyable to read.

The dolphins looked like they were surfing the waves that came off the front of the boat. Then they seemed to play a game of tag. Sometimes one dolphin would chase another. If he got close enough, he'd nip at the other's tail!

• The essay has correct grammar, spelling, and punctuation.

The scoring guide reminds you to check grammar, spelling, and punctuation. Look for any mistakes you often make, such as forming plural nouns incorrectly or using incorrect punctuation at the end of a sentence. Katy seems to have caught any mistakes she made in her first draft. Her essay doesn't have any errors.

Planning My Time

Before giving us a writing test prompt, my teacher tells us how much time we'll have to complete the test. First I'll think about how much time I'll have. Then I'll divide the time into the different parts of the writing process. I'll also make sure I give myself some time to study the writing prompt. Here's how I've divided my time into four steps.

Step 4:
Edit
5 minutes

Step 1:
Prewrite
25 minutes

Step 3:
Revise
15 minutes

Step 2:
Draft
15 minutes

Prewrite

Focus on **Ideas**

Writing Strategy   Study the writing prompt to find out what to do.

Once I have my writing prompt, I study it and make sure I know exactly what I'm supposed to do. Most writing prompts have a setup, a task, and a scoring guide. You should find these and label them on the writing prompt, just as I did. Then you can circle key words that tell what kind of writing you need to do. I circled *an essay that describes* because these words tell me what kind of writing I'll be doing. I circled the word *celebration* because that tells me what I'll be describing.

My Descriptive Test Prompt

Setup — Think about how we celebrate an important national holiday.

Task — Write (an essay that describes) a memorable (celebration) you witnessed and enjoyed.

Be sure

Scoring Guide
- your topic is clear and you use sensory details.
- your essay is organized in a natural sequence and uses transitions.
- you use first-person point of view.
- your essay has descriptive words and phrases.
- your sentences vary in length.
- your essay has correct grammar, spelling, and punctuation.

Next I'll think about how the scoring guide relates to the six writing traits I've studied in the rubrics. Not all of the traits are included in every scoring guide, but I need to remember them all to write a good essay.

Ideas

• **Be sure your topic is clear and you use sensory details.**

When I write my essay, it's important to focus on one topic. I need to think about details such as the sights, sounds, smells, tastes, and feel of things related to my essay's topic.

Organization

• **Be sure your essay is organized in a natural sequence and uses transitions.**

I want my reader to be able to follow along. Transitions can help me do that.

Voice

• **Be sure you use first-person point of view.**

I need to put myself in the story by using first-person words like *I*, *me*, and *us*.

Word Choice

• **Be sure your essay has descriptive words and phrases.**

I need to use word pictures so the reader can "see" the events I write about.

Sentence Fluency

• **Be sure your sentences vary in length.**

To make my essay flow, I will use a mix of long and short sentences.

Conventions

• **Be sure your essay has correct grammar, spelling, and punctuation.**

Whenever I write anything, I need to check my grammar, spelling, and punctuation!

Prewrite

Focus on **Ideas**

Writing Strategy   Respond to the task.

I know that writers gather information before they begin writing. When you write for a test, you can gather information from the writing prompt. Look at the task in the writing prompt. This is the part that explains what you are supposed to write. Remember, you won't have much time when writing for a test. That's why it's important to think about how you'll respond before you begin to write.

I know that I have to write an essay. I need to describe a celebration. Jotting down notes will help. I have to do this step quickly because the clock is ticking!

Task— Write an essay that describes a memorable celebration you witnessed and enjoyed.

Fireworks on New Year's Eve

- midnight
- cold night air
- Mom and Dad counting down
- exploding rockets
- sparks in the air
- lots of colors
- fireworks like flowers and fountains
- loud booming sounds
- people saying "ooh"
- spinning fireworks
- a burning smell
- smoke
- silence

Think about how you'll respond to the task part of your writing prompt before you write. Then jot down some notes to gather information.

Writing Strategy   Choose a graphic organizer.

Now I need to start organizing my ideas. I'll be describing something, so a Web would be a good graphic organizer. I can use my five senses to organize the details.

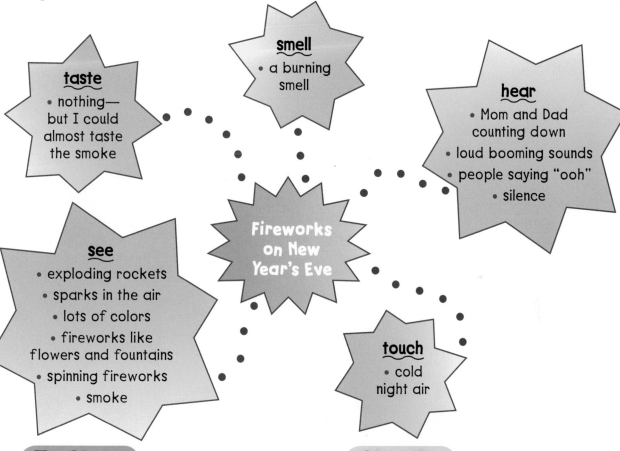

smell
• a burning smell

taste
• nothing— but I could almost taste the smoke

hear
• Mom and Dad counting down
• loud booming sounds
• people saying "ooh"
• silence

Fireworks on New Year's Eve

see
• exploding rockets
• sparks in the air
• lots of colors
• fireworks like flowers and fountains
• spinning fireworks
• smoke

touch
• cold night air

Reflect

Look at the graphic organizer. Does it include the details needed to write a good descriptive essay?

Apply

Choose the best graphic organizer for the assignment. Include important details about the topic, such as what you see, hear, smell, feel, or taste, in the organizer.

Prewrite

Writing Strategy Check the graphic organizer against the scoring guide.

In a test, you don't always get much time to revise. That makes prewriting more important than ever! So before I write, I'll check my Web against the scoring guide in the writing prompt.

smell
• a burning smell

hear
• Mom and Dad counting down
• loud booming sounds
• people saying "ooh"
• silence

taste
• nothing— but I could almost taste the smoke

Fireworks on New Year's Eve

see
• exploding rockets
• sparks in the air
• lots of colors
• fireworks like flowers and fountains
• spinning fireworks
• smoke

touch
• cold night air

Ideas

- has a clear topic and sensory details.

I'll use my Web as my guide when I write my draft. I'll use the sensory details to create word pictures for my reader.

Organization

- is organized and uses transitions.

Transitions are not part of my Web. I'll keep this in my mind as I write.

Voice

- uses first-person point of view.

I didn't include first-person point of view in my Web. As I write, I'll put myself in the essay.

Word Choice

- has descriptive words and phrases.

I'll use the ideas in my Web to create descriptive phrases.

Sentence Fluency

- has sentences that vary in length.

I'll have to check this after I write my draft. I'll make sure I have both short and long sentences in my essay.

Conventions

- has correct grammar, spelling, and punctuation.

I need to check my grammar, spelling, and punctuation when I edit my draft.

Reflect

Does the graphic organizer cover all the points of the scoring guide? What else should be included?

Apply

Before you begin writing, look back at the scoring guide in the writing prompt to make sure you know everything you need to do.

Draft

Writing Strategy Remember your purpose as you write.

The purpose of my essay is to describe the important details of an event. I'll begin with a good topic sentence. It will tell what the essay is about and when and where the event takes place. I'll include sensory details to describe the event.

[DRAFT]

Fireworks for the New Year
by Marta

On New Year's Eve, my town lit up the sky with the biggest display of fireworks anyone had ever seen. And why not. It was about to become a new year.

It was getting close to midnight. I shivered in the crisp, cold air. I pulled my hat over my ears and zipped my jacket up tight. my mom and dad started to count down: "ten, nine, eight, seven, six . . ." Then—WOW!

A rocket exploded in the sky. Red and gold sparks lit up the night. There was a gigantic boom. It was so loud I had to cover my ears. I could see smoke in the light from the sparks. A smell like something burning was in the air.

Then three more fireworks exploded at the same time. they were blue and green and opened out like a flower. There were more booms and the burning smell got stronger.

[DRAFT]

People were saying, "ooh!" and "ah!" My little brother got scared and Dad had to pick him up and hold him. We probably should have left him at home with a babysitter.

I couldn't believe all the colors. Purple and yellow and orange glowed in the sky. Each firework exploded a different way. Some went up like big water fountains and others spread out sideways and some even spun around in circles. The light was so bright I could see everyone around me, even though it was late at night.

It seemed like the explosions went on forever. I got used to the loud booms and the smell and didn't notice them after a while. Then the fireworks got bigger. Rocketes went up more and more fast. A giant silver explosion made it seem as bright as day.

Then the show stopped. The silence sounded strange after all the noise. The burning smell seemed to come back. I could almost taste the smoke that drifted across the field. The fireworks were over. A new year had arrived. It was time to go home and go to bed.

Reflect

Read the draft. Did Marta write a topic sentence with sensory details?

Apply

The purpose of the essay is to describe the important, memorable details of an event. Start with a topic sentence that includes sensory details.

Revise

Writing Strategy   Use transitions to guide the reader.

I've written my draft. Now I'll look back at the scoring guide and make sure I've included all the points I'll be graded on. The scoring guide reminds me to use transition words to organize my essay. Some transitions show the time order of events. Some examples are *at midnight, on Tuesday,* and *an hour later.* I'll look for places to add transitions to show when events happened.

[DRAFT]

added transition words

A rocket exploded in the sky. Red and gold sparks lit up the night. A split-second later came ~~There was~~ a gigantic boom. It was so loud I had to cover my ears. I could see smoke in the light from the sparks.

A smell like something burning was in the air.

Apply

Read your draft. Add transition words to show the time order of events.

Writing Strategy   Use first-person point of view.

Now I'll read my essay again. This time I'll check for first-person point of view. Using first person (*I, me, we, us*) helps to engage the readers because it sounds like I am talking directly to them. I found a few places where I could make my essay more personal by using first-person point of view.

[DRAFT]

Then three more fireworks exploded at the same time.

they were blue and green and opened out like a flower.
I heard
~~There were~~ more booms and the burning smell got stronger.

all around me

People were saying, "ooh!" and "ah!" My little brother got

scared and Dad had to pick him up and hold him. We probably

should have left him at home with a babysitter.

used first-person point of view

Reflect

Look at the revisions. What words does Marta use to put herself in the essay?

Apply

Make sure to use first-person point of view. Write your essay as if you are speaking directly to the reader.

Revise

Writing Strategy   Add descriptive words.

I've written my draft. Now I'll look back at the scoring guide and make sure I've included all the points I'll be graded on. The rubric reminds me that adding descriptive words and phrases always makes writing better. I want my reader to see, hear, smell, and feel the fireworks! I'll add some sound words for effect. Do you think they improve my description?

[DRAFT]

added words for effect

Boom! Ba-ba-boom!

A rocket exploded in the sky. Red and gold sparks lit up the night.

There was a gigantic boom. It was so loud I had to cover my ears. I

could see smoke in the light from the sparks. A smell like something

tickled my nose

burning ~~was in the air~~!

added descriptive words

Apply

Read your draft. Add words to paint a vivid picture that your reader can see, feel, hear, smell, and taste.

Writing Strategy Check the grammar, spelling, capitalization, and punctuation.

The scoring guide reminds me to use correct grammar and spelling. I also need to check my capitalization and punctuation. That's a lot to do, but I scheduled plenty of time to check for errors in these important areas. I'll read my draft carefully one more time.

Fireworks for the New Year
by Marta

[FINAL DRAFT]

On New Year's Eve, my town lit up the sky with the biggest display of fireworks anyone had ever seen. And why not? It was about to become a new year.

It was getting close to midnight. I shivered in the crisp, cold air. I pulled my hat over my ears and zipped my jacket up tight. my mom and dad started to count down: "ten, nine, eight, seven, six . . ." Then—WOW!

Boom! Ba-ba-boom!
A huge rocket exploded in the sky. Red and gold black sparks lit up the night. A split-second later came There was a gigantic boom. It was so loud I had to cover my ears. I could see a puff of smoke in the light from the sparks. A smell like something burning tickled my nose was in the air.

Apply

Every time you write for a test, you need to check your grammar, spelling, capitalization, and punctuation.

Descriptive Test Writing **463**

Then three more fireworks exploded at the same time. they were blue and green and opened out like a flower. ~~There were~~ I heard more booms, and all around me the burning smell got stronger. People were saying, "ooh!" and "ah!" My little brother got scared, and Dad had to pick him up and hold him. ~~We probably should have left him at home with a babysitter.~~

I couldn't believe all the colors. Purple and yellow and orange glowed in the sky. Each firework exploded a different way. Some went up like big water fountains, ~~and~~ others spread out sideways, ~~and~~ some even spun around in circles. The light was so bright I could see everyone around me, even though it was late at night.

It seemed like the explosions went on forever. I got used to the loud booms and the smell and didn't notice them after a while. Then the fireworks got bigger. Rocketes went up ~~more and more fast~~ faster and faster. A giant silver explosion made it seem as bright as day.

Then the show stopped. The silence sounded strange after all the noise. The burning smell seemed to come back. I could almost taste the smoke that drifted across the field. The fireworks were over. A new year had arrived. It was time to go home and go to bed.

Reflect

Check the essay against the scoring guide. Did Marta include everything in the scoring guide?

[FINAL DRAFT]

We're finished! With the help of the prompt and scoring guide, we wrote an exciting descriptive essay. Remember these important tips when you write for a test.

Test Tips

1. **Study the writing prompt before you begin to write.** Most writing prompts will have three parts: the setup, the task, and the scoring guide. Look for these three parts and label them. Use the helpful information they give you.

2. **Make sure you understand the task before you start to write.**
   - Read all three parts of the writing prompt carefully.
   - Circle key words in the task part of the writing prompt that tell you what kind of writing you need to do. The task might also tell you who your audience is.
   - Make sure you know how you'll be graded.
   - Say the assignment in your own words to yourself.

3. **Keep an eye on the clock.** Decide how much time you'll spend on each part of the writing process, and try to stick to your plan. Don't spend so much time on prewriting that you don't have enough time left to write.

4. **Reread your writing. Compare it to the scoring guide at least twice.** Remember the rubrics you've used all year? A scoring guide on a writing test is like a rubric. It reminds you of what is important.

5. **Plan, plan, plan!** You don't get much time to revise during a test, so planning is more important than ever.

6. **Write neatly.** Remember: If the people who score your test can't read your writing, it won't matter how good your essay is!

Appendix A
Grammar Practice

Kinds of Sentences

Know the Rule

A sentence that tells something is a **statement**. A statement ends with a period. A sentence that gives an order is a **command**. A command ends with a period. A sentence that asks something is a **question**. A question ends with a question mark. A sentence that shows strong feeling is an **exclamation**. An exclamation ends with an exclamation point. Choose the punctuation for the effect you want.

Examples:
I would like to visit Hawaii. *(statement)*
Get the map of Hawaii. *(command)*
Have you been to Hawaii? *(question)*
I can't wait to go to Hawaii! *(exclamation)*

Practice the Rule

Number a sheet of paper 1–10. Next to each number, write the kind of sentence.

1. Hawaii became a state in 1959.
2. Where is Hawaii located?
3. What is Hawaii's tallest mountain?
4. Name the eight main Hawaiian islands.
5. Hawaii has two national parks.
6. Where is Pearl Harbor?
7. Find the Hawaiian islands on a map.
8. Hawaii is in the Pacific Ocean.
9. What a beautiful place Maui is!
10. Find the cost of airfare to Hawaii.

Avoiding Run-ons and Comma Splices

Know the Rule

A **run-on sentence** is two complete sentences that run together without either a comma or a conjunction such as *and*. A **comma splice** occurs when two complete sentences are separated by only a comma. A conjunction after the comma is missing. To fix these types of sentence errors, add what is missing or make two separate sentences.

Examples:
I went to Paris I loved the city. *(incorrect)*
I went to Paris, **and** I loved the city. *(correct)*

I went to Paris, I loved the city. *(incorrect)*
I went to Paris. **I** loved the city. *(correct)*

Practice the Rule

Number a sheet of paper 1–10. Write **RO** after each run-on sentence. Write **CS** after each comma splice.

1. Paris is the capital of France it is located on the Seine River.
2. The Louvre is in Paris, it is one of the world's largest museums.
3. The Luxembourg Gardens is a large public park in Paris it was built in the seventeenth century.
4. The Eiffel Tower is a famous landmark my tour group from school decided to see it.
5. The Eiffel Tower has three levels we took the elevator ride to the top.
6. I loved Paris I especially liked walking around the city.
7. The food was delicious the people were very nice.
8. Our group was in Paris for two weeks, I never felt homesick.
9. The plane flight home was long I fell asleep.
10. My family met me at the airport, I was happy to be home.

Participles and Participial Phrases

Know the Rule

A **participle** is a verb form that acts like an adjective. In other words, a participle tells more about a noun or pronoun. A **participial phrase** is a phrase made up of a participle and the other words needed to complete the meaning.

Examples:
The young Jim Lovell's **failed** experiment taught him a lot. *(participle)*
The **exploding** rocket fell to the ground. *(participle)*
Exploding in the air, the rocket fell to the ground. *(participial phrase)*

Practice the Rule

Number a sheet of paper 1–10. Next to each number, write the sentence. Underline the participles and circle the participial phrases.

1. Excited, Lovell wanted to see if his rocket would fly.
2. The rocket, soaring upward, finally exploded and crashed.
3. Disappointed, Lovell was determined to figure out what went wrong.
4. Selected by NASA in 1962, Lovell was their youngest test pilot.
5. Heading for the moon, the crew realized they were on a grand adventure.
6. Amazed with space, the crew enjoyed a smooth flight.
7. Then, suddenly, exploding sounds filled the spacecraft.
8. Flashing lights lit up the control panel.
9. Understanding the situation, the crew sprang into action.
10. Trained pilots know how to deal quickly with problems.

Prepositional Phrases

Know the Rule

A **prepositional phrase** can tell *how, when, what, how much,* or *where* about another word in the sentence. A prepositional phrase begins with a preposition. Some common prepositions are *during, for, in, of, on, outside, over, under, to, with,* and *without.*

Examples:
One gymnast fell **during her performance**.
The other finished **without a mistake**.

Practice the Rule

Number a sheet of paper 1–10. Write each sentence. Underline each prepositional phrase. Circle each preposition.

1. During the week, Andre practices every day.
2. Andre has been practicing gymnastics for eight years.
3. Maria practices with Mario.
4. Mario met Maria outside the gym.
5. Maria's photo appeared in the local newspaper.
6. Mario is very committed to the sport.
7. He competed in a nationwide contest.
8. Mario's parents traveled with him.
9. He performed eight sets of exercises.
10. In the end, Mario won first prize.

Appositives and Appositive Phrases

Know the Rule

An **appositive** is a word or phrase that identifies, explains, or means the same thing as a noun. Appositives follow the nouns they identify and are usually separated from the rest of the sentence by commas.

Examples:

Wilheim Roentgen, **a German scientist,** discovered the x-ray.

Roentgen, **an only child,** was educated by his parents.

Practice the Rule

Number a sheet of paper 1–10. Beside the number write the appositive or appositive phrase.

1. Roentgen's invention, the X-ray, revolutionized medicine.

2. Doctors use the machine to find out if a fracture, a break in a bone, has occurred.

3. Jake Gladstone, the clumsiest boy in our class, fell off his bike.

4. His bike, a brand new model, slid on gravel.

5. Brian, my quick-thinking brother, decided to get Jake to the hospital.

6. The hospital, the tallest building in town, was built in 1950.

7. The doctor, an expert in bone injuries, ordered an x-ray for Jake.

8. Jake, a very impatient person, hated waiting around the emergency room.

9. While he waited, he learned that one machine, the PET scan, can tell doctors what's happening in a person's brain.

10. Another machine, the PillCam, takes pictures of a person's digestive system.

Plural Nouns

Know the Rule

A **singular noun** names one person, place, or thing (*grape*). A **plural noun** names more than one (*grapes*).

- To make most nouns plural, add *-s* to the singular noun (*apple, apples*).
- If the noun ends in *s, ch, sh, x,* or *z,* add *-es* (*peach, peaches*).
- For most nouns that end in a consonant and *y,* change the *y* to *i* and add *-es.* (*berry, berries*).
- For most nouns that end in a vowel plus *y,* just add *-s* (*toy, toys*).
- For most nouns that end in *f* or *fe,* change the *f* to *v* and add *-es* (*calf, calves*).
- For some nouns that end in *f,* just add *-s* (*staffs*).

Practice the Rule

Number a sheet of paper 1–10. Beside each number write the plural form of the noun to complete the sentence.

1. Many people look for _____ to save energy. (way)
2. Taking _____ instead of driving cars can save gasoline. (bus)
3. Getting to work by boat is available in some _____. (city)
4. Another thing people do is to check that their _____ are working properly. (chimney)
5. To save water, do not run _____ unless they are full. (dishwasher)
6. _____ can help by using their air conditioners less. (company)
7. You could also try turning up room _____. (temperature)
8. Riding in _____ is another way to save energy. (carpool)
9. _____ should check that their windows keep out cold air. (family)
10. Many people believe that saving energy will improve our _____. (life)

Personal Pronouns and Compound Personal Pronouns

Know the Rule

A **pronoun** is a word that takes the place of one or more nouns or pronouns. Use the following **personal pronouns** and **compound personal pronouns** to talk about yourself or about yourself and someone else:

- personal pronouns: *I, me, we, us*
- compound personal pronouns: *myself, ourselves*

Use the following **personal pronouns** and **compound pronouns** to refer to other people and things:

- personal pronouns: *she, her, it, he, him, you, they, them*
- compound personal pronouns: *herself, himself, itself, yourself, yourselves, themselves*

Example:
I made **myself** a sandwich.

Practice the Rule

Number a sheet of paper 1–10. Write each sentence. Underline each personal pronoun. Circle each compound personal pronoun.

1. Adrianna cooked the whole meal herself.
2. He decided to buy himself an ice cream cone.
3. Many people like to cook for themselves.
4. The meal she cooked for herself tasted awful.
5. The new oven cleans itself.
6. Did she teach herself to cook?
7. Frank made himself an iced coffee.
8. Robert splashed her with spaghetti sauce.
9. Latoya grew the tomatoes herself.
10. Rather than eat out, they decided to cook for themselves.

Past-Tense Verbs

Know the Rule

The **tense** of a verb lets you know whether something happens in the past, present, or future. **Past-tense verbs** show action that happened in the past. Many verbs in the past tense, though not all of them, end with *-ed*.

Examples:

A huge flaming object **dropped** on farmland in New Jersey.
The year **was** 1938.

Practice the Rule

Number a sheet of paper 1–10. For each sentence, write the past-tense verb.

1. A radio broadcast about an alien invasion once frightened a lot of people.
2. The broadcast aired on October 30,1938.
3. The program lasted for sixty minutes.
4. The program sounded like a real news bulletin.
5. It fooled many people.
6. People hid in cellars.
7. Some even wrapped their heads in towels.
8. They worried about poison gas.
9. The broadcast was a fake.
10. Later people protested the fake broadcast.

Present-Tense Verbs

Know the Rule

The **tense** of a verb lets you know whether something happens in the present, past, or future. **Present-tense verbs** show action that is happening now.

Examples:

Grizzly bears often **travel** alone.

The grizzly bear **is** North America's largest meat-eating animal.

Practice the Rule

Number a sheet of paper 1–10. Beside each number write the present-tense verb in each sentence.

1. The grizzly bear lives in the northern United States and in Canada.
2. The hind legs of grizzly bears are extremely powerful.
3. Sometimes grizzly bears walk on their hind legs.
4. Grizzly bears eat both plants and animals.
5. In preparation for winter, grizzly bears gain about 400 pounds.
6. Grizzlies dig dens for winter hibernation.
7. Normally grizzly bears avoid contact with humans.
8. Experts agree that the grizzly is an aggressive bear.
9. Despite their size and weight, grizzlies run very quickly.
10. Today only about 1,000 grizzlies live in the continental United States.

Future-Tense Verbs

Know the Rule

The **tense** of a verb lets you know whether something happens in the present, past, or future. **Future-tense verbs** show action that will happen. Verbs in the future tense use the helping verb *will*.

Examples:

Janine **will look** for books on her topic tomorrow.

She hopes the librarian **will help** her.

Practice the Rule

Number a sheet of paper 1–10. Beside each number write the future-tense verb in each sentence. Be sure to include both the helping verb and the main verb.

1. Manuel will need help picking a topic.
2. He will ask his older sister for help.
3. She will help him in the evening.
4. Peter will choose an interesting topic.
5. Monique will finish her paper on time.
6. I will write about Marco Polo.
7. I will read all about my topic.
8. I will check my paper for spelling mistakes.
9. Also, I will make a neat copy of my paper.
10. My classmates will enjoy my paper.

Helping Verbs

Know the Rule

Helping verbs come before the main verb in a sentence. Helping verbs work with the main verb to show time and mood. Helping verbs also start many questions.

Common Helping Verbs

am	was	has	can
is	were	have	may
are	will	had	must

Example:
Service dogs **are helping** people all across the country.

Practice the Rule

Number a sheet of paper 1–10. Write each sentence. Underline the helping verb once and the main verb twice.

1. Bessie, a golden retriever, is watching Jake very carefully.
2. Bessie has become Jake's key to freedom.
3. Jake must use a wheelchair to get around.
4. Bessie will help Jake with tasks.
5. Bessie's specialty is helping children with special needs.
6. Every day Bessie and her ten-year-old owner will learn more about each other.
7. Bessie was trained for many months at a special service dog center.
8. Was Jake's scent used for training Bessie?
9. Bessie is trained to follow Jake's scent.
10. Bessie can learn new things every day.

Present Perfect-Tense Verbs

Know the Rule

The **tense** of a verb lets you know whether something happens in the present, past, or future. **Present perfect-tense** verbs show that an action that happened in the past may still be taking place now, in the present. To form the present perfect tense, add the helping verb *has* or *have* to the past participle of a verb. The sentence *Joe has known Shana for three years* is in the present perfect tense. In other words, Joe met Shana three years ago, and he still knows her today.

Examples:
Brian **has practiced** every day this week.
The rest of us **have** not **practiced** every day.

Practice the Rule

Number a sheet of paper 1–10. Beside each number write the present perfect-tense verb. Be sure to include both the helping verb and the main verb.

1. Martha has attended every practice.
2. We have waited an hour for the beginning of practice.
3. We have rehearsed the play many times.
4. James has worked hard learning his lines.
5. People have performed in school plays for years.
6. Most times I have worked behind the scenes.
7. Jack has had a leading role only once.
8. There have been many successful school plays.
9. All her life Tina has thought of being in a professional play.
10. For years I have dreamed about getting a great role.

Adverbs

Know the Rule

An **adverb** is a word that describes a verb. It tells *how, when,* or *where* about a verb. Many adverbs end with *-ly*.

Examples:
The sauce cooked **slowly** on the stove.
Maria **often** makes spaghetti sauce.

Practice the Rule

Number a sheet of paper 1–10. Beside each number write the adverb and the verb it describes.

1. Yesterday Carmen bought some groceries.
2. First she cut the peppers.
3. Later she sliced the mushrooms.
4. She skillfully added spices.
5. Carmen used the hot pepper sparingly.
6. Manuel cheerfully set the table.
7. Soon the guests arrived.
8. Manuel greeted guests warmly.
9. Everything was properly prepared.
10. Everyone completely enjoyed the meal.

Prepositions and Prepositional Phrases

Know the Rule

A **preposition** is a word that shows the relationship between a noun or pronoun and another word in the sentence. In a sentence, prepositions are always followed by a word called the **object of a preposition**. A **prepositional phrase** begins with a preposition and ends with the object of a preposition. Some prepositional phrases help tell where something is.

Examples:

Go **to the back of the room.**

⟵ prepositional phrases

Common Prepositions

above	between	through
across	in	toward
behind	into	under
below	near	underneath
beneath	on	
beside	outside	

Practice the Rule

Number a sheet of paper 1–10. Write the sentences. Underline the prepositional phrase. Circle the preposition.

1. Find the blue box behind the bookcase.
2. Clara put the pencils on the shelf.
3. Jason walked across the hall.
4. Beneath the counter, he found the dog treats.
5. Julio waited near the door.
6. The book fell between two desks.
7. I waited outside the door.
8. I will check the supplies in the morning.
9. You will find the paper underneath the table.
10. Maria walked toward the supply closet.

Coordinating Conjunctions

Know the Rule

A **coordinating conjunction** connects words in a sentence. Common coordinating conjunctions are *and, but,* and *or*. Put a comma before a coordinating conjunction when it is used to form a compound sentence.
Examples:
Carla **and** Diane are taking art lessons.
Carla likes using watercolors, **but** she does not like using colored pencils.

Practice the Rule

Number a sheet of paper 1–10. Write each sentence. Circle the coordinating conjuction and underline the words or sentences it connects.

1. Kim and Barbara completed their assignment on Tuesday.
2. Ariella's watercolor painting is original and exciting.
3. I want to work in oils or pastels.
4. Our art teacher loves painting, but she does not like drawing.
5. I studied art for two years, but then I switched to photography.
6. I like to paint the sea and flowers.
7. Jackson or Cole will take you to the art fair.
8. The paper and paints are on the table.
9. I am taking art lessons and swimming lessons.
10. I want to work as an artist or an architect.

Interjections

Know the Rule

An **interjection** is a word that expresses strong emotion. It can stand alone, followed by an exclamation point. It can also begin a sentence. When an interjection begins a sentence, it is followed by a comma.

Examples:

Wow! Did you hear that wind?

Okay, let's get inside.

Common Interjections

ah	hurrah	ouch
bam	my goodness	phew
bravo	oh	rats
eek	oh dear	ugh
good grief	oh my	whoops
gosh	okay	wow
hey	oops	yikes

Practice the Rule

Number a sheet of paper 1–10. Beside each number write the interjection as it appears in the sentence and the punctuation that follows it.

1. Eek! The baseball just shattered the window.
2. Hey, we've got to get inside.
3. Good grief! The wind is ripping trees apart.
4. Rats! My tree house is ruined.
5. Ouch, a branch just hit my arm.
6. The storm is nearly over. Hurrah!
7. My goodness, we have a big mess to clean up.
8. You did a great job cleaning up. Bravo!
9. Oh dear, the wind is picking up again.
10. Oh my, here we go again!

Progressive Verbs

Know the Rule

Progressive verbs show that an action is happening, was happening, or will be happening. The action happens for a length of time. Progressive verbs are made from the *-ing* form of a verb along with a form of the verb *to be*.

Present Progressive	I *am walking*.	I am walking right now. I have not finished my walk.
Past Progressive	I *was walking* when it started to rain.	In the middle of walking, the rain began. My walk had not ended yet.
Future Progressive	I *will be walking* to school next year instead of taking the bus.	Over a period of time, I will walk to school many times.

Practice the Rule

Number a sheet of paper 1–10. Write the progressive form of the verb in parentheses that makes sense in each sentence.

1. Next year, Kelvin _____ how to play the saxophone. (learn)
2. Last year, he _____ the violin. (study)
3. Nisha cannot read while she _____ to music. (listen)
4. While Jayden _____ his guitar, a string broke. (tune)
5. I could see Amy's eyes move while she _____ her music. (read)
6. Jayden and Amy _____ to try out for the band this afternoon. (plan)
7. If they make it, they _____ together in the band! (play)
8. Mr. Mohr _____ music again next year. (teach)
9. Mr. Mohr _____ forward to teaching Jayden, Amy, and Kevin. (look)
10. The band members _____ that they will win the district band contest. (hope)

Homophones

Know the Rule

Homophones are words that sound the same but have different spellings and meanings.

Examples:

He **knows** the kind of flowers I like best.

The flowers tickle my **nose**.

Common Homophones	Meaning
eye	the organ of sight
I	personal pronoun referring to oneself
hear	to perceive sound
here	at or in this place
its	belonging to it
it's	it is
sea	a large body of salt water
see	to perceive with the eye
read	to have grasped the meaning of printed or written words
red	a color

Practice the Rule

Number a sheet of paper 1–5. Write the word that best completes each sentence correctly.

1. Last week I _____ everything I could about bees. (red/read)

2. Finally _____ decided to raise bees myself. (I/eye)

3. _____ in my yard, I have two bee hives. (Here/Hear)

4. I have a protective suit I _____ when working with my bees. (where/wear)

5. _____ of my favorite things is to watch my bees. (Won/One)

Using the Right Word

Know the Rule

Some words and phrases are often misused in writing. Using the correct word will make your writing less confusing for your readers.

Examples:

accept, except
Accept is a verb that means to receive: *I **accept** your apology.*

Except is usually a preposition that means excluding: *I liked all of the books **except** this one.*

than, then
Than is a conjunction used in comparisons: *I like chicken better **than** fish.*

Then is an adverb that indicates time: *First we'll cook, and **then** we'll eat.*

your, you're
Your is a possessive pronoun: *Where is **your** hat?*

You're is a contraction that means you are: ***You're** going to be late.*

could have, could of
Do not use **could** (*would, should*) **of** when what you mean is **could have**: *I **could have** won the contest.*

Practice the Rule

Number a sheet of paper 1–10. Write each sentence, correcting any words or phrases used incorrectly.

1. You're report is excellent.
2. I swim better then my brother.
3. Jen is busy every day accept Tuesday.
4. Bret could of done a better job.
5. Your a great baseball player.
6. Get yourself a snack and than begin your homework.
7. Please except my apologies for being late.
8. Marcus would of called, but he was at soccer practice.
9. Ali is taller then Mia.
10. Everyone handed in their homework accept Duncan.

Pronoun Antecedents

Know the Rule

A pronoun takes the place of a noun. The noun that a pronoun replaces is called its **antecedent**. When you write a pronoun such as *he, she, him, her, they, them,* or *it,* be sure that the antecedent—or word that the pronoun replaces—**is clear**. Also be sure that the pronoun agrees in number (singular or plural) and in gender (male or female) with the noun that it replaces.

Examples:

Melissa read an article about Alice Ramsey and **her** adventures.

Melissa was in the library when **she** read the article.

Practice the Rule

Number a sheet of paper 1–10. Write each sentence, using the correct pronoun. Underline its antecedent.

1. Melissa wrote in _____ journal about Alice Ramsey. (her/his)

2. Alice Ramsey lived a long time ago, but _____ adventures are still interesting to read about. (her/their)

3. Melissa decided to write _____ paper on Alice Ramsey. (her/their)

4. Melissa's two friends, Eileen and Kevin, wrote _____ papers on Eleanor Roosevelt. (his/their)

5. Melissa used the Internet for most of _____ research. (her/their)

6. Eileen and Kevin used the library for _____ research. (his/their)

7. Melissa learned a lot about Alice Ramsey and _____ life. (her/his)

8. Melissa's friends worked hard on _____ papers, too. (her/their)

9. Melissa presented _____ paper on Tuesday. (her/his)

10. Eileen and Kevin presented _____ papers on Wednesday. (his/their)

Comparative and Superlative Adjectives

Know the Rule

The **comparative form** of an **adjective** compares two people, places, or things. The **superlative form** compares three or more people, places, or things. For most short adjectives, add *-er* to compare two people, places, or things and *-est* to compare three or more. For most longer adjectives, use *more* to compare two persons, places, or things and *most* to compare three or more. Remember, the superlative form usually is preceded by the article *the*.

Comparing With Adjectives

- Adjectives ending with *e*:
  Drop the *e* and add *-er* or *-est*.

  wide
  wider
  widest

- Adjectives ending with a consonant and *y*:
  Change the *y* to *i* and add *-er* or *-est*.

  silly
  sillier
  silliest

- Some adjectives with two syllables and all adjectives with more than two syllables:
  Use *more* or *most* instead of *-er* or *-est*.

  impressive
  more impressive
  most impressive

Practice the Rule

Number a sheet of paper 1–8. Write each sentence, choosing the correct form of the adjective.

1. The cheetah is the world's (faster/fastest) land mammal.
2. The (speedier/speediest) insect is the hawk moth.
3. The (swifter/swiftest) mammal in the water is the killer whale.
4. Dinosaurs were big, but today's blue whales are even (most gigantic/more gigantic).
5. The (slower/slowest) animal on Earth is the three-toed sloth.
6. The (smaller/smallest) mammal on Earth is the bumblebee bat.
7. The pygmy shrew is just a little bit (bigger/biggest) than the bumblebee bat.
8. Which is (more beautiful/most beautiful), a cardinal or a robin?

Comparing With Adverbs

Know the Rule

You can use **adverbs** to compare two actions. Add *-er* to short adverbs to compare two actions. For most adverbs that end in *-ly*, use *more* to compare two actions.

Examples:

Comparing With Adverbs

One Action	Joe runs **fast**.
	Alexa swims **gracefully**.
Two Actions	Joe runs **faster** than Lee.
	Alexa swims **more gracefully** than Laetifa.

Practice the Rule

Number a sheet of paper 1–10. Beside each number write the comparative form of the adverb.

1. The new coach spoke _____ than last year's coach. (calmly)
2. Of the two competitors, Clarisse performed _____. (skillfully)
3. Wanda swam _____ than Dan. (rapidly)
4. Matt answered _____ than Peter. (politely)
5. Austin will complete his training _____ than Katie. (soon)
6. The winner completed his routine _____ than I did. (expertly)
7. The broad jump began _____ than the high jump. (late)
8. Austin speaks _____ than Matt. (softly)
9. Katie's relay team ran _____ than our team. (swiftly)
10. Mike cheered _____ than Matt. (loudly)

Comparing With Superlative Adverbs

Know the Rule

You can use the **superlative form** of adverbs to compare three or more actions. Add -est to short adverbs to compare three or more actions. For most adverbs that end in -ly, use most to compare three or more actions. Sometimes you will need to change the spelling of a word in order to add an ending. For example, you might need to change the y to i before adding -est.

Examples:

Of the five of us, Noah arrived **earliest**.

Of all the students in our class, Arun writes **most powerfully**.

Practice the Rule

Number a sheet of paper 1–10. Beside each number write the superlative form of the adverb.

1. Of the five girls, Angela spoke _____. (politely)
2. Of all the competitors, Ethan performed _____. (skillfully)
3. The teacher in our school who speaks _____ is Mr. Henderson. (calmly)
4. The person in our class who sings _____ is Rachel. (sweetly)
5. Of the ten members in our debating club, Andrew answers questions _____. (confidently)
6. Chloe and I arrived early, but Jayden arrived _____. (early)
7. Who has the _____ grades in our class? (high)
8. Recently five students were absent with the flu, but _____ only two students were absent. (recently)
9. Everyone works hard at math, but Emma works _____ of all. (hard)
10. Jason can run _____ of anyone in the class. (fast)

Abbreviations

Know the Rule

An **abbreviation** is a shortened form of a word. Most abbreviations begin with a capital letter and end with a period. An **initial** is a capital letter with a period after it. An initial takes the place of a person's name.

Common Abbreviations

Titles	Mr., Mister	Dr., Doctor	Sen., Senator
Addresses	St., Street	Rd., Road	P.O., Post Office
Initials	M. L. King Jr., Martin Luther King Junior	J. F. Kennedy, John Fitzgerald Kennedy	R. L. Stine, Robert Lawrence Stine
Months	Jan., January	Mar., March	Aug., August
Days	Mon., Monday	Thurs., Thursday	Sat., Saturday

Practice the Rule

Number a sheet of paper 1–10. Beside each number write the correct abbreviation for each underlined word.

1. <u>Doctor</u> Rodriguez
2. <u>Friday</u>
3. <u>Mister</u> Tully
4. <u>Nathaniel Anthony</u> D'Amore
5. Thomas Jones <u>Junior</u>
6. 53 Winter <u>Road</u>
7. <u>August</u> 14, 2012
8. 33 Temple <u>Street</u>
9. <u>Post Office</u>
10. <u>Saturday</u>

Capitalization

Know the Rule

Capitalize the first letter in proper nouns and proper adjectives.

Examples:

We are learning about **Mexico**.

Have you ever eaten at a **Mexican** restaurant?

Proper Nouns and Adjectives

Geographical Names	Holidays	Dates	Historic Documents, Periods, and Events	Organizations
Pacific Ocean	Fourth of July	April	Bill of Rights	American Red Cross
Mount Grey	Thanksgiving	Sunday	Colonial Era	Republican Party
Nile River	Father's Day	January	Great Depression	Warren Community Chorus
Canada	Labor Day	Wednesday	Revolutionary War	European Union

Practice the Rule

Number a sheet of paper 1–10. Beside each number write the sentence with capitalization errors corrected.

1. My friend from germany is coming to visit.
2. We learned about the great depression last month.
3. My project is due on monday.
4. The european union includes 27 countries.
5. This painting shows the english countryside.
6. My favorite holiday is thanksgiving.
7. Our test will be on the revolutionary war.
8. My mother belongs to the warren community chorus.
9. Let's get together on friday.
10. We will have a big party on the fourth of july.

Titles

Know the Rule

Capitalize the first word, the last word, and all the important words in a title. Verbs, such as *is* and *are*, are important words. Capitalize *the* only if it is the first word in a title. **Underline** the titles of books, magazines, newspapers, movies, works of art, and long musical compositions. If you are writing on a computer, put these titles in **italics**. Put **quotation marks** around the titles of shorter works, such as songs, stories, and poems.

Examples:
Charlotte's Web (book title)
Aladdin and the Wonderful Lamp (book title)
Sports Illustrated for Kids (magazine title)
"America the Beautiful" (song title)
"The Desert Scare" (story title)

Practice the Rule

Number a sheet of paper 1–10. Beside each number, write the sentence correctly.

1. Sarah, Plain and Tall is one of my favorite books.
2. Take the sky was the poem I chose to recite.
3. My mother reads the Chicago Tribune every morning.
4. I watched the movie National Velvet last night.
5. I wrote about the painting Cape Cod Afternoon.
6. A Wrinkle in time is a novel written by Madeline L'Engle.
7. The singing of The Star Spangled Banner closed the program.
8. The last piece of light is my favorite short story.
9. Cobblestone is a great history magazine.
10. Tomorrow I will start reading the book Summer of The Swans.

Commas in a Series

Know the Rule

A **series** is a list of three or more items in a sentence. A series can consist of single words, phrases, clauses, or sentences. Commas are used to separate items in a series. The last comma in the series goes before the word *and* or the word *or*.

Examples:
Three of the smartest dogs are **the border collie, the poodle, and the golden retriever**. (*phrases in a series*)
Every day **I take my dog to dog school, I give him plenty of exercise, and I play with him**. (*clauses in a series*)

Practice the Rule

Number a sheet of paper 1–10. Write the sentences. Add commas where they are needed.

1. Of the litter of puppies, Skidboot was the biggest most colorful and most energetic.

2. Skidboot chased chickens tore up trash, and ran after pets.

3. Mr. Hartwig taught Skidboot to fetch to jump and to obey commands.

4. Skidboot learned to fetch the phone to lead horses and to chase balls.

5. He also learned to sit to lie down and to wait.

6. Skidboot performed for local schools rodeos and state fairs.

7. He was a loyal obedient and smart dog.

8. Skidboot was a friend with a cold nose wagging tail and loyal spirit.

9. Skidboot won contests competitions, and people's hearts.

10. Skidboot brought joy amazement and pleasure to people's lives.

Commas After Introductory Phrases or Clauses

Know the Rule

Use a **comma** to show a pause in a sentence. When a sentence begins with an **introductory phrase** (a group of words without a subject and a predicate) or a **clause** (a group of words with a subject and a predicate), put a comma between it and the rest of the sentence.

Examples:

During the first week of June, we are going on a family picnic.

When we get to North Carolina, we will have to find a place to stay.

Practice the Rule

Number a sheet of paper 1–10. Write each sentence, adding commas where needed. If a sentence needs no comma, write **Correct**.

1. When we arrived at my aunt's house the picnic table was already set.
2. In the beginning, we were having a really good time.
3. When we sat down to eat there was food everywhere.
4. As I took a sip of my orange juice I spotted an ant.
5. Within minutes ants swarmed over all our food.
6. My aunt jumped up and screamed.
7. After a moment she calmed down.
8. Acting quickly my aunt grabbed our plates and put them inside.
9. Everything happened so quickly that I could hardly think.
10. Luckily for us the ants never returned.

Parentheses

Know the Rule

Use **parentheses** to set off an explanation, example, or other information in a sentence. Parentheses enclose information that is helpful but not necessary to the meaning of the sentence.

Examples:

The San Francisco earthquake **(1906)** killed more than 3,000 people.

An earthquake **(also known as a quake)** is caused by two blocks of earth deep under the ground suddenly slipping past each other.

Practice the Rule

Number a sheet of paper 1–10. Write each sentence, adding parentheses where needed.

1. The epicenter the point of Earth directly above the earthquake's origin is where the most damage occurs.

2. An earthquake's aftershocks the smaller earthquakes that occur later often cause additional damage.

3. Seismographs instruments that record earthquakes tell scientists how strong an earthquake is.

4. Tsunamis very large ocean waves caused by underwater earthquakes can destroy coastal regions.

5. More people died in the earthquake and tsunami in Japan in 2011 than died in the Kobe earthquake 1995.

6. The largest recorded earthquake was in Chile in 1960 May.

7. The 1960 earthquake caused damaging tsunamis in Hilo Hawaii.

8. It's a good idea to have an emergency kit flashlight, batteries, water, bandages ready just in case.

9. The magnitude the amount of energy released of an earthquake is measured by the Richter scale.

10. The Richter scale named for Charles Richter was invented in 1934.

Semicolons

Know the Rule

A **semicolon** can be used instead of a comma and a conjunction to join two related independent clauses. You can use a semicolon to fix a run-on sentence.

Example:

The plane took off; we were on our way to Venezuela.

Practice the Rule

Number a sheet of paper 1–10. Use a semicolon to combine each pair of sentences. Remember, the first word of the second independent clause should not be capitalized unless it is a proper noun.

1. Venezuela is the sixth largest country in South America. Brazil is the largest country.
2. Venezuela lies on the northern coast of South America. Its geography is unique.
3. Venezuela is close to the equator. As a result, the country has only two seasons.
4. The dry season lasts from December to April. The wet season lasts from May to November.
5. In ancient times, Indian tribes lived in Venezuela. They farmed, hunted, and fished for their food.
6. Christopher Columbus was the first European to visit Venezuela he arrived in 1498.
7. Caracas is Venezuela's capital. It sits next to a long valley that stretches from the east to the west.
8. On one side of the valley are the slopes of Avila National Park. On the other side are the hills of the southern suburbs.
9. Caracas grew during the years of the oil boom gleaming skyscrapers now line the city.
10. Caracas has great weather. The temperature is almost always like spring.

Colons

Know the Rule

Use a **colon**
- in a sentence before a list.
- between the hour and minutes in expressions of time.

Examples:
Jess grows three kinds of vegetables: tomatoes, peppers, and corn.
Please meet me at 2:10 P.M.

Practice the Rule

Number a sheet of paper 1–10. Write each sentence, adding colons where needed.

1. The bus will leave at 900 A.M.
2. Bring the following items sunglasses, good walking shoes, and lunch.
3. There were three sandwich choices for lunch tuna, cheese, and ham.
4. My travel bag held everything shirts, pants, a jacket, and shoes.
5. We saw some amazing things a waterfall, rare birds, and an antelope.
6. At 230 P.M. we took a break.
7. By 300 P.M. we were ready to continue our hike.
8. I realized I forgot some items bug spray, sunscreen, and extra water.
9. To get home, we traveled three ways a bus, a train, and a taxi.
10. We got home at 600 P.M.

More Practice

Kinds of Sentences

Label each sentence **statement, command, question,** or **exclamation**.

1. Bring the poster over here.
2. Have you finished your project?
3. Cal wrote about border collies.
4. His paper was so well done!
5. When is the next report due?

Avoiding Run-ons and Comma Splices

Write **RO** after each run-on sentence. Write **CS** after each comma splice.

1. Tornadoes form from powerful thunderstorms, they look like rotating funnel-shaped clouds.
2. Severe weather conditions can be scary tornadoes are one of nature's most violent storms.
3. A tornado warning means that a tornado has been seen, it also means that people should find shelter immediately.
4. My brothers and I saw a tornado once we were really scared.
5. Storm chasers go close to tornadoes, it's very dangerous.

Participles and Participial Phrases

Write the sentences. Underline the participial phrase and circle the participle.

1. Walking confidently, Marcus stepped up to the plate.
2. Excited, Marcus couldn't wait to show the fans his swing.
3. Understanding the situation, Marcus focused his attention on hitting the ball.
4. Cheering wildly, the fans jumped to their feet when Marcus hit a home run.
5. Marcus, trotting around the bases, waved at the fans.

More Practice

Prepositional Phrases

Write the prepositional phrase or phrases in each sentence.

1. Our trip began in Colorado.
2. We skated over the lake and hiked up the mountain.
3. Some of our friends stayed in the cabin.
4. After our hike we cooked a great supper.
5. We cooked fresh fish in a skillet.

Appositives and Appositive Phrases

Write the appositive phrase in each sentence.

1. Robert Fulton, an American engineer and inventor, developed the first commercially successful steamboat.
2. Fulton, a well-known portrait painter, had always been interested in mechanical inventions.
3. Fulton painted a portrait of Benjamin Franklin, one of the most famous Americans of his time.
4. Fulton designed his first working submarine, the *Nautilus*, between 1793 and 1797.
5. Fulton and Robert R. Livingston, the U.S. Ambassador to France, built a steamboat together.

Plural Nouns

Write the plural form of each noun.

1. letter
2. noise
3. wolf
4. puppy
5. turkey
6. porch
7. berry
8. roof

More Practice

Personal Pronouns and Compound Personal Pronouns

Write the pronouns in each sentence. Underline each personal pronoun. Circle each compound personal pronoun.

1. Felipe did the entire project himself.
2. He worked on it for four weeks.
3. Nadia did not do her project by herself.
4. She completed it with a partner.
5. Nadia and her partner were proud of themselves for working together well.

Past-Tense Verbs

Write the past tense of the verb in parentheses.

1. Andrew _____ his dog Buster yesterday morning. (walk)
2. Buster _____ the ball with Andrew for an hour. (chase)
3. Buster _____ high in the air to catch the ball. (jump)
4. Last week Andrew _____ Buster a bath. (give)
5. Yesterday Buster _____ in the dirt again! (roll)

Present-Tense Verbs

Write the present-tense verb or verbs in each sentence.

1. Dolphins spend most of their time beneath the surface of the water.
2. Because they have streamlined bodies, they swim very quickly.
3. Dolphins live in pods of up to a dozen dolphins.
4. They communicate with clicks, whistles, and other sounds.
5. Some dolphins perform tricks at aquariums.

More Practice

Future-Tense Verbs

Write the future tense of the verb in parentheses.

1. Carlos _____ his skateboarding this afternoon. (practice)
2. He _____ the skateboarding contest next month. (enter)
3. He hopes he _____. (win)
4. If he wins, he _____ a cash prize. (get)
5. Carlos _____ very happy if he wins. (be)

Helping Verbs

Write the helping and main verb in each sentence. Underline the helping verb once and the main verb twice.

1. The whole class is going to the Grand Canyon.
2. We will earn the money for the trip.
3. Our teacher is helping us.
4. We will have a great time.
5. Everyone should visit the Grand Canyon if possible.

Present Perfect-Tense Verbs

Write the present perfect-tense verb in each sentence.

1. Olivia has practiced horse jumping for five years.
2. She has worked hard with her horse Nina.
3. Nina has been a wonderful partner.
4. For years Olivia has dreamed of winning a horse-jumping contest.
5. Olivia has enjoyed working with Nina.

More Practice

Adverbs

Write the adverb or adverbs in each sentence. After each adverb, write the word that it describes.

1. Cesar carefully prepared his presentation.
2. First, he thoroughly researched his topic.
3. Then, he rehearsed his presentation.
4. He delivered his presentation skillfully and smoothly.
5. The class clapped loudly for Cesar.

Prepositions and Prepositional Phrases

Write the sentences. Underline the prepositional phrase. Circle the preposition.

1. We went to the game on Saturday.
2. In the morning, we packed our lunches.
3. During the second quarter, our team played much better.
4. At the end of the game, we cheered until we were hoarse.
5. Cold water felt good on our dry throats.

Coordinating Conjunctions

Write each sentence. Circle the coordinating conjuction and underline the words or sentences it connects.

1. Kara and Emilio love studying insects.
2. They learned that insects can live on the bodies of plants and animals.
3. Insects are everywhere, but most of the time we don't see them.
4. I love learning about insects and plants.
5. What should I study next, reptiles or birds?

More Practice

Interjections

Write the interjection and the punctuation that follows it.

1. Good grief! I really messed up that test.

2. Hey, how did you do on the test?

3. Oh dear, I should have studied harder.

4. Bravo! You got a perfect score.

5. Watch out! You almost ran into the table.

Progressive Verbs

Write the correct form of the verb in parentheses to show continuing action.

1. I _____ my garden next weekend. (plant)

2. While I _____ about my garden, I should order the seeds. (think)

3. A rabbit hopped by while I _____ my flowers. (water)

4. When the flowers _____, they are beautiful. (bloom)

5. This summer, I _____ my garden very much. (enjoy)

Homophones

Write the word that correctly completes each sentence.

1. I can _____ someone coming down the hallway. (here/hear)

2. _____ think it might be my friend Dana. (I/Eye)

3. I can _____ her coming down the hall. (sea/see)

4. _____ Dana! (Its/It's)

5. _____, Dana, how are you? (Hay/Hey)

More Practice

Using the Right Word

Write each sentence, correcting any words or phrases used incorrectly.

1. Your right; I should have studied harder.

2. You could of pestered me more to study.

3. You did better on the test then I did.

4. I like everything about school accept tests.

5. You did a good job on you're test, though.

Pronoun Antecedents

Write each sentence. Write the pronoun in parentheses that correctly completes each sentence. Underline the pronoun's antecedent.

1. Alysa wrote _____ paper on Amelia Earhart. (his/her)

2. She learned that Earhart took _____ first flying lessons in California. (her/their)

3. In 1931 Earhart married George Putnam, and together _____ formed a successful partnership. (she/they)

4. Brian and Rafael wrote _____ papers on Roberto Clemente. (his/their)

5. Clemente played all of _____ professional baseball games with the Pittsburgh Pirates. (his/their)

Comparative and Superlative Adjectives

Write the form of the adjective in parentheses that best completes each sentence.

1. Miguel is _____ than Alma. (tall)

2. Sarah is the _____ person in our class. (friendly)

3. Li is a _____ runner than Alonzo. (fast)

4. The _____ speaker in our class is Natasha. (confident)

5. Vikram has a _____ voice than Ali. (soft)

More Practice

Comparing With Adverbs

Write the form of the adverb in parentheses that best completes each sentence.

1. My dog runs _____ than yours. (quickly)

2. The competition began _____ than we thought it would. (late)

3. The winning dog performed _____ than the runner-up. (skillfully)

4. My dog barks _____ than yours. (often)

5. Your dog eats _____ than my dog. (noisily)

Comparing With Superlative Adverbs

Write the form of the adverb in parentheses that best completes each sentence.

1. This year we got off to the _____ start ever. (quick)

2. Of all the hikers, Ramon climbed _____. (fast)

3. We started _____ in the morning this year than we did last year. (early)

4. Of all of us, Liza screamed _____ when she saw the snake. (loud)

5. The _____ we can get home is 4 P.M. (soon)

Abbreviations

Write the correct abbreviation for each underlined word below.

1. <u>Friday</u>

2. <u>Mister</u> Owens

3. 227 Commercial <u>Street</u>

4. 18 Meadow <u>Road</u>

5. <u>Doctor</u> Chen

6. <u>Eileen Marie</u> McCoy

7. <u>December</u>

8. <u>Monday</u>

More Practice

Capitalization

Write the paragraph, correcting all errors in capitalization.

My favorite holiday is the fourth of july. This year, my family is traveling to new mexico to celebrate the day. We will leave on sunday and return on saturday. We plan to visit the museum of indian arts and culture.

Titles

Write each sentence, correcting errors in the use of titles.

1. Last month we read the book the cricket in times square.
2. Showery Times is my favorite poem.
3. Next month we will study the painting Golden Sun Flowers.
4. Baseball Youth is a magazine with great stories and articles about young baseball players.
5. How many times have you seen the movie stuart little?

Commas in a Series

Write the sentences. Add commas where they are needed.

1. Adrianna Leon and I went hiking together.
2. Leon carried the camera Inez carried the food and I lugged the water.
3. Leon's camera is small light and durable.
4. Leon took pictures of mountains lakes and birds.
5. We saw crows hawks and blue jays.

More Practice

Commas After Introductory Phrases or Clauses

Write the sentences. Add commas where they are needed.

1. After the race ended we went out to eat.
2. By the time the food arrived we were starving.
3. In the beginning we hardly talked at all.
4. After we had eaten we were much more talkative.
5. On the way home we stopped to see Nana.

Parentheses

Write the sentences. Add parentheses where they are needed.

1. Eleanor Roosevelt 1884–1962 became First Lady of the United States in 1933.
2. Before she became First Lady, Mrs. Roosevelt worked with the Women's Trade Union League WTUL to improve working conditions for women and children.
3. Her mother Anna Hall Roosevelt died when Eleanor was only eight.
4. Her husband Franklin D. Roosevelt got polio in 1921.
5. In 1939, Mrs. Roosevelt defended Marion Anderson 1897–1993 when the singer was not allowed to perform at Constitution Hall.

Semicolons

Write the sentences. Add semicolons where they are needed.

1. I researched my paper for three hours now I can begin writing.
2. The first page will introduce my topic the second page will explain it.
3. I presented my paper everyone in the class thought it was good.
4. I will keep my paper in a safe place I may want to refer to it someday.
5. Mom and Dad were proud of my report they hung it on the refrigerator.

More Practice

Colons

Write the sentences. Add colons where they are needed.

1. Bring the following to class tomorrow paper, pencils, and colored markers.

2. The sale will begin at 10 00 A.M.

3. Mia's class will sell the following items books, toys, and games.

4. All school sales will end at 2 00 P.M.

5. Here is how to study your spelling words read the words, say the words, and write the words.

Transitions

Transitional words and phrases can help make the meaning of your writing clearer by connecting sentences and paragraphs. Below are words that you can use to make it easier for readers to understand what you are trying to say.

Words and Phrases That Can Show Time Order

about	after	as soon as	at	before
during	finally	first	second	third
later	meanwhile	next	soon	then
until	today	tomorrow	yesterday	

Words and Phrases That Can Show Likenesses and Differences

Likenesses: also both in the same way
likewise similarly

Differences: although however in contrast instead
on the other hand unlike yet

Words and Phrases That Can Show Cause and Effect

because	as a result	however	since	thus
therefore				

Words and Phrases That Can Show Location

above	across	around	behind	below
beneath	beside	between	down	in back of
in front of	inside	near	next to	on top of
outside	over	under		

Words and Phrases That Can Conclude or Summarize

finally	in conclusion	lastly	therefore

Prepositions

Prepositions link nouns, pronouns, and phrases to other words in a sentence. There are many prepositions in the English language. These are some of the most common ones:

at	after	against
around	among	below
before	between	beside
beyond	from	inside
into	onto	over
past	through	underneath
upon	within	

Appendix B
Rubrics

4-Point Rubrics

5-Point Rubrics

6-Point Rubrics

	4	3	2	1
Ideas	The topic is just the right size—not too big or too small. Descriptive details introduce and develop the setting, narrator, characters, and plot. Carefully selected ideas completely satisfy the needs of the reader.	The topic is the right size. Details introduce and develop the setting, narrator, characters, and plot. The ideas selected by the author frequently meet the needs of the reader.	The topic is too big or too small. Some details develop the setting, narrator, characters, and plot. The ideas selected by the author sometimes meet the needs of the reader.	The writing is not a narrative. Details are unrelated or not included.
Organization	The narrative unfolds logically and naturally. Transition words and phrases help sequence the events. A strong beginning leads to a satisfying conclusion.	Some events are not connected or are out of order. Transition words and phrases are needed to help sequence the events. The beginning and the conclusion work, but may not be strong.	The narrative does not unfold logically and naturally. Events are out of order. Transition words and phrases are confusing or missing. The beginning or the conclusion is weak.	The writing is disorganized and very difficult to follow. Transition words and phrases are not used. No beginning or conclusion is evident.
Voice	The voice, mood, and tone are just right for the purpose. Dialogue, if used, reveals each character's voice clearly.	The voice, mood, and tone are just right in places, but inconsistent. Dialogue, if used, somewhat reveals the characters' voices.	The voice sounds disinterested. Mood and tone are weak. Dialogue, if used, does not uniquely distinguish the characters' voices.	Voice is flat. Mood and tone are absent. Dialogue, if used, does not sound right for some of the characters.
Word Choice	Words and phrases consistently help the reader "see" the characters and "experience" the events. Nouns and verbs are clear and precise, supported by a few carefully selected modifiers.	Some words and phrases help the reader picture characters and events, but some are too general. Certain nouns and verbs are weak, requiring too much help from modifiers. Modifiers are satisfactory.	Many words and phrases are too general. They keep the reader from picturing the characters and events clearly. Nouns and verbs lack clarity or precision. Too many or too few modifiers are used, and many of them are weak.	Many words are not used correctly. They distract the reader.
Sentence Fluency	Varied sentence beginnings, lengths, and patterns make the writing flow smoothly. Several particularly well-crafted sentences add style and interest. The paper is effortlessly read aloud with inflection or feeling.	There is some variation in sentence beginnings, lengths, and patterns. The sentences are correct, and one or two sentences add style. The paper can be read aloud with inflection or feeling.	Many sentences have the same beginnings, lengths, and patterns. This interrupts the flow of the writing. The sentences are mostly correct, but it is difficult to read the paper with inflection.	Sentences are poorly written or incorrect. The writing does not flow.
Conventions	Spelling, grammar, punctuation, and capitalization are correct. The narrative contains no errors.	There are a few grammatical errors that may cause the reader to pause momentarily, but meaning is clear.	Many errors are present, and some confuse the reader.	The writing has not been edited. Serious errors make the narrative hard to understand.

Informative/Explanatory Writing Rubric

	4	3	2	1
Ideas	The topic is introduced clearly. Information and examples develop the main idea(s). Carefully selected ideas completely answer the reader's main questions.	A topic is introduced. Most of the information and examples develop the main idea(s). The ideas chosen by the author frequently answer the reader's main questions.	A topic is introduced, but little of the information or examples develops the main idea(s). Some of the reader's questions are answered.	A topic is not introduced. Information and examples are incomplete or unrelated to the topic.
Organization	Information is organized into a strong and thoughtful introduction, a body, and a satisfying conclusion. Varied and appropriate transitions connect the ideas.	Information is organized into an introduction, a body, and a conclusion. More or better transitions are needed.	Information is not well organized. The introduction, body, and conclusion may be poorly developed. Transitions are confusing or not helpful.	The writing is not organized. Introduction and conclusion may both be missing. Transitions are not used.
Voice	The voice sounds interested and informative. It fully connects with the audience and conveys the writer's purpose well.	The voice sounds informative and mostly connects with the audience. It conveys the purpose some of the time.	The voice sounds informative in places. It conveys the purpose, but often fades out.	Voice is weak or absent. It does not connect with the audience or convey the writer's purpose.
Word Choice	Precise language and domain-specific vocabulary are used. Definitions are complete and helpful. Nouns and verbs are clear and precise, supported by a few carefully selected modifiers.	Some precise language, domain-specific vocabulary, and definitions are used. Some nouns and verbs are weak, requiring help from modifiers. Modifiers are satisfactory.	Little precise language and domain-specific vocabulary is used. Definitions are missing or incorrect. Nouns and verbs lack clarity or precision. Too many or too few modifiers are used, and many of them are weak.	Precise language and domain-specific vocabulary are not used.
Sentence Fluency	Clear, concise sentences make the text flow smoothly. Sentence beginnings, lengths, and patterns are varied for effect. The paper is effortlessly read aloud with inflection.	One or two sections of the writing do not flow smoothly. In these sections, several sentences may have the same beginnings, lengths, or patterns. The paper can be read with inflection.	In many places, the writing does not flow smoothly due to repetitive sentence beginnings, lengths, and patterns. It is difficult to read the paper with inflection.	Sentences are incomplete or incorrect.
Conventions	The text contains no errors. Spelling, grammar, punctuation, and capitalization are correct.	The text contains some errors in spelling, grammar, punctuation, and capitalization. One or two errors may cause the reader to pause momentarily, but meaning remains clear.	Many errors are present. Some errors are basic or repeated. The errors interfere with meaning in places.	The writing has not been edited. Serious errors make the writing hard to understand.

	4	3	2	1
Ideas	The writer states a clear opinion. The perfect details and facts are chosen to support the writer's reasons.	The writer states an opinion. Some details and facts are well chosen to support the writer's reasons.	The writer states an opinion, but few details are well chosen to support the writer's reasons.	The writer does not state an opinion. Reasons are not provided.
Organization	The text is organized logically and creatively. Helpful, appropriate, even unique transitions link the writer's opinion and reasons. A compelling conclusion clearly supports the opinion statement.	The text is organized logically. More or better transitions are needed to link the opinion and reasons. The beginning and the conclusion are functional. The conclusion relates to the opinion statement.	The text is not organized logically. Transitions may not show how the writer's ideas are related. Either the beginning or the conclusion is weak. The conclusion may not relate to the opinion statement.	The text is not organized as an opinion. Transitions are not used. Ideas are hard to follow. No beginning or conclusion is evident.
Voice	The voice is clearly convincing and totally fits the writer's purpose. The mood and tone are appropriate and engage the audience.	The voice is convincing and fits the writer's purpose. The mood and tone are engaging some of the time.	The voice is convincing in some places. The mood and tone are incorrect or inconsistent. They lose the audience.	The voice is weak or absent. The tone is not appropriate.
Word Choice	Precise words and fair language convey the writer's opinion. No biased words or phrases are used. Nouns and verbs are clear and precise, supported by a few carefully selected modifiers.	Some words are too general. One biased word or phrase may be used. Some nouns and verbs are weak, requiring help from modifiers. Modifiers are satisfactory.	Most words are weak. A few biased words or phrases may be used. Nouns and verbs lack clarity or precision. Too many or too few modifiers are used, and many of them are weak.	Words are weak, biased, or used incorrectly.
Sentence Fluency	A variety of sentence patterns adds interest and style. Great variation in sentence beginnings and lengths makes the writing flow very smoothly. The paper is effortlessly read aloud with inflection.	Some sentence patterns are varied and add interest. Some variation in sentence lengths and beginnings is evident. The writing flows smoothly in some places, but not in others. The paper can be read with inflection.	Too many sentences share the same pattern. The writing does not flow smoothly due to a lack of variation in sentence lengths and/or beginnings. It is difficult to read the paper with inflection.	Sentences are poorly written or incomplete. The writing is hard to follow.
Conventions	The text contains no errors. Spelling, grammar, punctuation, and capitalization are correct.	There are some errors in spelling, grammar, punctuation, and capitalization. One or two of these errors may cause the reader to pause momentarily, but meaning remains clear.	Many errors are present. Some errors are basic or repeated. The errors interfere with meaning in places.	The writing has not been edited. Serious errors make the writing hard to understand.

Descriptive Writing Rubric

	4	3	2	1
Ideas	The topic is clear, focused, and complete. Sensory details and examples are related to and develop the main ideas. The description helps the reader experience what is being described very clearly.	The topic is clear but may not be focused or complete. Sensory details and examples develop most of the main ideas. The description sometimes helps the reader experience what is being described.	The topic is not clear or focused. Details and examples develop some of the main ideas. The reader cannot always experience what is being described.	The topic is not clear. Details and examples are unrelated or missing. The reader cannot experience what is being described.
Organization	The description is well organized into a strong introduction, body, and conclusion. Details support the topic. Appropriate transitions connect the ideas and guide the reader.	Most of the description is organized. The introduction, body, and conclusion are functional. Most of the details support the topic. More or better transitions are needed to connect the ideas and guide the reader.	Some of the description is organized. The introduction, body, or conclusion may be weak. Few of the details support the topic. More and better transitions are needed to connect the ideas and guide the reader.	The description is not organized and does not have an introduction or conclusion. Details are missing. Transitions are not used.
Voice	The writer's voice connects strongly with the audience. The mood and tone match the purpose perfectly.	The writer's voice connects with the audience in places. The mood and tone match the purpose, but are inconsistent.	The writer's voice does not fit the purpose or the audience well. The mood and tone are inappropriate or inconsistent.	The writer's voice is weak or absent. It does not connect with the audience.
Word Choice	Precise, descriptive language and creative comparisons create a clear picture of the subject. Nouns and verbs carry the descriptive load with help from a few carefully chosen modifiers.	Some of the language is precise, but some is vague. Some of the comparisons create a clear picture of the subject. Many nouns and verbs depend upon modifiers for specificity. Modifiers are satisfactory.	Most of the language is not descriptive. Comparisons are ineffective. Nouns and verbs lack clarity or precision. Too many or too few modifiers are used, and many of them are weak.	The language is very basic and limited. Comparisons are not used.
Sentence Fluency	A variety of sentence beginnings, lengths, and patterns keeps the description interesting. It is effortless to read aloud with inflection or feeling. The writing flows very smoothly.	Some sentences share the same beginnings, lengths, or patterns. Some of the writing flows smoothly. The paper can be read aloud with inflection or feeling.	Several sentences in a row have the same beginnings, lengths, or patterns. The flow of the writing may slow or stall in parts. The paper is difficult to read aloud with inflection or feeling.	Sentences are not varied or interesting. The writing does not flow. The description is very difficult to read.
Conventions	The description contains no errors. Spelling, grammar, punctuation, and capitalization are correct.	The description contains some errors in spelling, grammar, punctuation, and capitalization. One or two of these errors may cause the reader to pause momentarily, but meaning remains clear.	Many errors are present. Some errors are basic or repeated. The errors interfere with meaning in places.	The writing has not been edited. Serious errors make the writing hard to understand.

	5	4	3	2	1
Ideas	The topic is just the right size—not too big or too small. Descriptive details introduce and develop the setting, narrator, characters, and plot. Carefully selected ideas completely satisfy the needs of the reader.	The topic is the right size. Most details introduce and develop the setting, narrator, characters, and plot. Carefully selected ideas satisfy most of the reader's needs.	The topic is the right size. Some details introduce the setting, narrator, characters, and plot. The ideas selected by the author frequently meet the needs of the reader.	The topic is too big or too small. Some details develop the setting, narrator, characters, and plot. The ideas selected by the author sometimes meet the needs of the reader.	The writing is not a narrative. Details are unrelated or not included.
Organization	The narrative unfolds logically and naturally. Transition words and phrases help sequence the events. A strong beginning leads to a satisfying conclusion.	One or two events in the middle are not connected or are out of order. Transition words and phrases help sequence most of the events. The beginning or the conclusion is strong.	Some events are not connected or are out of order. Transition words and phrases are needed to help sequence the events. The beginning and the conclusion work, but may not be strong.	The narrative does not unfold logically and naturally. Events are out of order. Transition words and phrases are confusing or missing. The beginning or conclusion is weak.	The writing is disorganized and very difficult to follow. Transition words and phrases are not used. No beginning or conclusion is evident.
Voice	The voice, mood, and tone are just right for the purpose. Dialogue, if used, reveals each character's voice clearly.	The voice, mood, and tone are just right most of the time. Dialogue, if used, reveals the characters' voices.	The voice, mood, and tone are just right in places, but inconsistent. Dialogue, if used, somewhat reveals the characters' voices.	The voice sounds disinterested. Mood and tone are weak. Dialogue, if used, does not uniquely distinguish the characters' voices.	Voice is flat. Mood and tone are absent. Dialogue, if used, does not sound right for any of the characters.
Word Choice	Words and phrases consistently help the reader "see" the characters and "experience" the events. Nouns and verbs are clear and precise, supported by a few carefully selected modifiers.	Words and phrases frequently help the reader "see" most of the characters and "experience" most of the events. Nouns and verbs are mostly clear and precise. Most modifiers are carefully selected.	Some words and phrases help the reader picture some characters and events, but some are too general. Certain nouns and verbs are weak, requiring too much help from modifiers. Modifiers are satisfactory.	Many words and phrases are too general. They keep the reader from picturing the characters and events clearly. Nouns and verbs lack clarity or precision. Too many or too few modifiers are used, and many of them are weak.	Many words are not used correctly. They distract the reader.
Sentence Fluency	Varied sentence beginnings, lengths, and patterns make the writing flow smoothly. Several particularly well-crafted sentences add style and interest. The paper is effortlessly read aloud with inflection or feeling.	Most sentence beginnings, lengths, and patterns are varied. One or two sentences add style. The paper is easily read aloud with inflection or feeling.	There is some variation in sentence beginnings, lengths, and patterns. Modifiers are satisfactory. some are too general. Certain nouns and verbs are correct but ordinary. The paper can be read aloud with inflection or feeling.	Many sentences have the same beginnings, lengths, and patterns. This interrupts the flow of the writing. The sentences are mostly correct but ordinary. It is difficult to read the paper with inflection.	Sentences are poorly written or incorrect. The writing does not flow.
Conventions	Spelling, grammar, punctuation, and capitalization are correct. The narrative contains no errors.	There are a few minor errors, but they do not make the narrative difficult to read.	There are a few grammatical errors that may cause the reader to pause momentarily, but meaning is clear.	Many errors are present, and some confuse the reader.	The writing has not been edited. Serious errors make the narrative hard to understand.

Informative/Explanatory Writing Rubric

	5	4	3	2	1
Ideas	The topic is introduced clearly. Information and examples develop the main idea(s). Carefully selected ideas completely answer the reader's main questions.	The topic is introduced clearly. Most of the information and examples develop the main idea(s). Almost all of the reader's main questions are answered.	A topic is introduced. Some of the information and examples develop the main idea(s). The ideas chosen by the author frequently answer the reader's main questions.	A topic is introduced, but little of the information or examples develops the main idea(s). Some of the reader's questions are answered.	A topic is not introduced. Information and examples are incomplete or unrelated to the topic.
Organization	Information is organized into a strong and thoughtful introduction, a body, and a satisfying conclusion. Varied and appropriate transitions connect the ideas.	Information is organized into an introduction, a body, and a conclusion. Most transitions are varied and appropriate.	Information is organized into an introduction, a body, and a conclusion. More or better transitions are needed.	Information is not well organized. The introduction, body, and conclusion may be poorly developed. Transitions are confusing or not helpful.	The writing is not organized. Introduction and conclusion may both be missing. Transitions are not used.
Voice	The voice sounds interested and informative. It fully connects with the audience and conveys the writer's purpose well.	The voice sounds informative and mostly connects with the audience. It conveys the purpose fairly well.	The voice sounds informative and connects with the audience somewhat. It conveys the purpose some of the time.	The voice sounds informative in places. It conveys the purpose, but often fades out.	Voice is weak or absent. It does not connect with the audience or convey the writer's purpose.
Word Choice	Precise language and domain-specific vocabulary are used. Definitions are complete and helpful. Nouns and verbs are clear and precise, supported by a few carefully selected modifiers.	Precise language and domain-specific vocabulary are used. Most definitions are complete and helpful. Nouns and verbs are mostly clear and precise. Most modifiers are carefully selected.	Some precise language, domain-specific vocabulary, and definitions are used. Some nouns and verbs are weak, requiring help from modifiers. Modifiers are satisfactory.	Little precise language and domain-specific vocabulary is used. Definitions are missing or incorrect. Nouns and verbs lack clarity or precision. Too many or too few modifiers are used, and many of them are weak.	Precise language and domain-specific vocabulary are not used.
Sentence Fluency	Clear, concise sentences make the text flow smoothly. Sentence beginnings, lengths, and patterns are varied for effect. The paper is effortlessly read aloud with inflection.	Most of the sentences flow smoothly. The sentence beginnings, lengths, and patterns are varied. The paper is easily read aloud with inflection.	One or two sections of the writing do not flow smoothly. In these sections, several sentences may have the same beginnings, lengths, or patterns. The paper can be read with inflection.	In many places, the writing does not flow smoothly due to repetitive sentence beginnings, lengths, and patterns. It is difficult to read the paper with inflection.	Sentences are incomplete or incorrect.
Conventions	The text contains no errors. Spelling, grammar, punctuation, and capitalization are correct.	The text contains very few errors in spelling, grammar, punctuation, or capitalization. The meaning remains clear.	The text contains some errors in spelling, grammar, punctuation, and capitalization. One or two errors may cause the reader to pause momentarily, but meaning remains clear.	Many errors are present. Some errors are basic or repeated. The errors interfere with meaning in places.	The writing has not been edited. Serious errors make the writing hard to understand.

Opinion Writing Rubric

	5	4	3	2	1
Ideas	The writer states a clear opinion. The perfect details and facts are chosen to support the writer's reasons.	The writer states a clear opinion. Most details and facts are well chosen to support the writer's reasons.	The writer states an opinion. Some details and facts are well chosen to support the writer's reasons.	The writer states an opinion, but few details support the writer's reasons.	The writer does not state an opinion. Reasons are not provided.
Organization	The text is organized logically and creatively. Helpful, appropriate, even unique transitions link the writer's opinion and reasons. A compelling conclusion clearly supports the opinion statement.	The text is organized logically. One or two more transitions are needed to link the opinion and reasons. The beginning is strong, and the conclusion supports the opinion statement.	The text is organized logically. More or better transitions are needed to link the opinion and reasons. Either the beginning and the conclusion are functional. The conclusion relates to the opinion statement.	The text is not organized logically as an opinion. Transitions may not show how the writer's ideas are related. Either the beginning or the conclusion is weak. The conclusion may not relate to the opinion statement.	The text is not organized as an opinion. Transitions are not used. Ideas are hard to follow. No beginning or conclusion is evident.
Voice	The voice is clearly convincing and totally fits the writer's purpose. The mood and tone are appropriate and engage the audience.	The voice is convincing and fits the writer's purpose. The mood and tone are appropriate and engaging most of the time.	The voice is somewhat convincing and fits the writer's purpose. The mood and tone are engaging some of the time.	The voice is convincing in some places. The mood and tone are incorrect or not inconsistent. They lose the audience.	The voice is weak or absent. The tone is not appropriate.
Word Choice	Precise words and fair language convey the writer's opinion. No biased words or phrases are used. Nouns and verbs are clear and precise, supported by a few carefully selected modifiers.	Most words are precise and fair. No biased words or phrases are used. Nouns and verbs are mostly clear and precise. Most modifiers are carefully selected.	Some words are too general. One biased word or phrase may be used. Some nouns and verbs are weak, requiring help from modifiers. Modifiers are satisfactory.	Most words are weak. A few biased words or phrases may be used. Nouns and verbs lack clarity or precision. Too many or too few modifiers are used, and many of them are weak.	Words are weak, biased, or used incorrectly.
Sentence Fluency	A variety of sentence patterns adds interest and style. Great variation in sentence beginnings and lengths makes the writing flow very smoothly. The paper is effortlessly read aloud with inflection.	Most sentence patterns are varied and add interest. Variation in sentence beginnings and lengths makes the writing flow smoothly. The paper is easily read aloud with inflection.	Some sentence patterns are varied and add interest. Some variation in sentence lengths and beginnings is evident. The writing flows smoothly in some places, but not in others. The paper can be read with inflection.	Too many sentences share the same pattern. The writing does not flow smoothly due to a lack of variation in sentence lengths and/or beginnings. It is difficult to read the paper with inflection.	Sentences are poorly written or incomplete. The writing is hard to follow.
Conventions	The text contains no errors. Spelling, grammar, punctuation, and capitalization are correct.	The text contains very few errors in spelling, grammar, punctuation, or capitalization. The meaning remains clear.	There are some errors in spelling, grammar, punctuation, and capitalization. One or two of these errors may cause the reader to pause momentarily, but meaning remains clear.	Many errors are present. Some errors are basic or repeated. The errors interfere with meaning in places.	Many errors have not been edited. Serious errors make the writing hard to understand.

Descriptive Writing Rubric

	5	4	3	2	1
Ideas	The topic is clear, focused, and complete. Sensory details and examples are related to and develop the main ideas. The description helps the reader experience what is being described very clearly.	The topic is clear and focused. Most sensory details and examples are related to and develop the main ideas. The description helps the reader experience what is being described most of the time.	The topic is clear but may not be focused or complete. Sensory details and examples develop most of the main ideas. The description sometimes helps the reader experience what is being described.	The topic is not clear or focused. Details and examples develop some of the main ideas. The reader cannot always experience what is being described.	The topic is not clear. Details and examples are unrelated or missing. The reader cannot experience what is being described.
Organization	The description is well organized into a strong introduction, body, and conclusion. Details support the topic. Appropriate transitions connect the ideas and guide the reader.	Most of the description is organized, featuring an introduction, body, and conclusion. Most details support the topic. One or two more transitions are needed to connect the ideas and guide the reader.	Most of the description is organized. The introduction, body, and conclusion are functional. Some of the details support the topic. More or better transitions are needed to connect the ideas and guide the reader.	Some of the description is organized. The introduction, body, or conclusion may be weak. Few of the details support the topic. More and better transitions are needed to connect the ideas and guide the reader.	The description is not organized and does not have an introduction or conclusion. Details are missing. Transitions are not used.
Voice	The writer's voice connects strongly with the audience. The mood and tone match the purpose perfectly.	The writer's voice connects with the audience most of the time. The mood and tone match the purpose.	The writer's voice connects with the audience in places. The mood and tone match the purpose, but are inconsistent.	The writer's voice does not fit the purpose or the audience well. The mood and tone are inappropriate or inconsistent.	The writer's voice is weak or absent. It does not connect with the audience.
Word Choice	Precise, descriptive language and creative comparisons create a clear picture of the subject. Nouns and verbs carry the descriptive load with help from a few carefully chosen modifiers.	Most of the language is precise. Most comparisons create a clear picture of the subject. Nouns, verbs, and modifiers are mostly strong.	Some of the language is precise, but some is vague. Some of the comparisons create a clear picture of the subject. Many nouns and verbs depend upon modifiers for specificity. Modifiers are satisfactory.	Most of the language is not descriptive. Comparisons are ineffective. Nouns and verbs lack clarity or precision. Too many or too few modifiers are used, and many of them are weak.	The language is very basic and limited. Comparisons are not used.
Sentence Fluency	A variety of sentence beginnings, lengths, and patterns keeps the description interesting. It is effortless to read aloud with inflection or feeling. The writing flows very smoothly.	Most of the sentences feature varied beginnings, lengths, and patterns, making the writing interesting. Most of the writing flows smoothly. The paper is easy to read aloud with inflection or feeling.	Some sentences share the same beginnings, lengths, or patterns. Some of the writing flows smoothly. The paper can be read aloud with inflection or feeling.	Several sentences in a row have the same beginnings, lengths, or patterns. The flow of the writing may slow or stall in parts. The paper is difficult to read aloud with inflection or feeling.	Sentences are not varied or interesting. The writing does not flow. The description is very difficult to read.
Conventions	The description contains no errors. Spelling, grammar, punctuation, and capitalization are correct.	The description contains very few errors in spelling, punctuation, or capitalization. Grammar is correct, and meaning is clear.	The description contains some errors in spelling, grammar, punctuation, and capitalization. One or two of these errors may cause the reader to pause momentarily, but meaning remains clear.	Many errors are present. Some errors are basic or repeated. The errors interfere with meaning in places.	The writing has not been edited. Serious errors make the writing hard to understand.

	6	5	4	3	2	1
Ideas	The topic is just the right size—not too big or too small. Descriptive details introduce and develop the setting, narrator, characters, and plot. Carefully selected ideas completely satisfy the needs of the reader.	The topic is the right size. Most details introduce and develop the setting, narrator, characters, and plot. Carefully selected ideas satisfy most of the reader's needs.	The topic is the right size. Some details introduce and develop the setting, narrator, characters, and plot. The ideas selected by the author frequently meet the needs of the reader.	The topic is too big or too small. Some details develop the setting, narrator, characters, and plot. Some ideas selected by the author are unrelated. The author did not consider the needs of the reader.	The topic is undeveloped. Too few details develop the narrative. Some details are not included.	The writing is not a narrative. Details are not included.
Organization	The narrative unfolds logically and naturally. Transition words and phrases help sequence the events. A strong beginning leads to a satisfying conclusion.	One or two events in the middle are not connected or are out of order. Transition words and phrases help sequence most of the events. The beginning or the conclusion is strong.	Some events are not connected or are out of order. Transition words and phrases are needed to help sequence the events. The beginning and the conclusion work, but may not be strong.	The narrative does not unfold logically and naturally. Events are out of order. Transition words and phrases are confusing or missing. The beginning or the conclusion is weak.	The narrative does not unfold logically. Events are out of order. Transition words and phrases are not used. The beginning or the conclusion is missing or problematic.	The writing is disorganized and very difficult to follow. No beginning or conclusion is evident.
Voice	The voice, mood, and tone are just right for the purpose. Dialogue, if used, reveals each character's voice clearly.	The voice, mood, and tone are just right most of the time. Dialogue, if used, reveals the characters' voices.	The voice, mood, and tone are just right in places, but inconsistent. Dialogue, if used, somewhat reveals the characters' voices.	The voice sounds disinterested. Mood and tone are weak. Dialogue, if used, does not uniquely distinguish the characters' voices.	The voice, mood, and tone are not consistent. Dialogue, if used, does not sound right for some of the characters.	Voice is flat. Mood and tone are absent. Dialogue is not used.
Word Choice	Words and phrases consistently help the reader "see" the characters and "experience" the events. Nouns and verbs are clear and precise, supported by a few carefully selected modifiers.	Words and phrases frequently help the reader "see" most of the characters and "experience" most of the events. Nouns and verbs are mostly clear and precise. Most modifiers are carefully selected.	Some words and phrases help the reader picture characters and events, but some are too general. Certain nouns and verbs are weak, requiring too much help from modifiers. Modifiers are satisfactory.	Many words and phrases are too general. They keep the reader from picturing the characters and events clearly. Nouns and verbs lack clarity or precision. Too many or too few modifiers are used, and many of them are weak.	Most words do not help the characters and events come alive for the reader. Nouns and verbs are vague, unclear, or confusing. Modifiers may be missing entirely.	Many words are not used correctly. They distract the reader.
Sentence Fluency	Varied sentence beginnings, lengths, and patterns make the writing flow smoothly. Several particularly well-crafted sentences add style and interest. The paper is effortlessly read aloud with inflection or feeling.	Most sentence beginnings, lengths, and patterns are varied. One or two sentences add style. The paper is easily read aloud with inflection or feeling.	There is some variation in sentence beginnings, lengths, and patterns. The sentences are correct but ordinary. The paper can be read aloud with inflection or feeling.	Many sentences have the same beginnings, lengths, and patterns. This interrupts the flow of the writing. The lengths and beginnings do not vary, making the writing robotic or rambling.	All or almost all the sentences follow the same pattern. Lengths and beginnings do not vary, making the writing robotic or rambling.	Sentences are poorly written or incorrect. The writing does not flow.
Conventions	Spelling, grammar, punctuation, and capitalization are correct. The narrative contains no errors.	There are a few minor errors, but they do not make the narrative difficult to read.	There are a few grammatical errors that may cause the reader to pause momentarily, but meaning is clear.	Many errors are present, and some confuse the reader.	Several serious errors make the narrative hard to understand.	The writing has not been edited.

Informative/Explanatory Writing Rubric

	6	5	4	3	2	1
Ideas	The topic is introduced clearly. Information and examples develop the main idea(s). Carefully selected ideas completely answer the reader's main questions.	The topic is introduced clearly. Most of the information and examples develop the main idea(s). Almost all of the reader's main questions are answered.	A topic is introduced. Some of the information and examples develop the main idea(s). The ideas chosen by the author frequently answer the reader's main questions.	A topic is introduced, but little of the information or examples develops the main idea(s). Some of the reader's questions are answered.	A topic is introduced, but examples do not develop the main idea(s). The author did not think about what questions the reader might have.	A topic is not introduced. Information and examples are incomplete or unrelated to the topic.
Organization	Information is organized into a strong and thoughtful introduction, a body, and a satisfying conclusion. Varied and appropriate transitions connect the ideas.	Information is organized into an introduction, a body, and a conclusion. Most transitions are varied and appropriate.	Information is organized into an introduction, a body, and a conclusion. More or better transitions are needed.	Information is not well organized. The introduction, body, and conclusion may be poorly developed. Transitions are confusing or not helpful.	Information is only partly organized. The introduction or the conclusion is missing. Transitions are not used.	The writing is not organized. Introduction and conclusion may both be missing. Transitions are not used.
Voice	The voice sounds interested and informative. It fully connects with the audience and conveys the writer's purpose well.	The voice sounds informative and mostly connects with the audience. It conveys the purpose fairly well.	The voice sounds informative and connects with the audience somewhat. It conveys the purpose some of the time.	The voice sounds informative in places. It conveys the purpose, but often fades out.	The voice consistently sounds flat. It may sound uninformed or uninterested. It does not convey the purpose.	Voice is weak or absent. It does not connect with the audience or convey the writer's purpose.
Word Choice	Precise language and domain-specific vocabulary are used. Definitions are complete and helpful. Nouns and verbs are clear and precise, supported by a few carefully selected modifiers.	Precise language and domain-specific vocabulary are used. Most definitions are complete and helpful. Nouns and verbs are mostly clear and precise. Most modifiers are carefully selected.	Some precise language, domain-specific vocabulary, and definitions are used. Some nouns and verbs are weak, requiring help from modifiers. Modifiers are satisfactory.	Little precise language and domain-specific vocabulary is used. Definitions are missing or incorrect. Nouns and verbs lack clarity or precision. Too many or too few modifiers are used, and many of them are weak.	Some domain-specific vocabulary is used incorrectly. Clarification and definition are not provided for the reader. Nouns and verbs are vague, unclear, or confusing. Modifiers may be missing.	Precise language and domain-specific vocabulary are not used.
Sentence Fluency	Clear, concise sentences make the text flow smoothly. Sentence beginnings, lengths, and patterns are varied for effect. The paper is effortlessly read aloud with inflection.	Most of the sentences flow smoothly. The sentence beginnings, lengths, and patterns are varied. The paper is easily read aloud with inflection.	One or two sections of the writing do not flow smoothly. In these sections, several sentences may have the same beginnings, lengths, or patterns. The paper can be read with inflection.	In many places, the writing does not flow smoothly due to repetitive sentence beginnings, lengths, and patterns. It is difficult to read the paper with inflection.	All or almost all the sentences have similar beginnings, lengths, or patterns. The writing sounds robotic or rambling.	Sentences are incomplete or incorrect.
Conventions	The text contains no errors. Spelling, grammar, punctuation, and capitalization are correct.	The text contains very few errors in spelling, punctuation, grammar, or capitalization. The meaning remains clear.	The text contains some errors in spelling, grammar, punctuation, and capitalization. One or two errors may cause the reader to pause momentarily, but meaning remains clear.	Many errors are present. Some errors are basic or repeated. The errors interfere with meaning in places.	Serious errors stop the reader frequently and make the writing hard to understand.	The writing has not been edited.

Opinion Writing Rubric

	6	5	4	3	2	1
Ideas	The writer states a clear opinion. The perfect details and facts are chosen to support the writer's reasons.	The writer states a clear opinion. Most details and facts are well chosen to support the writer's reasons.	The writer states an opinion. Some details and facts are well chosen to support the writer's reasons.	The writer states an opinion, but few details are well chosen to support the writer's reasons.	The writer's opinion is not clear. Facts are inaccurate or unrelated to the writer's reasons.	The writer does not state an opinion. Reasons are not provided.
Organization	The text is organized logically and creatively. Helpful, appropriate, even unique transitions link the writer's opinion and reasons. A compelling conclusion clearly supports the opinion statement.	The text is organized logically. One or two more transitions are needed to link the opinion and reasons. The beginning is strong, and the conclusion supports the opinion statement.	The text is organized logically. More or better transitions are needed to link the opinion and reasons. The beginning and the conclusion are functional. The conclusion relates to the opinion statement.	The text is not organized logically. Transitions may not show how the writer's ideas are related. Either the beginning or the conclusion is weak. The beginning or conclusion may not relate to the opinion statement.	The text is not organized logically. Transitions are not used. Ideas are hard to follow. The beginning or the conclusion is missing.	The text is not organized as an opinion. No beginning or conclusion is evident.
Voice	The voice is clearly convincing and totally fits the writer's purpose. The mood and tone are appropriate and engage the audience.	The voice is convincing and fits the writer's purpose. The mood and tone are appropriate and engaging most of the time.	The voice is somewhat convincing and fits the writer's purpose. The mood and tone are engaging some of the time.	The voice is convincing in some places. The mood and tone are inconsistent. They lose the audience.	The voice is flat and does not fit the writer's purpose. The mood and tone do not engage the audience.	The voice is weak or absent. The tone is not appropriate.
Word Choice	Precise words and fair language convey the writer's opinion. No biased words or phrases are used. Nouns and verbs are clear and precise. Most modifiers are carefully selected.	Most words are precise and fair. No biased words or phrases are used. Nouns and verbs are mostly clear and precise. Most modifiers are carefully selected.	Some words are too general. One biased word or phrase may be used. Some nouns and verbs are weak, requiring help from modifiers. Modifiers are satisfactory.	Most words are weak. A few biased words or phrases may be used. Nouns and verbs lack clarity or precision. Too many or too few modifiers are used, and many of them are weak.	Many words are overused and ineffective. Several biased words and phrases are used. Nouns and verbs are vague, unclear, or confusing. Modifiers may be missing.	Words are weak, biased, or used incorrectly.
Sentence Fluency	A variety of sentence patterns adds interest and style. Great variation in sentence beginnings and lengths makes the writing flow very smoothly. The paper is effortlessly read aloud with inflection.	Most sentence patterns are varied and add interest. Variation in sentence beginnings and lengths makes the writing flow smoothly. The paper is easily read aloud with inflection.	Most sentence patterns are varied and add interest. Some variation in sentence lengths and beginnings is evident. The writing flows smoothly in some places, but not in others. The paper can be read with inflection.	Some sentence patterns are varied and add interest. Some variation in sentence lengths and beginnings is evident. The writing flows smoothly in some places, but it is difficult to read the paper with inflection.	Too many sentences share the same pattern. The writing does not flow smoothly due to a lack of variation in sentence lengths and/or beginnings.	Almost all sentences are alike. The writing is boring and does not flow smoothly.
Conventions	The text contains no errors. Spelling, punctuation, and capitalization are correct.	The text contains very few errors in spelling, grammar, punctuation, or capitalization. The meaning remains clear.	The text contains some errors in spelling, grammar, punctuation, or capitalization. One or two of these errors may cause the reader to pause momentarily, but meaning remains clear.	There are some errors in spelling, grammar, and punctuation. One or two of these errors interfere with meaning in places.	Many errors are present. Some errors are basic or repeated. The errors make the writing hard to understand.	Serious errors stop the reader frequently and make the writing hard to understand.

Descriptive Writing Rubric

	6	5	4	3	2	1
Ideas	The topic is clear, focused, and complete. Sensory details and examples are related to and develop the main ideas. The description helps the reader experience what is being described very clearly.	The topic is clear and focused. Most sensory details and examples are related to and develop the main ideas. The description helps the reader experience what is being described most of the time.	The topic is clear but may not be focused or complete. Sensory details and examples develop most of the main ideas. The description sometimes helps the reader experience what is being described.	The topic is not clear or focused. Details and examples develop some of the main ideas. The reader cannot always experience what is being described.	The topic and main ideas are not clear. Few sensory details and examples are included. The reader has to work to experience what is being described.	The topic is not clear. Details and examples are unrelated or missing. The reader cannot experience what is being described.
Organization	The description is well organized into a strong introduction, body, and conclusion. Details support the topic. Appropriate transitions connect the ideas and guide the reader.	Most of the description is organized, featuring an introduction, body, and conclusion. Most details support the topic. One or two more transitions are needed to connect the ideas and guide the reader.	Most of the description is organized. The introduction, body, and conclusion are functional. Some of the details support the topic. More or better transitions are needed to connect the ideas and guide the reader.	Some of the description is organized. The introduction, body, or conclusion may be weak. Few of the details support the topic. More and better transitions are needed to connect the ideas and guide the reader.	The description is not well organized. The introduction or conclusion is missing or problematic. Details are missing. Transitions are misused or missing.	The description is not organized and does not have an introduction or conclusion. Details are missing. Transitions are not used.
Voice	The writer's voice connects strongly with the audience. The mood and tone match the purpose perfectly.	The writer's voice connects with the audience most of the time. The mood and tone match the purpose.	The writer's voice connects with the audience in places. The mood and tone match the purpose, but are inconsistent.	The writer's voice does not fit the purpose or the audience well. The mood and tone are inappropriate or inconsistent.	The writer's voice does not fit the purpose or the audience. The mood and tone are inappropriate.	The writer's voice is weak or absent. It does not connect with the audience.
Word Choice	Precise, descriptive language and creative comparisons create a clear picture of the subject. Nouns and verbs carry the descriptive load with help from a few carefully chosen modifiers.	Most of the language is precise. Most comparisons create a clear picture of the subject. Nouns, verbs, and modifiers are mostly strong.	Some of the language is precise, but some is vague. Some of the comparisons create a clear picture of the subject. Many nouns and verbs depend upon modifiers for specificity. Modifiers are satisfactory.	Most of the language is not descriptive. Comparisons are ineffective. Nouns and verbs lack clarity or precision. Too many or too few modifiers are used, and many of them are weak.	The language is not descriptive. Comparisons are confusing. Nouns and verbs are vague, unclear, or confusing. Modifiers may be missing.	The language is very basic and limited. Comparisons are not used.
Sentence Fluency	A variety of sentence beginnings, lengths, and patterns keeps the description interesting. It is effortless to read aloud with inflection or feeling. The writing flows very smoothly.	Most of the sentences feature varied beginnings, lengths, and patterns. Most of the writing flows smoothly. The paper is easy to read aloud with inflection or feeling.	Some sentences share the same beginnings, lengths, or patterns. Some of the writing flows smoothly. The paper can be read aloud with inflection or feeling.	Several sentences in a row have the same beginnings, lengths, or patterns. The flow of the writing may slow or stall in parts. The paper is difficult to read aloud with inflection or feeling.	Many sentences have the same beginnings, lengths, or patterns. The writing does not flow smoothly.	Sentences are not varied or interesting. The writing does not flow. The description is very difficult to read.
Conventions	The description contains no errors. Spelling, grammar, punctuation, and capitalization are correct.	The description contains very few errors in spelling, punctuation, or capitalization. Grammar is correct, and meaning is clear.	The description contains some errors in spelling, grammar, punctuation, and capitalization. One or two of these errors may cause the reader to pause momentarily, but meaning remains clear.	Many errors are present. Some errors are basic or repeated. The errors interfere with meaning in places.	Serious errors stop the reader frequently and make the writing hard to understand.	The writing has not been edited.

Index

draft, continued

in narrative, 16–17, 38–39, 60–61, 86–87, 112–113

in opinion, 250–253, 276–277, 298–299, 320–321, 344–345

E

edit

in descriptive, 371, 393, 415, 439, 463–464

in informative/explanatory, 139, 161, 183, 208–209, 233–234

in narrative, 21, 43, 65, 91, 117–118

in opinion, 257, 281, 303, 325, 349–350

editorial, 264–285

ending, 85

events, 120, 297

evidence, 314, 322, 398

examples and details, 398

exclamatory sentences, 90, 467

expository writing. *See* informative/explanatory writing

F

fact, 120, 296, 297, 300

figurative language, 422, 434

five-column chart, 203

five parts. *See* friendly letter

formal and informal language, 158, 255, 298

formatting, 86, 94, 286, 289, 290, 295, 304

four-paragraph organizer, 319

fragments, 8, 13, 21, 23

friendly letter

five parts of, 286, 289, 290, 295, 304–305

punctuating, 303

writing, 286–307

frequently confused words. *See* homophones

G

genres

descriptive writing, 352–465

character sketch, 376–397

descriptive paragraph, 354–375

poem, 422–443

poetry review, 398–421

test writing, 444–465

informative/explanatory writing, 120–235

compare-and-contrast essay, 122–143

how-to essay, 166–187

research report, 144–165

summary, 188–213

test writing, 214–235

narrative writing, 2–119

adventure story, 48–71

biographical sketch, 26–47

personal narrative, 4–25

play, 72–97

test writing, 98–119

opinion writing, 236–351

book review, 308–329

editorial, 264–285

friendly letter, 286–307

opinion essay, 238–263

response to literature, 308–329

test writing, 330–351

***good* and *well*,** 259

grammar, usage & mechanics

abbreviations, 305, 490, 505

action verbs, 63, 184, 211

adjectives, 259, 402, 406, 407, 413, 415, 416, 417, 487, 491

adverbs, 242, 247, 257–259, 327, 479, 488, 489, 502, 505

apostrophes, 52, 65, 67, 140, 211

appositives, 159, 471, 499

articles, 358, 363, 371, 373

capitalization, 13, 148, 153, 161–163, 303, 305, 490–492, 506

colons, 497, 508

comma splices, 468, 498

commas, 66, 78, 83, 91–93, 303–304, 380, 393, 395, 468, 493–494, 506

comparative adjectives, 415, 417, 487, 504

complete subject and predicate, 22

compound personal pronouns, 473, 500

compound sentences, 280, 380, 385, 393, 395, 468

compound subject and predicate, 22

coordinating conjunctions, 393–395, 468, 481, 502

direct quotations, 66, 308

double negatives, 194, 209, 210

forms of *be*, 30, 35, 43, 45

friendly letter, parts of, 286, 289, 290, 295, 304–305

future-tense verbs, 476

good and *well*, 259

transitions, continued
    signal words, 33, 56, 448
    time-order words, 38, 460, 506
    transitional words and phrases, 38, 315, 323, 368, 506

U

using the right word, 485, 504. *See also good* and *well;* homophones

V

variety of sentences, 12, 30, 34, 42, 56, 64, 78, 82, 90, 104, 126, 130, 148, 152, 160, 170, 174, 182, 220, 242, 246, 290, 294, 302, 312, 324, 336, 358, 362, 380, 384, 392, 402, 406, 414, 450

verb tense
    future, 476, 501
    past, 268, 273, 281, 282, 474, 500
    present, 44, 475, 500
    present perfect, 478, 501
    progressive, 483
    See also subject-verb agreement

verbs, 44, 52, 56, 63, 198, 199, 268, 271, 312, 316, 320, 503
    action, 63, 184, 211
    forms of *be*, 30, 35, 43, 45
    helping verbs, 476–478, 501
    irregular verbs, 45, 282–283
    linking verbs, 45, 211
    modal auxiliaries, 476–478

visuals, 95, 261, 329, 397

voice
    in draft, 60–61, 178–179, 298–299, 410–411

    in revise, 19, 40, 115, 137, 158, 231, 255, 278, 347, 369, 390, 461

W

web, 155–157, 225, 365, 367, 455, 456

word choice
    descriptive details, 12, 20, 362, 370, 382, 386, 387, 428, 430, 432, 434, 436, 449, 462
    domain-specific vocabulary, 130, 138, 194, 198, 204
    figurative language, 422, 434
    in draft, 86, 204, 320, 434
    in revise, 20, 41, 63, 116, 138, 159, 181, 232, 256, 279, 301, 348, 370, 391, 413, 462
    precise language, 103, 116, 138, 148, 152, 159, 170, 174, 181, 204, 205, 219, 232
    sensory details, 354, 356–360, 364, 366, 400, 424, 448, 455

word picture, 370

words (of a character), 376, 387

writer's terms
    adverbs, 257
    appositives, 159, 471
    attribute chart, 133
    beginning, 89
    body, 276
    cliché, 391
    commas, 91, 303
    comparative adjectives, 488
    conclusion, 276
    details, 16
    detail sentences, 366
    dialogue, 60, 88
    direct quotations, 65

fact, 296
first-person point of view, 19
five-column chart, 203
formal tone, 158
four-paragraph organizer, 319
homophones, 139
interview, 36
introduction, 276
lead, 136
loaded words, 256
main-idea table, 275
metaphor, 434
negatives, 209
network tree, 297, 409
opinion, 248, 318
order of importance organizer, 249
outline, 177
paragraph, 156
past-tense verbs, 281
play format, 86
plural nouns, 371
prepositional phrases, 439
pronouns, 183, 325
punctuating a friendly letter, 303
reasons, 250, 274
run-on sentences, 393
sentence types, 90
sequence chain, 15
simile, 434
spider map, 387
stage directions, 88
story map, 59, 85
subject-verb agreement, 43
supporting details, 206
third-person point of view, 40
three-column chart, 433
timeline, 37
tone, 158, 278
topic sentences, 366